Rice University

THE CAMPUS GUIDE

Rice University

Stephen Fox
Photographs by Paul Hester
Foreword by Lars Lerup

Princeton Architectural Press
NEW YORK | 2001

This book has been made possible through the generous support
of the Graham Foundation for Advanced Studies in the Fine Arts.

Princeton Architectural Press
37 East 7th Street
New York, NY 10003
212.995.9620

For a free catalog of other books published by Princeton Architectural Press,
call toll free 1.800.722.6657 or visit our web site at www.papress.com

Series editor: Jan Cigliano
Series concept: Dennis Looney
Copy editor: Heather Ewing
Design: Sara E. Stemen
Layout: Mary-Neal Meador
Maps: Jane Garvie
Special thanks to Nettie Aljian, Ann Alter, Amanda Atkins, Nicola Bednarek,
Mia Ihara, Clare Jacobson, Mark Lamster, Anne Nitschke, Lottchen Shivers,
Tess Taylor, Jennifer Thompson, and Deb Wood of Princeton Architectural Press
—Kevin C. Lippert, *publisher*

Library of Congress Cataloging-in-Publication Data
Fox, Stephen, 1950–
        Rice University : an architectural tour / by Stephen Fox ; photographs by Paul
        Hester ; foreword by Malcolm Gillis
            cm. — (The campus guide)
        Includes bibliographical references (p.) and index.
        ISBN 1-56898-246-1 (pbk. : alk. Paper)
        1. Rice University—Buildings—Guidebooks.   2. Rice University—Pictorial
        works.   I. Hester, Paul.   II. Title.   III. Campus guide (New York, N.Y.)

LD6053 F69 2001
378.764'1411—dc21   CIP
                                                                                      00-060646

Printed in China

05 04 03 02 01   5 4 3 2 1

How to Use This Book

This guide is intended for visitors, alumni, and students who wish to have an insider's look at the most historic and interesting buildings on campus—from the magnificent Academic Court and Court of Engineering, designed by Cram, Goodhue & Ferguson in 1912, to the more recent Jones Graduate School of Management by Robert A. M. Stern, Alice Pratt Brown Hall by

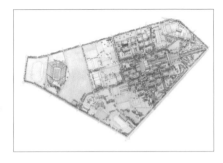

Ricardo Bofill, and James A. Baker III Hall by Hammond Beeby & Babka.

The book is divided into eight Walks, arranged geographically by area around the campus and the Houston community. Each Walk, or section, is introduced by a historical overview and a three-dimensional map that identifies the buildings on the Walk, then is followed by informative profiles and photographs of each building or site. Walk Eight, the last, is conceived as a drive around Houston, including the Museum of Fine Arts, Houston; Shadyside, the neighborhood landscaped by George E. Kessler, Autry House by Cram & Ferguson; and Shorthand House by François de Menil.

Many buildings on the campus are homes to students, faculty and their families, and staff members—day and night. Please do not enter classrooms or residential buildings. Buildings and services open to the public include:

Admissions Office, admi@rice.edu

Brown Fine Arts Library, Fondren Library: 8:30AM–11:00PM Monday–Thursday, 8:30AM–9:00PM Friday, 9:30AM–9:00PM Saturday, 12:30PM–11:00PM Sunday; 713.348.4832

Campus Police, 713.348.6000

Department of Architecture, Anderson Hall, 713.348.4864

Department of Art & Art History, Sewall Hall, 713.348.4815

Rice Media Center, 713.348.4882; media@rice.edu

Rice Players, 713.348.7529 reservations

Rice Student Center: 7AM–1AM Monday, 7AM–2AM Tuesday–Thursday, 7AM–9PM Friday, 9AM–12AM Saturday, 12PM–12AM Sunday

Rice University Art Gallery: 11AM–5PM Tuesday–Saturday, 11AM–8PM Thursday, 12PM–5PM Sunday, closed Monday and all university holidays; 713.348.6069; ruag@rice.edu

Shepherd School of Music, Alice Pratt Brown Hall, 713.348.4854; concert hall office 713.348.4933

Tours: 11AM and 3PM Monday–Friday

Further Information from:
Rice University
6100 Main Street
Houston, Texas 77005
713.348.0000
www.rice.edu

It is hard to avoid thinking about Arcadia when reflecting on the American university campus, or more specifically the American archetype of privileged precincts—Thomas Jefferson's University of Virginia. Rice University shines in this light. In fact it is astonishing how many visitors to Rice, even those with different convictions than the classical, express their admiration for this campus: "it is so beautiful." To maintain this winsome yet fixed smile in the eye of a cultural storm takes stubbornness and determination. At Rice there is plenty of both.

The anatomy of this determination has changed over the years and resulted in some digressions from the smile. Stephen Fox more than anyone is prepared and able to look the anatomy right in the eye. As it turns out, Fox's scrutiny is unflinching and not entirely flattering. Yet behind Fox's observations lies warmth, affection, and admiration that stems from his own deep commitment to the architectural enterprise. Hard earned and stubborn has been Fox's study of the Houston scene. Any city of Houston's complexity should be so lucky to have a chronicler of Fox's intelligence and critical eye.

To maintain the integrity of this privileged precinct in a city of great diversity—largely the result of an unbound entrepreneurial spirit—may be easier than if inserted in a planned city. Rice remains different by being planned. This has not gone unnoticed. Mild-mannered protests by neighbors suggest that Rice ought to get beyond its hedges. This may be well intentioned but ultimately threatening to the physical integrity of the campus. Rice has intelligently addressed this by turning the zone along the hedge into a public precinct that caters to joggers whom daily and ritualistically circumscribe the campus. Stubbornly, Rice refuses to succumb to the paranoia of the gated community.

Issues of this kind continually threaten the integrity of our Arcadia. The mechanical beasts—automobiles—that dominate the rest of the city are a daily headache. Much likes snakes in Paradise, cars slither through and disrupt the tranquillity and now for the first time parking is going underground, sump pumps included. Enemies are not just civilization, but occasionally entirely natural.

Black birds used to invade the campus and occupy the many trees for weeks. The resulting ruckus and excremental debris led the campus to solicit help from experts—to no avail. Nature's last laugh was on a group of illustrious guests partying under the campus trees. Suddenly a waiter dropped a tray and the birds descended en masse to partake while simultaneously bombarding the guests (cleaners must have had a field day). Having accomplished their mission the birds have since flown across town, a place where they might prefer its glass-box architecture.

As this book goes to press, Rice has entered a building boom. In ensuing years, thousands of construction workers will mingle with the regular population. Culturally it will serve us well. Having construction next to academic pursuits shows that building a university is an ongoing enterprise where thinking and building go hand in hand.

Lars Lerup
William Ward Watkin Professor and Dean
School of Architecture, Rice University

Introduction

The campus of Rice University is significant for its architecture and planning. It is also significant for its landscape architecture and its influence on the planning and architectural standards of the portion of Houston that surrounds it. Edgar Odell Lovett, the first president of the Rice Institute (as the university was known until 1960), retained the Boston architects Cram, Goodhue & Ferguson in 1909 to prepare a master plan for the development of the campus, a flat site of 277 acres south of the town of Houston. Ralph Adams Cram's General Plan of 1910 envisioned a spatial armature of evergreen live oak trees and privet hedges to shape the space and direct movement and vision across this site. Cram's first buildings were designed in a bold, colorful neo-Byzantine style, a style he asserted was appropriate for an institution of high culture in a hot, humid, southern setting. Cram's first buildings, completed in 1912 when the university opened, propelled Rice to instant renown.

Cram's buildings and spaces have powerfully affected the imaginations of succeeding generations. In the 1910s and 1920s, the countryside around Rice developed as the City Beautiful civic arena of Houston, in which Mediterranean-style architecture and allées of live oak trees together created a harmonious garden-city landscape. Despite a brief rejection of the General Plan in the postwar 1940s, the most imaginative buildings at Rice in the 1950s were those that sought to translate the spatial and material attributes of Cram's architecture into modern architectural terms. In the late 1970s, postmodernism impelled a reappraisal of the General Plan.

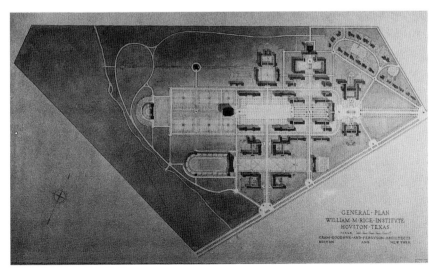

General Plan of the William M. Rice Institute. Cram, Goodhue & Ferguson, architects, 1910, William Ward Watkin, draftsman (Woodson Research Center, Fondren Library, Rice University)

James A. Baker III Hall, Hammond, Beeby & Babka

Outstanding buildings by James Stirling, Michael Wilford, and César Pelli in the early 1980s made possible the reconciliation of current building programs with the organizing principles of the Cram plan. During the 1990s Rice embarked on an extensive building campaign in which high-profile architects such as Ricardo Bofill and the Taller de Arquitectura, Cambridge Seven Associates, John Outram, Hammond, Beeby & Babka, Alan Greenberg, and Antoine Predock designed new buildings.

The architecture of Rice University represents an extraordinary assertion of will. It was designed to represent the identity of a cultural institution that, because it was newly created, had no identity, and to situate this institution in a historical tradition of high culture that was largely invented. Ralph Adams Cram and Edgar Odell Lovett "socially constructed" an identity for this the new university (to use a term drawn from the discourse of anthropology) by using space to shape consensus on what was distinctive about Rice as a community of learning, scholarship, and culture. Because Cram shaped spaces that proved to be emotionally compelling, they transcend the fictions he and Lovett devised. The substantiality of Cram's brick and stone, neo-Byzantine style buildings, and the ways in which they fix place spatially in conjunction with the ranks of live oak trees and hedges installed under his direction, belie their made-up origin.

Cram's General Plan evokes the progressive era in American thought and politics at the turn of the twentieth century in its combination of mythic appeal and rational action, of bold invention and conservative idealism. Rice's campus, because it represents such a clear case of landscape invention and social construction, possesses a historical significance that is as compelling as its architectural beauty. It is the attribute of beauty (more mythic than discursive in its appeal) that Cram counted on to ensure that the long term construction of Rice's campus be carried out in fulfillment of the spatial-organizational principles of the General Plan. Rice stands out among other historically significant American university campuses of the progressive era for the consistency with which Cram's and Lovett's vision has been adhered to for the next one hundred years. Rice presents a fascinating study of the ways in which twentieth-century architects have engaged history and identity through design.

The Origins of Rice University

The William M. Rice Institute for the Advancement of Literature, Science and Art was granted a charter by the State of Texas on May 19, 1891. William M. Rice (1816–1900), who obtained the charter, was a Houston commission merchant and investor. Rice emigrated to the Republic of Texas from Massachusetts in 1838 and settled in the three-year-old town of Houston in 1839. By 1860 Rice's business acumen had made him one of the richest men in Texas. After the Civil War, he and his wife, Elizabeth Baldwin Rice, retired to New York, although Rice's business interests were centered in Houston. According to his biographer, Andrew Forest Muir, the Rices, who were childless, began in the late 1870s to entertain the idea of endowing an institution for the care and education of children. During the late 1880s and early 1890s Rice's conception of this institution evolved, and in May 1891 he asked a number of Houston business and professional men to serve as trustees of the William M. Rice Institute. With the help of a Houston business associate, Emanuel Raphael, and his attorney James A. Baker, Rice drafted a charter of incorporation. This defined the institute as non-sectarian and specified that it was to consist of a public library; an institution for the advancement of literature, science, art, philosophy, and letters; a polytechnic school; and collections of scientific apparatus and works of art, all "for the cultivation and other means of instruction of the white inhabitants of the City of Houston and the State of Texas."[1] Rice conveyed $200,000 to the institute as an endowment but declined to implement the institute during his lifetime. In June 1892 William and Elizabeth Baldwin Rice supplemented this gift with the transfer of productive rural real estate in Texas and Louisiana, the property occupied by the Capitol Hotel in downtown Houston, and a seven-acre tract in the 1500 and 1600 blocks of Louisiana Street in Houston, which they intended to be the site of the William M. Rice Institute.

Libbie Baldwin Rice died in July 1896, three months after suffering a stroke. Following her death, a will of which her husband was unaware was filed for probate. Libbie Rice left her half of her husband's estate to her relatives and various philanthropies. Her ability to dispose of her husband's assets rested on a determination of whether she was legally a resident of Texas (a state that recognized a wife as possessing a community property interest in her husband's estate) or a resident of New York (which did recognize community property). Rice and attorney Baker contested the will on the grounds that the Rices were legal residents of New York. At the end of 1899, Rice, who was living at his apartment on Madison Avenue in New York, became the target of a murder plot involving his valet and a lawyer from Texas engaged in the litigation over Mrs. Rice's will. On September 23, 1900, the valet, acting on instructions from the lawyer, chloroformed the 84-year-old Rice while he was sleeping. The lawyer produced a will that he had forged, naming him as Rice's residuary legatee and leaving the Rice Institute an insignificant bequest. From Houston, James Baker launched an investigation. Within two weeks, the lawyer and valet were arrested and charged with forgery and murder; the valet confessed to the conspiracy and both were convicted.

Baker, whom Rice had named chairman of the institute's board of trustees, saved Rice's fortune for the Rice Institute by exposing the forgery and murder and by forcing a settlement over Mrs. Rice's will that preserved the integrity of William M. Rice's financial corpus. When Rice's estate was finally settled in April 1904, the Rice Institute inherited assets totaling slightly more than $4.6 million. Two of Rice's nephews, William M. Rice, Jr. (his uncle's namesake) and Benjamin Botts Rice, the sons of Rice's brother and business associate F. A. Rice, were elected to the board. Not until 1907 did the trustees begin the search for a scholar who could give shape to the founder's vision. The trustees solicited recommendations from university presidents, including Woodrow Wilson, then president of Princeton University. William M. Rice, Jr., the only trustee to have attended college, had been a classmate of Wilson's in the class of 1879 at Princeton. Wilson recommended Edgar Odell Lovett (1871–1957), professor of mathematics at Princeton. In November 1907 the trustees invited Lovett to become president of the Rice Institute. Lovett accepted and assumed the presidency in March 1908, a position he would hold for 38 years.

Beginning the Rice Institute

Lovett was Rice University's intellectual architect. He designed the curriculum, recruited the faculty and students, and administered the planning and

Board of Trustees of the William M. Rice Institute, 1911. Edgar Odell Lovett is standing, second from left; James A. Baker, chairman of the board, is seated at the right (Woodson Research Center)

construction of the university's campus. Rather than planning a university on the seven-acre site that the founder had set aside on Louisiana Street, the trustees, at Lovett's suggestion, acquired six tracts totaling 277 acres during 1908 and 1909. These lay on the flat coastal plain south of Houston, one-and-a-half miles outside the city limit along an extension of Houston's Main Street. While property acquisition was underway, Lovett made a round-the-world tour to inspect universities and technological institutes in Europe and Japan. Sustaining his ambitions for the Rice Institute was William M. Rice's endowment; by 1912, the year instruction began at Rice, this had expanded to nearly $10 million, making it the seventh most richly endowed university in the United States.

During the summer of 1909 Lovett interviewed architects and in August awarded the commission for a master plan of development and the design of four buildings to Cram, Goodhue & Ferguson of Boston. Ralph Adams Cram (1863–1942) and his partner Bertram Grosvenor Goodhue (1869–1924) were two of the most highly regarded architects in the U.S. Cram was a traditionalist, known for his advocacy of Gothic architecture. Goodhue was known for his exquisite drawing skills and a penchant for stylistic exoticism. Frank W. Ferguson (1861–1926) was the firm's technical specialist and business manager. Cram and Goodhue formed their partner-ship in 1891. In 1903, after winning the competition for replanning the U.S. Military Academy at West Point, Cram, Goodhue & Ferguson had estab-lished a second office in New York, headed by Goodhue.

Since 1906 Cram had been consulting architect to Princeton University. Whether this influenced Lovett's choice is unclear. Fredericka Meiners, in her history of Rice's first fifty years, suggested that Lovett selected Cram despite this connection, because he did not want to appear to be imitating Princeton. Cram's challenge at Princeton was to reshape an eighteenth- and nineteenth-century campus to represent its transformation from a church-related college into a twentieth-century university. Cram materialized this transformation with neo-Gothic architecture, most extravagantly at Princeton's Graduate College (1913). His "social construction" of a modern university as a medieval English college reflected the American progressive movement's dependence on historical models when it came to architecture. American progressives sought to manage modernization by constructing it not as a radical disruption but as a continuation of "tradition." Cram was a brilliant proponent of this paradoxical practice. The commission for Rice propelled him to new heights in the invention of tradition.

The General Plan

During September and October 1909 Cram and his associates in Boston produced one proposal for the campus site, while Goodhue and his associates worked on another in New York. Cram and Goodhue traveled to Houston in November 1909 to present President Lovett and the trustees with these plans and to inspect the site for which they had been made. Following their two presentations, Cram and the Boston office refined the site plan, which was approved by President Lovett in May 1910. It was based on the scheme that Goodhue had submitted, although he was not associated with the Rice project after November 1909. The ink and watercolor drawing of the approved plan, which Cram's draftsman William Ward Watkin prepared in July 1910, is an extraordinary document.

Cram's General Plan—Cram, Goodhue & Ferguson's name for the master plan—represents several "layers" of planning. In terms of functional organization, it grouped buildings by academic discipline (humanities, sciences, engineering) and use (academic, residential, athletic). The General Plan organized related-use functions along the main axis and parallel east-west axes that structured view and movement. These axes were intersected at right angles by north-south cross-axes to construct a matrix of directed views and implied lines of movement. The long, thin, slab shapes of the buildings (which were optimal for the hot, humid climate) also reinforced axial extension. Centrality and symmetry marked important buildings, such as the Administration Building (now Lovett Hall), located at key points in the plan. Trees and hedge rows were specified in the General Plan as the components defining lines of view and movement volumetrically. More so than

The Rice Institute, 1920. Main Boulevard stretches across the lower left; *the Harry C. Wiess House in Shadyside,* lower right corner; *the tree line in the distance markes the course of Harris Gully.* ("The Flying Owls," Woodson Research Center)

buildings, hedge rows and trees planted in allées reshaped the vast, immeasurable, and monotonous space of the flat coastal plain, imposing rhythm, measure, direction, sequentiality, and hierarchy—what might in literary terms be called a narrative structure. As Rice's tree canopies matured, the allées of trees transformed the two-dimensional diagram of the General Plan, and the unpromising campus site, into a complex sequence of varied spaces that, like the chapters of a novel, the verses of a song, or the stanzas of a poem, were capable of telling stories to make sense of place.

Cram, Goodhue & Ferguson structured the General Plan with a single major axis, three-quarters of a mile in length. Beginning at the main entrance to the campus, it was aligned to parallel the longest dimension of the property (now Rice Boulevard). The main axis bisected the Academic Court, framed by the Administration Building and flanked by classroom buildings devoted to the humanities (eventually the sites of the Physics Building and Sewall, M. D. Anderson, and Rayzor Halls). The General Plan depicts the main axis as bisecting a freestanding auditorium, the Commencement Hall (centered where the axis now crosses the north-south street between Herring Hall and the Baker Institute), then proceeding westward to form the spine of the Persian gardens. A secondary axis, south of the main axis, regulated the organization of the Residential Group for Men (the site of what became Baker, Will Rice, and Hanszen Colleges). Its east end was to be fixed by a student center (now the site of a parking lot facing Lovett

College); its west end by a gymnasium and stadium (where the playing field between Hanszen College and the Rice Gymnasium is located). The north-south cross axes began at Entrance 3 and 4 on Main Street. The cross axes linked the Residential Group with the Academic Court and terminated in the Court of Engineering (site of the Mechanical Laboratory and Power House) and the Graduate Court (where Hamman Hall and George R. Brown Hall would eventually be built). Because the main and secondary axes were deliberately not coordinated with the alignment of Main Street, Cram, Goodhue & Ferguson created a self-contained campus that was disconnected from the city that would one day engulf it.

Looking south along the first cross-axis from the Court of Engineering, 1912. Administration Building, left; Institute Commons, right (now Baker College) (Woodson Research Center)

Looking north along the first cross-axis from Entrance Three, 1915. South Hall (now Will Rice College) and the Institute Commons and East Hall (now Baker College), left; Mechanical Laboratory and Power House, center; Physics Building (obscured by trees) and Administration Building in the Academic Court, right (Woodson Research Center)

The Academic Court framed by Italian cypress trees and privet hedge parterres, 1920. In the distance are components of the Residential Group for Men (F. J. Schlueter photo, Woodson Research Center)

The Architecture of the General Plan

When the institute opened, it was Cram's audacious architecture that astounded viewers, not the magnitude of the General Plan or the allées of live oak trees (to the extent the trees had been planted, they were only saplings.) The buildings that Cram, Goodhue & Ferguson produced embodied Lovett's ambitions for Rice. Designed in a style contrived expressly for Houston, they exerted an almost hypnotic effect on the imaginations of Houstonians. As Cram wrote in his autobiography, published in 1936:

> We wanted something that was beautiful, if we could make it so, Southern in its spirit, and with some quality of continuity with the historic and cultural past. Manifestly the only thing to do was to invent something approaching a new style . . . and to develop a psychological excuse for it. . . . I reassembled all the elements I could from South France and Italy, Dalmatia, the Peloponessus, Byzantium, Anatolia, Syria, Sicily, Spain and set myself the task of creating a measurably new style that, while built on a classical basis, should have the Gothic romanticism, pictorial quality and structural integrity.[2]

Through architecture Cram sought to construct an identity for the Rice Institute that legitimized its implicit assertion to continuity with the high cultural traditions of western Europe.

Cram's effort can be seen in a broader historical context. Since the 1890s progressive American architects had discovered that the United States possessed a host of regional architectural cultures, often of non-Anglo-American origin, exemplified by the Pueblo and Spanish architectures of New Mexico, the Spanish architecture of California, and the French and Spanish architectures of Louisiana. Bertram Goodhue was a pivotal figure in this process of identifying regional architectural vernaculars and adapting them to contemporary uses, a feat he achieved with his spectacular neo-Spanish designs for the Panama-California Exposition in San Diego of 1914. Cram took this procedure a step further by inventing a historical regional architectural style at Rice. His construction of "tradition" through invention underscored the essential modernity of his techniques. William Ward Watkin, who came to Houston in August 1910 to administer construction of the institute's first four buildings, subsequently identified a book of measured drawings, *The Monastery of St. Luke of Stiris, in Phocis, and the Dependent Monastery of St. Nicholas in the Fields, near Skripou, in Boeotia,* published in London in 1901 by British architects Robert Weir Schultz and Sidney Howard Barnsley, as the primary source of formal information used by Cram's associates to detail the buildings at Rice.

Although the cultural connections between twentieth-century Texas and medieval Greece were, at the least, tenuous, the practice of adopting exotic historic models in search of a Texan style architecture had precedent in various late-nineteenth-century Texan buildings, often designed by architects from the northeastern United States. In 1891 Bertram Goodhue produced a medieval Italian style design for a church in Dallas, Texas, which was never built. In 1909, through the intervention of Edward M. House, future advisor to Woodrow Wilson and son of the Houston banker Charles House, the University of Texas at Austin retained New York architect Cass Gilbert to design a new library. Gilbert's library of 1910, although based on Italian Renaissance models, incorporated Spanish decorative detail. The library commission then served as the point of departure for a campus master plan undertaken by Gilbert in 1910 and 1914. Like Cram, Gilbert envisioned a series of courts controlled by axes and cross-axes and linked by arcades. Gilbert's Italian and Spanish historical references were not as exotic as Cram's, but they were just as contrived with regard to Texas. New York architect Henry Hornbostel also designed a complex of buildings in a free rendition of Italian architecture for Emory University in Atlanta, of which only two buildings were constructed in 1916. Hornbostel made the Italian connection on the basis of setting and climate rather than on any historical cultural connection between Italy and Atlanta.

Gilbert at the University of Texas and Hornbostel at Emory paralleled Cram's practice at Rice. They were celebrated metropolitan architects called on by provincial elites to envision new futures for local cultural institutions. Through recourse to architectural exoticism they constructed historical narratives that discovered and explored cosmopolitan connections between southern hometowns and "southern," non-Anglo-Saxon worlds. Their bold styles, monumental scale, and systematic integration of building, landscape, and open space asserted the institutions' singularity and superiority and legitimized the right of their leaders to exercise cultural authority. Cram provided Edgar Odell Lovett with buildings and a setting that compelled the trustees of the Rice Institute to commit to Lovett's ambitious vision of the kind of university Rice might be. Architecture legitimized Lovett's authority by bringing widespread attention (of a kind that no Texan cultural institution had experienced before) to the institute's buildings.

The Lovett Years, 1912–1946

Between 1912 and 1916, when Rice graduated its first class, President Lovett expanded the faculty and student body (the entering class consisted of 77 students). The Physics Building of 1914 was constructed alongside the Administration Building facing the Academic Court; two dormitories, East Hall and West Hall, were added to the Residential Group. Improvements to the grounds included the planting of live oak and cedar elm trees during 1913 in accordance with the General Plan. Cram, Goodhue & Ferguson (which became Cram & Ferguson after Goodhue withdrew from the partnership in late 1913) directed these improvements with William Ward Watkin (1886–1952). Watkin had formed such a productive working relationship with President Lovett during the construction of the institute that when Rice

Rice Memorial Center

Baccalaureate, 1928. In the distance is the low tower of Cohen House with the campanile of the Edward Albert Palmer Memorial Chapel rising behind it; Hermann Hospital in Hermann Park, right (Woodson Research Center)

opened he was appointed instructor in architectural engineering. Watkin founded Rice's architecture department, and was head of the department until his death in 1952. He was also curator of grounds as well as architect or associate architect for new buildings. Watkin formed a strong, proprietary attachment to the university and he ensured continuity with Cram's architectural and planning intentions.

During the 1920s Houston's economy and population soared. Between 1920 and 1930, Houston grew from the third largest Texas city to the first. World War I had created a massive demand for oil that enriched the oil companies headquartered in Houston or with regional offices there. This wealth added a new layer to the city's economic elite. The emergence of an oil elite was especially visible in the development of the Main Boulevard civic arena surrounding Rice during the 1920s. The construction of the Museum of Fine Arts, Autry House, Hermann Hospital, and the residential enclave of Shadyside, represented the translation of oil wealth into civic benefaction and domestic refinement. With his commissions, Watkin was active in extending the architectural narrative of Cram's campus buildings and his techniques for shaping space urbanistically into this area. This was the most privileged sector of Houston and its coordinated development was based on the model Rice provided.

Yet at Rice there was little new construction during the 1920s. In 1921 the institute's endowment stood at $12.8 million. By 1929 it had increased to only $14.8 million. Rice's trustees were extremely conservative. They represented the older, pre-oil layers of Houston's elite and while they recognized the need to seek new sources of funding, they did not develop the means to do so. The slow growth of the endowment placed constraints on the number of students that could be admitted, although enrollment grew from 860 students in 1921 to 1,400 by the early 1930s. The faculty expanded from 40 in 1920 to 70 by 1930. Although Cram & Ferguson prepared schematic designs for a house for the president in 1924, a library in 1927, and a classroom building in 1929, only two projects proceeded to completion: the Chemistry Building of 1925 and the Founder's Memorial of 1930, a bronze statue of William M. Rice by the English sculptor John Angel atop a granite base. Cram & Ferguson shared design responsibility for the Chemistry Building with William Ward Watkin. Watkin served as the architect for Cohen House, the institute's faculty club. This was the first building at Rice to be built by an outside donor, George S. Cohen, a Houston retail merchant. Watkin also designed a Field House in 1920, which was demolished in 1951.

Rice's influence spread beyond Houston. In 1924 Watkin and the Fort Worth, Texas, architects Sanguinet, Staats & Hedrick designed a master plan for a new state-supported university in Lubbock, Texas—what is today Texas Technological College. The ambitious scale of Watkin's master plan reflected the influence of Bertram Goodhue's studies for the Rice general plan. The design of Texas Tech's original buildings, especially such details as the sallyport of the administration building of 1925 and the use of arcaded exterior passages, was notably similar to Rice. Cram & Ferguson designed a series of buildings in the late 1920s and 1930s that appear to be indebted to their work at Rice. McCormick Hall at Princeton (1925) and the monastery and chapel of St. John The Evangelist in Cambridge, Massachusetts (1928, 1936) are based on their dormitories at Rice. They developed Doheny Memorial Library at the University of Southern California of 1932 in Los Angeles from their design for the Administration Building.

Although the Depression led to a decline in the institute's income and consequently in the size of the faculty and the number of students admitted .Yet Houston's economy rebounded markedly after 1935. This was reflected at Rice in the second structure to be built with outside funding: the first Rice Stadium of 1938 by William Ward Watkin, adjacent to Watkin's Field House at Main Boulevard and University Boulevard. In 1940 and 1941 Cram & Ferguson and Watkin separately worked on schematic designs for a new institute library. The war years brought major changes to Rice, even while campus planning was deferred. In 1941 President Lovett resigned, but because of the war he remained as president until a replacement was recruited in 1946. James A. Baker died in 1941 and Ralph Adams Cram in 1942. When Lovett stepped down, three other elderly trustees retired. The

trustees elected to replace those who died or retired in the 1940s were
Houston businessmen in their 40s and 50s; a number were executives of oil
corporations or independent oilmen. They brought new ideas on administrative structure, institutional planning, and management that were reflected in
a building campaign that began with the term of the institute's second president, William V. Houston.

The Houston Years, 1946–1960

President Houston (pronounced How-ston), who had been a professor of
physics at the California Institute of Technology—its campus designed by
Bertram Grosvenor Goodhue—was not involved with architecture in the
personal way that President Lovett had been. Harry C. Wiess, president of
Houston's major local oil corporation, the Humble Oil & Refining Company
(now Exxon) and a former client of William Ward Watkin's, was elected a
trustee in 1944. Wiess was the first chair of a new trustees' committee on
buildings and grounds. During the four years before his death in 1948 Wiess
exercised the kind of involvement with campus planning and construction
that Lovett and Watkin had during Lovett's administration. In 1943 Wiess
had been one of a number of Houston businessmen who made substantial
contributions to Rice to enable it to buy part ownership of an oil field in
Starr County, Texas. The Rincón Field provided Rice with its first major
infusion of new funding since William M. Rice's original bequest. This made
it possible for Rice to double the number of buildings on campus between
1946 and 1950 by building M. D. Anderson Hall, the Abercrombie Engineering Laboratory, Fondren Library, a President's House, the Wiess Hall
dormitory (now Wiess College), Rice Stadium, and the Rice Gymnasium
and Autry Court. As the practice of naming of new buildings for donors
implied, Rice's postwar trustees actively sought the financial support of
Houston's elite in expanding the university. They created a new body, the
board of governors (of which the trustees were voting members), to expand
Rice's outreach to its alumni and to Houston's elite.

 The Houston architectural firm of Staub & Rather designed all
these projects except Rice Stadium and the Rice Gymnasium. John F. Staub
was Houston's most accomplished eclectic architect; his partner J. T. Rather,
Jr., was a Rice architecture alumnus who later served on Rice's board of governors in the 1950s. Staub had supplanted Watkin as Harry Wiess's architect
in the 1920s. Although Watkin was nominally involved as consulting architect for Anderson Hall, the Abercrombie Laboratory, and Fondren Library,
he did not participate in their planning or design. Staub & Rather appeared
deliberately to break with the architectural and planning order of Cram's
General Plan. The decision to build the Fondren Library across the main
axis, blocking the transition from the Academic Court to the Great Square,

was the most dramatic instance of rejection and it was endorsed by the faculty. Staub & Rather's buildings symbolically repudiated the paternalism of the later Lovett era. Architecturally, however, they did not represent a new vision. Rather, who designed all the buildings except the Fondren Library and the President's House, demonstrated an awareness of modern architecture in his designs. His buildings were nevertheless firmly anchored in the conservative formal conventions of modernistic institutional architecture of the 1930s and 1940s.

Rice Stadium, by a slightly younger generation of Rice architecture alumni—Hermon Lloyd, W. B. Morgan, and Milton McGinty—was a work of modern design. Built under the auspices of another of the younger trustees, George R. Brown, who in 1950 became the first Rice alumnus to be elected chairman of the board of trustees, Rice Stadium did not so much reject the General Plan as transcend it. The 70,000-seat stadium reflected Houston's rise as the prototypical postwar American suburban city. The stadium was a work of monumental infrastructure engineering, its immense surface parking lots underlying the primacy of the automobile. Rice Gymnasium and Autry Court, a much lesser work of architecture, suggested that the General Plan was irrelevant to the way Rice would continue to grow. The trustees selected the design on the basis of competitive bidding among general contractors—contractors submitted their own architectural designs as part of the process. It was sited for easy access to parking rather than for its spatial connections to the rest of the campus.

What transformed this potentially drastic pattern of campus development was modern architecture.

The most conservative architecture built at Rice during the 1950s was the most modern. What made it conservative was that the architects involved—Lloyd & Morgan and George Pierce-Abel B. Pierce—designed their modern buildings with careful regard for the General Plan. The Nuclear Research Laboratory of 1952 (subsequently the Bonner Nuclear Laboratory; demolished in 1994 to provide a site for Duncan Hall) by George Pierce-Abel B. Pierce set the pattern for the Pierce and Lloyd firms' subsequent work. Lloyd & Morgan's Mary Gibbs Jones College of 1957 (the first dormitory for female students at Rice) and Pierce-Pierce's Earth Sciences group and Hamman Hall of 1958 were planned as thin, slab-shaped buildings that sought modernist analogues to the Cram buildings and to the spatial patterns of the General Plan. The additions that Wilson, Morris, Crain & Anderson made to Cram's East, South, and West hall dormitories in 1957 to transform them into Baker, Will Rice, and Hanszen colleges were not as architecturally rigorous as the Lloyd & Morgan and Pierce-Pierce buildings, but they reinforced and extended the shape of the General Plan. Rice's modern buildings of the 1950s make an intriguing counterpoint to the two most architecturally significant university campuses designed in Texas in the 1950s. Trinity University in San Antonio of 1950–1955, by the San Antonio architects O'Neil Ford and Bartlett Cocke, with William W. Wurster and Sam B. Zisman as consultants, embodied the rationalist ethos of site specificity, constructional economy, and rejection of symmetry and centrality. The University of St. Thomas in Houston of 1957–1959, by the New York architect Philip Johnson, represented an application of the discipline of Ludwig Mies van der Rohe to a small campus in an inner-city neighborhood. Rice's modern buildings exhibited architectural similarities to those at Trinity and St. Thomas. What made them distinctive was that they continued an existing architectural narrative, and translated that narrative into modernist terms. Rice's modern architecture of the 1950s contrasted with "traditional" architecture built on campus at mid-century: the Rice Memorial Center of 1958 by another Rice architecture alumnus, Harvin C. Moore, and Staub, Rather & Howze's Rayzor Hall of 1962, begun the year that President Houston retired.

Exercising a more subtle but pervasive effect on the campus was a new landscape overlay installed in phases between 1957 and 1960. Designed by Robert F. White, professor of landscape architecture at Texas A&M University and his associates Fred Klatt and George S. Porcher, these installations systematically suburbanized campus space. J. T. Rather, as a member of the committee on buildings and grounds, worked with White on replacing streets aligned on the cross-axes with exposed aggregate-surfaced sidewalks, removing hedge rows (including the Cape Jasmine hedges in the Academic Court and all the hedges in the Court of Engineering), and installing new planting. White diversified the tree stock of the Rice campus. He planted a wide variety of deciduous oak trees as well as loblolly pines, ornamental trees such as mimosa, crape myrtle, and Japanese yew, and ground covers such as liriope and Asiatic jasmine. White did not attempt to shape space with massed ranks of trees. Instead he spaced trees out so that even in the rare instances where they were aligned their canopies would not grow together to shape space.

The Pitzer Years, 1961–1968

Rice recruited another California scientist, Kenneth S. Pitzer, dean of chemistry at the University of California, Berkeley, to succeed President Houston. Pitzer's tenure was brief but expansive. He arrived in the summer of 1960 just after Rice made the momentous change from "Rice Institute" to "Rice University." President Pitzer challenged the board of governors to prepare to expand systematically the faculty, the curriculum, and the student body. In 1963 the board of governors initiated legal action to eliminate the racial exclusionary clause from William M. Rice's charter and to enable the university to charge tuition. Between 1961 and 1966 Rice undertook its first Five Year Plan of academic expansion; this resulted in the construction of two new laboratory buildings (Ryon and Space Science), two classroom buildings (Herman Brown and Sewall), and three new residential colleges (Margarett Root Brown for women, and Lovett and Richardson for men) between 1965 and 1971. Allen Center, an administrative office building, and a major addition to the Fondren Library were completed in the late 1960s.

The architecture of the 1960s contrasts with the exuberant expansionary spirit of the university. The buildings were, with one exception, works of modern architecture, most designed by Houston architects who had worked on the campus in the 1950s. Unlike Rice's modern architecture of the 1950s, that of the 1960s seems formulaic and disconnected to the sites where it was built. Because these buildings did not disrupt the scale of the campus, and because they were sited, finished, and externally detailed so as not to conflict with the campus setting, they did not inflict the sort of damage that the Fondren Library, the Rice Gymnasium, and the Rice Memorial Center had. Yet with the suburbanization of campus space that began in earnest in the late 1950s, these buildings represented a collective loss of energy and intensity.

The major exception was the one "traditional" building, Sewall Hall, completed in 1971 next to the Administration Building and across the Academic Court from the Physics Building. The donor, Blanche Harding Sewall, had stipulated that Sewall Hall reflect the design of Cram's Physics Building. The architects, Lloyd, Morgan & Jones, adhered to this directive with diligence. Rather than designing a stylistic pastiche, they produced a building whose composition, detailing, and spatial planning matched the quality and care of Cram, Goodhue & Ferguson's.

Two years elapsed between the time of President Pitzer's resignation to become president of Stanford University and the installation of a successor. The board of governors sought to name William H. Masterson, professor of history and dean of humanities at Rice, a Houstonian, and a cousin of the Rev. Harris Masterson, Jr., the founder of Autry House, as president. A rebellion of the faculty and students led to Masterson's almost immediate withdrawal. During this period, two architectural events occurred that might have, but did not, send Rice's buildings in a new direction. One was the construction of two metal-surfaced temporary buildings on the edge of the stadium parking lot. These were the Rice Museum of 1969 and the Media Center of 1970, designed by the Houston architects Howard Barnstone and Eugene Aubry and built by the Houston collectors and patrons Dominique Schlumberger and John de Menil. Dominique and John de Menil constructed these buildings to house the Institute for the Arts, which they brought to Rice from the University of St. Thomas. The two metal sheds embodied what the cultural anthropologist Pamela Smart has called "the Menil aesthetic."[3] Their sense of spontaneity highlighted the lack of energy in most of Rice's buildings of the 1960s.

In 1969–1970 eminent architect Louis I. Kahn prepared a schematic design for an art, architecture, music, and performance complex for Rice. Inasmuch as Sewall Hall, which was to contain the art and art history department and teaching gallery, was under construction and the Rice Museum was completed, the scope of Kahn's commission remains somewhat ambiguous. Kahn's proposal, never executed, was sweeping. He inserted a long string of studio buildings, running from the eventual site of the Humanities Building as far west as Herring Hall, was slotted between the trees Cram, Goodhue & Ferguson aligned to define the south side of the Great Square. Kahn proposed that two performance halls be built where the General Plan called for the Commencement Hall to go. He called for the demolition of the Rice Memorial Center and to replace it with an art museum. He designed a new university center alongside the Rice Memorial Chapel (which was to remain), backing up to the Fondren Library along the second cross-axis. Kahn also proposed that underground parking be built where Baker Hall and the Jamail Plaza were eventually sited. The grandeur of Kahn's scheme seems to have been its undoing, as the board of governors did not ask him to proceed further. What can be deduced from the project is how the scale of Cram's campus, and the landscape armature of the General Plan, inspired Kahn. His scheme implicitly criticized the lack of boldness and vision that characterized Rice architecture in the 1960s.

The Hackerman Years, 1970–1984

The board of governors obtained consensus from faculty, students, and alumni in calling Norman Hackerman, professor of chemistry at the University of Texas at Austin and president of that university from 1967 to 1970, as Rice's fourth president. The student body had increased to 3,000 students. The first half of the Hackerman administration led to completion of buildings planned in the late 1960s. During these years the trustees who had joined Rice's board in the 1940s and 1950s began to retire. Their replacements seemed more aware of the potential that architecture possessed for representing the university's ambitions In 1979 the faculty of the school of architecture and its dean, O. Jack Mitchell, recommended that James Stirling, Michael Wilford & Associates of London—architects who were not Rice alumni—be hired to design the architecture building. The board of governors assented to this choice. The presence of the Houston business-woman and Rice alumna, Josephine E. Abercrombie, as chair of the board's building and grounds committee, lent authority to this decision. That

Stirling & Wilford's addition to Anderson Hall, one of the Staub & Rather buildings, received international recognition on its completion in 1981 alerted the university's authorities to the potential that ambitious patronage had for obtaining public notice. During Mrs. Abercrombie's tenure, which lasted through three university presidents, into the term of Rice's present president, Malcolm Gillis, Rice renewed a level of architectural patronage the university had not ventured since President Lovett's time.

Herring Hall by César Pelli & Associates of 1984 confirmed the board's wisdom in retaining well-known architects to design Rice's buildings. In 1983 the building and grounds committee commissioned Pelli's firm to undertake a Master Plan for Growth. The board asked Pelli to make recommendations for accommodating new construction for reinforcing spatial attributes of the General Plan. Stirling & Wilford and Pelli, with their respective architectural designs, demonstrated the continuing relevance of the General Plan. Both firms made it clear that past divergences from the plan could be reconstructed through remedial planning efforts built into the design of new buildings. Stirling & Wilford revealed the value of rehabilitating an existing building, rather than demolishing and replacing it. Pelli demonstrated that it was possible to generate an architectural language from Rice's buildings that was respectful but not imitative. The impact of the architectural movement called postmodernism, which took shape in the 1970s in reaction to the sterility of mainstream modern American architecture , was especially evident in the interest that Stirling & Wilford and Pelli displayed for renewing the architectural history of Rice.

The Rupp Years, 1985–1993

During the tenure of George Rupp, who came to Rice after serving as dean of the Divinity School at Harvard University and leaving to become president of Columbia University, attitudes and practices regarding architecture and planning at Rice that took shape under Josephine Abercrombie's direction continued. In 1988 Dean W. Currie came from the Harvard Business School to serve as the university's vice president of finance and administration. Working with Mrs. Abercrombie's committee, Currie reinforced the university's support for hiring exceptional architects. The Cambridge Seven of Cambridge, Massachusetts, designed George R. Brown Hall in 1991. Following the lead of Stirling & Wilford's additions to Anderson Hall and Pelli's Herring Hall, the Cambridge Seven's building reorganized a problematic space in the Court of Science in conformance with Cram's General Plan. Alice Pratt Brown Hall of 1991, built to house the Shepherd School of Music and designed by Ricardo Bofill and the Taller de Arquitectura of Barcelona, opened a new sector of the campus, a westward extension of the main axis

Herring Hall; César Pelli, architect, 1984

into what the General Plan had designated the Persian gardens. The campus of Rice and its architecture, especially the Administration Building and Herring Hall, provided the setting for President George Bush to confer with the chiefs of government and state of Canada, France, Germany, Italy, Japan, the United Kingdom, and the European Union when he was host for the 1990 Economic Summit of Industrialized Nations at Rice in July 1990.

The Gillis Years, 1993–present

Rice's sixth president, Malcolm Gillis, had been professor of economics and dean of arts and sciences at Duke University. Although Josephine Abercrombie retired from the board of trustees in 1994, the building and grounds committee, under her successor D. Kent Anderson, maintained the level of patronage she instituted. During the Gillis administration the campus has undergone a sustained building boom. Duncan Hall by the British architects John Outram & Associates, James A. Baker III Hall by Hammond, Beeby & Babka of Chicago, and Butcher Hall by Antoine Predock represent three trends in Rice's architectural production of the 1990s. Duncan Hall, like Bofill's Alice Pratt Brown Hall, is an eccentric building. It situates itself, architecturally, in a discourse on myth and symbol constructed by John Outram. While Outram acknowledges Rice's design heritage, Duncan Hall's connection to its location at Rice seems tenuous. Baker Hall is a neo-traditional building. It represents the end of postmodernism, eschewing interpretation for mimesis. Butcher Hall, in the tradition of Rice's modern architecture of the 1950s as well as Stirling & Wilford's and Pelli's buildings, it encapsulates the idiosyncrasies of Rice's architectural heritage. Rather than confirming tradition thematically, it explores the construction of continuity by making spatial connections with the buildings and landscapes around it.

At the turn of the twenty-first century, Rice University completed a new humanities building in 2000 by Alan Greenberg of Washington, D.C., and has new residential colleges by Machado & Silvetti of Boston and Michael Graves of Princeton under construction. New York architect Robert A. M. Stern is designing a two-building complex for the Jones School of Management. These projects divide along the ideological lines of constructing continuity and stylistic thematization.

Rice University in the year 2000 has 4,300 students and an endowment of $2.8 billion. It has achieved a reputation for excellence based on the caliber of its students and faculty. Its institutional identity is embodied in the campus and buildings. Ralph Adams Cram's architecture and his General Plan were the instruments with which President Edgar Odell Lovett broadcast his own ambitions. By ensuring that the architecture and planning of the institute were, as Rice's diploma reads, "to all high emprise dedicated. . . ." Lovett ensured that despite its distance from metropolitan centers of culture, Rice would have a presence in the world.

1.   Andrew Forest Muir, "William Marsh Rice and His institute," *Rice University Studies*, 58 (Spring 1972): 152.

2.   Ralph Adams Cram, *My Life in Architecture*, Boston: Little, Brown & Company, 1936, 126.

3.   Pamela Smart, "Sacred Modern: An Ethnography of an Art Museum," Ph.D. dissertation, Rice University, 1998, 19, 65, 69.

Entrance One and the Academic Court

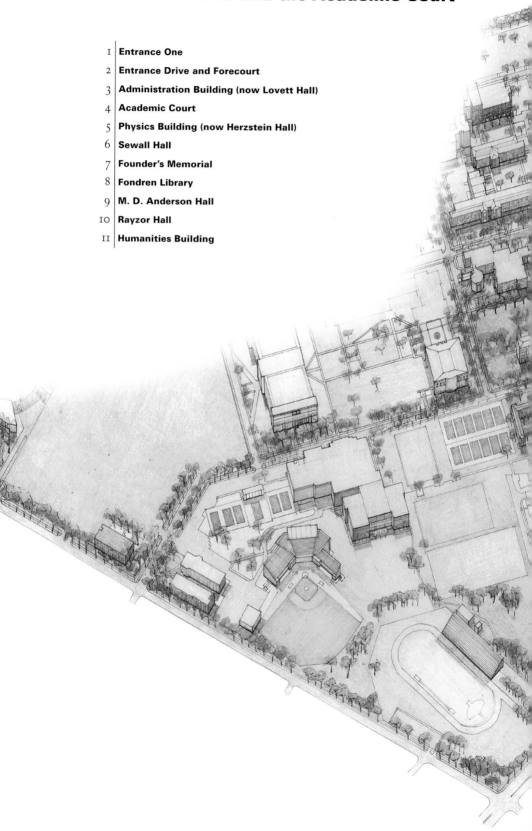

In the impressive sequence of spaces that begins at Entrance One on Main Boulevard, landscape and architecture work together to shape space, direct movement, and frame vision. This spatial sequence is no less an invention than Ralph Adams Cram's neo-Byzantine architectural style. It represents the ability of Cram and his colleagues to envision the transformation of the Texas coastal plain into a park and garden where rhythm, proportion, and measure regulate nature as efficiently and harmoniously as they do buildings.

It took four decades for this landscape to mature and six decades for the architectural components of the Academic Court to be built out. During this period, both the natural and built elements of the landscape were revised. The enclosure of the Academic Court by the Fondren Library in the late 1940s and the suburbanization of plantings in 1960 (and again in 1980) diminished the scope of Cram's vision. Yet this vision was so intensely focused and resilient that it withstood the alterations and digressions that occurred. Visitors' impressions are still apt to be formed by the extraordinary formal consistency of the entrance sequence and the Academic Court rather than by the lapses of history.

Cram (and behind him President Edgar Odell Lovett) shaped attitudes and opinions with his systematic integration of building, site planning, and landscape design at Rice. He constructed impressions of authority, power, and richness that endowed the Rice Institute with an institutional legitimacy it might not have possessed had its setting not stimulated such awe. When the Administration Building was renamed Lovett Hall in honor of Edgar Odell Lovett in 1947, following his retirement, the Latin inscription on the dedicatory plaque—paraphrasing a quotation from Horace translated as "He has built a monument more lasting than bronze"—implicitly acknowledged the fusion of institutional identity and cultural ambition in the architecture and landscape architecture of Rice.

The construction of enduring cultural monuments was of overriding concern to American elites during the progressive era. The sequence of spaces from Entrance One to the Academic Court is historically significant because it gives physical form to this cultural preoccupation and demonstrates how it gave rise to power-filled landscape constructions that exerted ideological authority and shaped public consensus on what was good, true, and beautiful. In Houston, this spatial sequence became a model for creating new landscapes of civic power during the 1920s. It continues today to work its magic on visitors, alumni, students, and faculty, who are apt to experience it not as representing the essence of Houston, as Ralph Adams Cram intended, but as the antithesis of Houston.

1. **Entrance One** *Cram, Goodhue & Ferguson, 1912*

The entry sequence from Main Boulevard at Entrance One demonstrates
Ralph Adams Cram's virtuosity. He masterfully choreographed movement
and perception in order to imbue the raw space of the Texas coastal plain
with shape and meaning. When Rice opened in 1912 the brick gate piers
and the screen walls that link them stood in isolation. Amur River privet
hedges in front of the gate piers had been installed (in a slightly different
configuration than the hedges of dwarf yaupon now there), but there was
no Main Boulevard and no allée of live oak trees. The allée that now
canopies the entrance drive consisted of saplings. Only to the left of the
drive was there a stand of trees. Otherwise, the landscape was open, a condition that persisted for several decades while Cram's plantings matured.

The screen wall and gate piers are arced in plan, delineating a
space at Main and Sunset Boulevard where none had existed. They constitute a landmark, announcing the presence of the university. They beckon
visitors in, disengaging them from Main Boulevard and reorienting them to
the ideal, planned space of the university campus inside the wax leaf ligustrum hedges that ring the campus. The yaupon hedges in front of the gate
piers fill up empty space with their green mass, giving shape to the diago-
nals and arcs of Cram's planning geometry. Their clipped tops raise the
horizon line of the flat site, creating a new, artificial layer of horizontal space
that introduces the themes of spatial gradation and layering. These themes
are elaborated in the wall and piers. They are built of rose-colored brick,
founded on a stepped, double-level base course of pink Llano granite.

Entrance One

Integrated into the base course of the gate piers are rounded, protruding granite wheel guards. The upper zones of the piers and walls are striated with courses of oversized brick laid in Flemish bond with thick mortar joints, imbuing the wall surfaces with rhythm and measure (although this is obscured by the fig ivy that blankets most of the wall surface). Limestone shields bracketing the main gate exhibit the totem of Rice, the owl of Athena. Heralder, Pierre de Chaignon la Rose of Cambridge, Massachusetts, designed these shields, incorporating chevrons from coats of arms he traced to families named Houston and Rice with the classical Athenian emblem of wisdom.

This description implies the steps by which Cram, Goodhue & Ferguson used architecture to systematically configure Rice space and sys-tematically integrate the phenomenal and the ideological. The architects externalized the underlying geometry of the campus plan with architecture and artificially manipulated nature. They built Cram's Byzantine stylistic references into the detailing of the granite and brick gate piers and screen wall using materials indigenous to Texas: the Llano granite was quarried in Llano County, near Austin, and the brick was made from clay deposits along Buffalo Bayou in Houston. With deft sleight-of-hand, they designed an asymmetrical screen wall that reads as symmetrical (Main Boulevard counts as the third, virtual, gateway). In the coded language of heraldry, they conjoined civic identity and a mythic symbol of wisdom. The con-struction of "Rice-ness" as a fusion of the exotic, the indigenous, and the aspiring is posited at the university's gateway, establishing the themes that are subsequently developed as one proceeds through the campus. The present lanterns replace Cram, Goodhue & Ferguson's simple globe-shaped light diffusers.

2. Entrance Drive and Forecourt

Cram, Goodhue & Ferguson, 1912; Robert F. White & Associates, 1960

The entrance sequence begins at Entrance One, and is structured in stages that transform the approach to the Administration Building into a ceremo-nial procession. Cram, Goodhue & Ferguson specified that southern mag-nolia trees be planted just behind the gate piers, followed by double rows of live oak trees planted twenty-five feet on center for approximately 800 feet. Installed by the Houston nurseryman Edward Teas, these trees imposed on the landscape what it lacked in its natural state: a grandly scaled sense of rhythm and measure. As the canopies of the live oaks matured, they trans-formed the entrance drive into a tunnel of directed movement and vision. Today, this tunnel tightly frames a vista of the Sallyport, the arched passage that penetrates the Administration Building. Lamp standards specified by

Entrance Drive and Forecourt

Cram, Goodhue & Ferguson punctuate the allée of oaks. Flanking the drive-way are brick-lined paths surfaced with decomposed granite, imbuing the landscape with the rosy coloration of the brick and granite wall and piers. In late February and early March Formosa azaleas planted between the trees are in full flower. Their neon intensity elevates the reddish coloration of the granite and brick to a higher pitch. With the magnolia trees and the allée of oak trees, the azaleas create "Southern-ness," an attribute Cram sought to build into his architecture.

The entrance park is a grove of academe. Its combination of ordered street trees framing more random planting, its subtle integration of landscape with materials associated with the buildings, its shade, its cool, and above all its strongly formed space exert a mythical appeal. In an ideo-logical way these attributes create a material and natural sense that, inside the hedges, one has entered an enchanted landscape removed from the profane city. They empower the imagination to interpret Rice as an ideal landscape, commencing a narrative structure of high idealism—President Lovett's term, which he incorporated into the text of Rice's diploma, was "high emprise"—with which the architects and their client sought to give the campus coherence and consistency.

The tree canopy is so thick that it is not until one emerges from beneath it that the Administration Building comes fully into view. This point of transition marks the next stage in the entrance sequence. Today, a broad, flat plane of grass surfaces the forecourt in front of the Administration Building. This was installed in a major reconfiguration of the campus's landscapes in 1960 in place of Cram's original forecourt, a gravel-surfaced expanse that was only half the width of the Administration Building. From the time Rice opened, the gravel forecourt was used as a parking lot, subverting the ceremonial experience of entering the campus but offering a necessary space the General Plan did not make provision for. The grass forecourt, designed by Robert F. White, professor of landscape architecture at Texas A&M University, frames the full 300-foot long expanse of the Administration Building. White moved the southern magnolia trees from behind the gate piers to this new green to stand in isolation, displaying huge, aromatic white flowers that bloom each May. Flatness and openness, the characteristics of the landscape as Cram found it, were put to service here to construct a forceful contrast with the oak tunnel, impressing upon first-time visitors the power and magnificence of Cram's exotic architecture. This experience is enhanced today for those arriving by car, as White's grass forecourt moves vehicles off-axis and forces them to circulate around the edge of the court. The General Plan called for the construction of buildings facing the north and south sides of the forecourt (today the location of parking lots screened by hedges). These were to be the women's residential college (the only one) to the north (to the right of the Administration Building), and the Fine Arts Building to the south (to the left of the Administration Building): expansive, symmetrical, two-story buildings configured around interior courtyards.

3. Administration Building (Lovett Hall)

Cram, Goodhue & Ferguson, 1912

The Administration Building, which the trustees of the Rice Institute named for Edgar Odell Lovett in 1947, is Ralph Adams Cram's masterpiece at Rice and one of the most important buildings of his career. It teaches an inexhaustible stream of lessons about what architecture can accomplish.

The Administration Building was designed to operate at a variety of scales. It works visually at the scale of the landscape, thanks to the reciprocal relationship that exists between its symmetrical east elevation, the grass forecourt, and the allée of oak trees through which it is approached. It also operates at this scale because in the atmospheric intensity of Houston, its rose coloration reads as a distinct horizontal layer between the green layer of the forecourt, the softer gray-green of its copper-surfaced roof, and the blue of the sky. Cram, Goodhue & Ferguson subtly emphasized horizontality in the layered construction of the building's exterior walls, progressing upward from a granite plinth, to a thick base course of Ozark marble, to the increasing prominence of brick, striated with courses of oversized brick, before concluding in a frieze of turquoise and malachite-colored tiles above the arches of the loggias. As an architectural component of the constructed

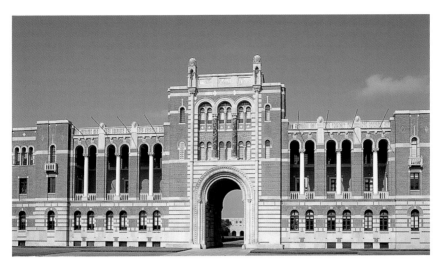

Administration Building (Lovett Hall)

landscape of the General Plan, the Administration Building engages the main axis, which penetrates the building through the monumental arched portal that Cram called the Sallyport, a term derived from military architecture. The Administration Building defers to the continuity of the axis as the maker of Rice space by arching over it to facilitate its forward progress.

At fifty feet in width, the Administration Building is very narrow, given its 300-foot length. President Lovett insisted that all buildings at Rice be designed for maximum permeability by the prevailing southeast breeze; therefore, the long, thin, bar shape of the Administration Building became normative for the configuration of Cram, Goodhue & Ferguson's buildings. To inhibit a perception of exaggerated linearity and flatness, the architects layered the front elevation with advancing planes and receding voids, articulated with shadows. The arched, double-height loggias to either side of the Sallyport harbor wells of shadow. These give a sense of volumetric depth to the long, planar front of the building. The thickness of the Sallyport establishes another layer of depth, one that breaks through the building mass to daylight. The subdivisions of the east front of the Administration Building architecturally reiterate the measured rhythms introduced at Entrance One and amplified in the allée of live oak trees along the entrance drive.

The architects externalized interior spatial arrangements to induce (and rationally justify) variations in the east front of the Administration Building, animating the long facade. This introduces a second level of scale gradation, most evident in the outermost bays, where triple-arched windows rise up between the first and second-floor levels. These rising windows introduce a sense of dynamic movement keyed to the organization of interior space. They are stationed at the landing level of secondary stairs in each wing of the Administration Building. The shadowed, two-story-high loggias with their green-veined white Brocadillo marble columns mark the two most important interiors in the Administration Building. To the north (right) of the Sallyport, the loggia opens off the original location of the institute's library on the second floor. To the south (left) of the Sallyport, the loggia opens off a two-story high room, the Faculty Chamber, originally a convocation hall. In the tower above the Sallyport, behind the powerful screen of purple Negallo marble columns, are third and fourth floor spaces. The third floor originally contained the board of trustees' meeting room and the fourth floor President Lovett's office suite. Today both spaces are used as administrative offices. Note that the narrow, arched, third-floor window to the left of the central bay is fitted with a grilled screen instead of a steel-framed casement window, qualifying the symmetry that gives the east front of the Administration Building its solemn authority.

Cram, Goodhue & Ferguson used facing materials to give the Administration Building a third level of scale gradation that enables it to project a sense of monumentality. The pavement of pink granite slabs immediately in front of the Sallyport, which runs inside the Sallyport, imparts a sense of material density and durability that is translated into the detailing of the wall surfaces, with their Byzantine layering of stone and brick. At close hand, the rosy hue underlying the pale gray surface of the Ozark marble is apparent. The Ozark marble blocks are largest at the bottom of the wall, where they step up in two stages from the narrow granite plinth. The blocks decrease in size as the wall rises and they are intersected with courses of sand-struck brick. The selection and detailing of building materials contributed to the reiteration of proportional order in the landscape. The orchestration of materials, decoration, and iconography reinforces the centrality of the axis; the richest parts of the building cluster around the main axis. Following the preface and introduction afforded by Entrance One, the main drive and forecourt, the Administration Building constitutes the opening chapter of Cram's narrative.

The meanings that this narrative is supposed to convey seem rather fragile, probably because they are so blatantly fictitious. Cram provided no explanatory key to the iconography, so visitors are left to speculate as to how systematic the narratives were intended to be. Yet meaning was a critical concern to President Lovett and his architects. *The Book of the Opening*, a three-volume work published to commemorate the dedication of the Rice Institute in October 1912, contains a chapter by President Lovett entitled "The Meaning of the New Institution." The seamlessness that Cram, Goodhue & Ferguson's architecture and site planning exhibit was essential. Beauty, wonder, and awe had to so captivate onlookers that they would demand that the story continue.

The Princeton art historian, E. Baldwin Smith, in two books published in the 1950s, *Architectural Symbolism of Imperial Rome and the*

Administration Building (Lovett Hall)

Middle Ages (1950) and *The Dome* (1956), characterized the architectural components visible in the Administration Building—columns, cornices, and arches that construct symmetrical frames—as symbols of power drawn from the iconography that identified gods, heroes, and kings in classical antiquity. The architecture is representative of the "idea" of Rice University. It constructs "Rice-ness" in historically allusive codes.

At the entrance to the Sallyport, the marble cornerstone of the Administration Building, installed in March 1911, is inscribed with a passage in Greek from Eusebius of Caesarea, the Byzantine churchman and biographer of Constantine, *The Book of the Opening* translates this quotation as "'Rather,' said Democritus, 'would I discover the cause of one fact than become king of the Persians.'" Ancient dedication to scientific discovery and indifference to status (a favorite theme of Progressive era rhetoric), filtered through a Christian source, were layered into the choice of this inscription. Cram directed Pierre de Chaignon la Rose to research medieval Byzantine inscriptions so that the lettering of the cornerstone would be "authentic" rather than classical-era Greek lettering. The shield of Rice and the shield of Texas join it. Note the proliferation of Texan Lone Stars in the column capitals and keystones.

The rolled soffits of the inset arches framing the Sallyport are filled with architectural sculpture executed in a medieval Byzantine style. Most

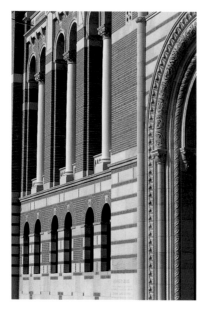

Detail, Administration Building (Lovett Hall)

distinctive are the corbelled heads that uphold the innermost arch. These are two of the four classmen; the other two uphold the west arch, facing the Academic Court. Each figure represents a different class: the senior with his mortarboard and tassel on the east face and the foolish freshman on the west face are the most identifiable. This whimsical collegiate iconography constructs Rice identity in a more pointed way than the historically allusive sculpture. The figures build in tradition, around which neophytes bond on the basis of a new, in-group identity instilled as part of the ritual of Rice's freshman "O-Week" orientation.

Nomenclature is layered into this process of constructing identity. The name "Sallyport" was assigned to this monumental vaulted passage from the time it was designed. By virtue of naming, it became not simply a generic space but a specific, symbolic place on the Rice campus. The Sallyport is a second gateway to Rice, reiterating the landmarking function of the screen wall at Entrance One. It directs visitors' access to the center of the Rice campus, where the story begins. It also identifies the Administration Building, by extension, as a city wall, which must be penetrated to gain access to the heart of the community.

Upon approaching and entering the Sallyport, visitors are shifted back onto the main axis. The spatial definition of the axis changes, however, as it penetrates the Administration Building. Space constricts at the ground plane (the Sallyport is nineteen feet, four inches wide) and is projected vertically upward (the vaults are thirty feet high). The west-facing arch of the Sallyport—looking into the Academic Court toward the Founder's Memorial—frames a vista of the sky and the ground plane that seems to emphasize their immeasurable expanse. Cram used architecture to pay homage to the natural setting that so impressed him when he first visited Houston, yet which his General Plan so insistently reshaped. The stone-lined surfaces of the Sallyport give the space acoustic resonance. Even at the level of sound, Cram, Goodhue & Ferguson constructed place-specific perceptual characteristics. The architects' ability to create variety within unity, an attribute that critics recognized in them, was brought into play in the Sallyport as they concentrated visitors' awareness at this stage of move-ment along the main axis. For instance, they stationed Breccia Paradiso marble colonnettes between first-floor windows in the Sallyport, riveting visual attention on their heavily abraded surfaces.

Cram had hoped that in some future phase the Sallyport's vaulted ceiling could be surfaced with decorative tile work. Within the arch formed by the vault above the triple-arched stair windows there are inset tile roundels. These roundels were fabricated, as was all the exterior and inte-rior decorative tile work on the Administration Building, by Henry Chapman Mercer and the Moravian Pottery and Tile Works of Doylestown, Penn-sylvania, one of the most important art tile studios in the United States in the first decades of the twentieth century. The wall-hung bronze light fix-tures with their milk-glass diffusers were designed by Cram, Goodhue & Ferguson. The steel casement windows, fabricated by the Hope Metal Casement Window Company of Birmingham, England, remain in place. Note at the inside corners of the Sallyport how the overlapping intersection of wall planes is resolved to form a rich layering of surfaces. In the Gothic tradition of building, in which Cram worked, this sort of conjunction main-tains the clarity of the individual planes while demonstrating how they cohere to shape space volumetrically.

At the west edge of the Sallyport, visitors can continue along the main axis into the Academic Court or they can turn into the pair of vaulted passages that Cram called "cloisters." His use of monastic terminology to characterize these arcaded outdoor passages represents another semantic layer of "community"—one that was not ultimately adopted in everyday use at Rice. However until 1949, when the library moved out of the Administration Building, students socialized casually in the cloisters and the Sallyport during the school day.

In the cloisters Cram, Goodhue & Ferguson articulated hierarchies of use with their organization of space. At Entrances B and C (the two entryways flanking the Sallyport), the cloister bays through which visitors approach the paneled oak entrance doors are solidly walled with exedras (the concave wall surface opposite the entrance doors) and capped with domical ceiling vaults. The use of curved space is meant to arrest pedestrian movement along the cloister walkways and mark the points of entry to what were the two most important spaces in the building, the faculty chamber at Entrance B and the library at Entrance C. Walking into these exedral bays from the Sallyport, a noticeable change in acoustic resonance occurs, underscoring the singularity of each space. The precision with which Cram, Goodhue & Ferguson orchestrated perceptual changes in a continuing sequence is apparent as one walks into the long run of the cloister. Eight bays, ceiled with plastered groin vaults of Guastavino tile construction, run to either end of the Administration Building. Each bay is eleven feet six inches square in plan and eighteen feet high at the apex of the vault. In conjunction with the massive, load-bearing columns of Llano granite supporting the cloister arches, the vaults impose an authoritative frame for surveying the landscape of the Academic Court, which, until construction of the Fondren Library in the late 1940s, was completely open. The paving of the cloister walks with brick framed by marble stretchers reiterates the proportional composition of the building's stone and brick wall surfaces as well as the square-sectioned space of each vaulted bay. The marble lintels framing the heads of the basement windows and the marble sills of the first-floor windows, which curve up at the edges to receive the jambs, reinforce the sense of substantiality that the Administration Building radiates. Walking past these openings, one is conscious of the depth of the wall and how depth implies structural durability and institutional permanence. Proximity to the building's surfaces make one aware of how Cram, Goodhue & Ferguson embedded the ideological attribute of "permanence" into their construction and the extent to which construction was both a material and an ideological activity. Given the insistence with which the architects reinforced every architectural move, it is amazing to experience the unobtrusiveness of their layers of detailing.

The cloisters not only frame views of the adjacent landscape, they construct a one-point perspective view along their length, which repeats the type of vista constructed at the entrance allée and the Sallyport. Repetition of the one-point perspective conditions visitors to internalize this point of view, which Cram used over and over to spatially compose the coastal plain and civilize it. It is the inventive variations that Cram, Goodhue & Ferguson devised to prevent this repetition from becoming monotonous that, in historical perspective, seem so admirable.

The cloister columns terminate in capitals carved with figural sculpture. Four of the twelve column capitals are carved with intertwined serpents and birds. Four more are carved with portrait faces representing fifteen European men (and Thomas Jefferson) identified in *The Book of the Opening* as "founders, leaders, and pioneers" of fields of knowledge related to literature, science, and art. Four more capitals feature playful collegiate icons of the 1912 period: the bookworm (in Rice terminology, the "weenie"), the cheerleader, and the football player (the "jock"). The alternating high-mindedness and humor the capitals exhibit construct a Rice identity that is intellectually ambitious *and* self-deprecating. The portrait heads and all of the most demanding carving on the Administration Building were the work of Oswald J. Lassig, an immigrant Austrian stone carver. Lassig was a member of the crew of stone carvers recruited to work on the first buildings at Rice. Discovering his special abilities, John A. Roberts, the superintendent for the general contractor William Miller and Sons, promoted Lassig to the role of architectural sculptor.

Near either end of the cloisters are Entrances A and D, which lead to the secondary stairs lit by the rising arched windows on the east front of the Administration Building. Looking up inside these stairways, one sees the plastered undersides of the stair treads. Here, as in Cram, Goodhue & Ferguson's other buildings at Rice, the "negative" exposure of construction provided economical surface articulation. Note the doorplates of the interior doors closest to Entrance A, with their intertwined peacocks. Cram, Goodhue & Ferguson designed not only the hardware and lighting fixtures of the original buildings but the furniture, although very little of the latter survives. The architects designed the cloister light fixtures, with their elongated glass diffusers.

Entrances B and C are more richly finished internally. All of the first-floor spaces in the Administration Building are ceiled with vaults (almost all those in office spaces are masked by suspended acoustical ceilings installed in 1964 when the building was centrally air-conditioned). The floors of the first and second-story vestibules are paved with intricately patterned compositions of Moravian tiles and plaques of Verde Antico and Cippolino marble. The stairs connecting the first and second floors at Entrances B and C are notable for another instance of ingenious "negative" detailing: the handrails are continuous curved-section slits let into the marble-cased wall of each stairwell so that no projecting handrail is required.

The second-floor library space no longer exists. It is now the president's office and has been subdivided into a suite of rooms. At Entrance B, the university's welcome center is located on the first floor. Here visitors may obtain information about Rice. Above it (but not generally accessible to visitors) is the faculty chamber, now the Founders Room. In 1970, this beautifully proportioned two-story room was remodeled by the New York interior decorator William Pahlmann for use by Rice's board of governors as meeting and entertainment space, though Pahlmann's trash-and-treasure approach to furnishing and finishes was not consonant with the dignity of the space. The Founders Room was partially remodeled to serve as a conference room where President George Bush welcomed six heads of state and government to the sixteenth Economic Summit of Industrialized

Administration Building (Lovett Hall)

Nations at Rice in July 1990. The faculty chamber still awaits full restoration of its original architectural nobility. Above the entrance vestibule is a third-floor level musicians' balcony overlooking the faculty chamber.

The stair at Entrance C leads to President Lovett's office suite in the fourth-floor tower (also not accessible to visitors). This suite retains two fireplace hoods designed by Cram, Goodhue & Ferguson as well as the panoramic vista that Lovett had of his domain. No president of Rice since Lovett has chosen to walk up four flights of stairs, however.

The west elevation of the Administration Building regulates the design of the Academic Court. The three levels of scale visible on the east façade of the Administration Building operate here as well, but the design is completely different. The 300-foot length of the building determines the width of the Academic Court. Its symmetry responds to the thrust of the main axis and is reciprocated in the symmetrical organization of the Academic Court. The Brocadillo marble columns that rise above the cloister columns rhythmically mark this symmetry at the scale of the landscape. Within the big-scale frame the columns provide, the organization of the building's interior is registered in the disposition of openings. To the north of the Sallyport (the left) the second-floor library and third-floor classrooms are indicated by the line of French doors screened with bronze balcony rails and the line of double-arched windows above. To the south (right) of the Sallyport, there is a running arcade of triple-arched windows separated by colonnettes of Norwegian rose marble at the third floor level, above more widely spaced pairs of French doors at the second-floor level, signaling the presence of the faculty chamber inside. Inset within the first-floor cloister, the size and sill-level of windows change to distinguish room use. As with the colossal columns, the frame is regular, the interstices variable. While on its east front, the base of the Administration Building is solid and the upper zone is opened with loggias, on the west front the base is opened up with the cloister arcades and the upper zone is solidly walled. This reversal gives the Academic Court side of the Administration Building a more accessible feeling, dialectically identifying it as the "inside" face of the building.

Like the east front of the Administration Building, the west front emphasizes gateway symbolism. The monumental arch and the marble columns, surmounted by terminal blocks inset with panels of dark, varie-gated Vert Tyrios marble, cause the Administration Building to figure in the landscape like an elongated Roman commemorative arch. Not only is this symbolism tied to the act of entering the Academic Court from Entrance One, it has been ritually linked to graduation since the university's first com-mencement in 1916. During President Lovett's administration, commence-ment was held in the Academic Court, with graduates receiving their diplomas from the president in front of the Sallyport, which became a sym-bolic point of departure for reentering the city and the world.

There is abundant programmatic iconography on the west front of the building. To either side of the Sallyport are stone panels of draped female figures in high relief, identified as *science* and *art*. Modeled by the New York sculptor C. Percival Dietsch and carved by Oswald Lassig, they bear inscriptions by Aristotle and Plotinus. Spaced between the French doors on the Faculty Chamber wing are three marble tablets. Representing *letters, science,* and *art,* the tablets contain relief portraits of Homer, Newton, and Leonardo da Vinci and inscriptions from Pindar, the Book of Job, and (under da Vinci) President Lovett. Lassig also carved the tablets.

Decoding the Administration Building makes one aware of Cram's, and Lovett's, architectural ambitions. In addition to facilitating the activities that occur within it, the building symbolically performs the narratives Lovett and Cram constructed to give Rice University historical legitimacy and cultural authority. It constructs a "tradition" of architecture for Houston. It is a visual encyclopedia of scientific knowledge, a compendium of allegor-ical symbols, and a comic "bestiary" of student life. The Administration Building is a powerhouse. It sets the precedent for and regulates all that is to follow.

Academic Court

4. **Academic Court**

Cram, Goodhue & Ferguson, 1912; Robert F. White & Associates, 1960

Cram, Goodhue & Ferguson conceived the Academic Court—which the
Administration Building, the Physics Building, Sewall Hall, Anderson Hall,
Rayzor Hall, and Fondren Library face—as an Italian garden. In the General
Plan, it was to be 500 feet long, centered on the main axis, and extending to
what is now the front of the Fondren Library. At that point, triple rows of
live oak trees, whose vestiges can be seen on either side of the library build-
ing, were to have carried the line of building façades facing the Academic
Court westward another 650 feet, bounding what the architects called the
Great Square. Buildings were to have stepped back behind the triple rows
of live oaks, as the humanities building and Herring Hall do. The Great
Square, as seen from the Administration Building, was to be defined by the
massed canopies of trees and the dark reservoirs of shade beneath them.
Cram, drawing on Goodhue's general plan scheme, masterfully deployed
nature to build at the scale of the landscape and control the westward pro-
gression of the axis in a way that buildings could not have done adequately.
Cram and Goodhue evoked Thomas Jefferson's design of the University of
Virginia, where Jefferson opened one end of the lawn of his academical
village to a vista of the distant landscape. Although Cram, Goodhue &
Ferguson had no Blue Ridge Mountains to work with, they paid homage to
the immense scale of the Texas coastal plain by constructing one-point
perspectival frames that expanded outward to encompass ever widening

cones of vision. The controversial decision to build the Fondren Library across the main axis in 1946 foreclosed this extraordinary vista.

In its present form the Academic Court reflects the remodeling of 1960 that simplified Cram, Goodhue & Ferguson's landscape design. Until then, those walking through the Sallyport of the Administration Building were diverted off axis onto a pair of walks surfaced with decomposed granite. These framed a central landscaped island containing a parterre of Cape Jasmine hedges which burst forth each spring around Commencement time with exaltingly perfumed gardenia blossoms; four additional layers of Amur River privet hedges flanked the central parterre of Cape Jasmine. The light standards in front of the Administration Building mark the alignment of what had been an outer pair of walks parallel to the central pair. The outermost sidewalks in front of the Physics Building and Sewall Hall preserve original alignments. Along these are the Italian cypress trees shown in Cram, Goodhue & Ferguson's earliest renderings of the Administration Building. Houston's clay soil, colloquially known as "gumbo," is singularly inhospitable to Italian cypresses. Despite massive sub-surface intervention, the trees must be replaced constantly. Japanese yews were substituted for the cypresses in 1962, but cypresses were reinstalled in 1980. Cram, Goodhue & Ferguson wanted a reflecting basin where the central parterre was located. As late as 1913, in their rendering of the Physics Building, they showed a long reflecting basin there, bridged by cross walks. However, President Lovett had vetoed reflecting basins in 1910 because he feared they would provide breeding grounds for mosquitoes.

As historical photographs make clear, the original inscription of parallel walks, hedge parterres, Italian cypress trees, and building facades projected the alignment of the main axis westward. The redundancy of parallel east-west lines represented Cram, Goodhue & Ferguson's effort to fill up the empty space they had to work with. The hedge parterres constructed a new, "natural" datum that elevated the horizontal plane to waist level, investing the flat landscape with depth, just as Cram, Goodhue & Ferguson invested the walls of their buildings with depth. A central reflecting basin would have introduced an additional layer of "negative" depth through its pattern of reflections when seen at a distance. The cypress trees projected the rhythm and measure of the facades of the Administration and Physics Buildings into the landscape. The systematic integration of landscape and building constructed a new sort of space, in scale with the landscape but possessing a sense of direction, depth, proportion, and, by inference, purpose, lacking in the campus site's prior condition.

The cross-axis originating at Entrance Three intersects the main axis in the Academic Court. This alignment was originally marked by a street. The street was eliminated in 1959, in part because through-campus automobile traffic generated by the Texas Medical Center was resulting in

Academic Court

morning and afternoon rush hours in the Academic Court. As with the replacement of the central Cape Jasmine parterres with a broad central walkway of exposed aggregate concrete on axis with the Sallyport, so the simultaneous elimination of the cross street and its replacement with grass suburbanized the Academic Court. The Academic Court was further streamlined in 1980 when the privet hedges were replaced by symmetrical pairs of single-layer hedges of dwarf yaupon. As such changes illustrate, once the architects' original multi-layered spatial structure begins to be vitiated, the coastal plain reasserts its monotony and the rhythmic proportioning of space that Cram, Goodhue & Ferguson constructed is drained of its power.

The Academic Court constructs Rice space through ritual occupation, in terms of both everyday and ceremonial uses. Photographs document the Baccalaureate ceremonies held in front of the west face of the Administration Building and the annual spring Garden Party that President and Mrs. Lovett staged. In 1960 Commencement was moved to the forecourt in front of the Administration Building but in 1985 it was returned to the Academic Court. The casual daily occupation of the Academic Court is symbolized by the diagonal paths through the grass between sidewalks and—a phenomenon that began in the 1980s—Houston brides having their wedding photographs made there.

5. Physics Building (Herzstein Hall)

Cram, Goodhue & Ferguson, 1914

The Physics Building was the first building to be built after the opening of the institute in 1912. Cram wanted to reserve the Academic Court for the liberal arts. President Lovett planned to initially emphasize science and engineering in the institute's curriculum, and he insisted that the Physics Building be built facing the Academic Court. This occasioned another display of architectural virtuosity. Cram, Goodhue & Ferguson constructed multiple identities for the Physics Building related to its proximity to different sectors of the campus. The Physics Building exhibits the architects' dialectical-material approach to the construction of architectural meaning.

The long south elevation of the Physics Building faces the Academic Court. The architects treated this as the building's honorific face and as an extension of the Administration Building; they engaged in a perceptual sleight-of-hand to assert the dependence of the Physics Building on the Administration Building, and, simultaneously, the Physics Building's autonomy. The Physics Building complements the Administration Building by forming one arm of a U-shaped figure. The arms (Sewall Hall forms the corresponding arm) embody the idea of the "headship" of the Administration Building and enclose the east end of the Academic Court, so that the building group works at the scale of the landscape.

The three bays at the west end of the front of the Physics Building give it the extra "weight" it needs to hold down its end of this U-shaped building group. However, these bays upset the symmetry of the front of the Physics Building, which Cram, Goodhue & Ferguson asserted when they placed twin Venetian Gothic pinnacles—rising above the roof line at either end of the cloister run—to frame the center cloister arch. And indeed, this emphasis was intentional, as the architects signaled by making the arches step down in height on either side of the central arch, which is marked by a projecting marble balcony with a pair of stone owls poised on its rail. Cram, Goodhue & Ferguson had it both ways: the Physics Building asserts its independent identity through symmetry even as it is integrated into the larger building group through asymmetry.

This dialectic also regulates the use of materials and ornament on the building. The base course and piers of the Academic Court facade are Tennessee marble banded with brick laid in Flemish bond with thick mortar joints. Figured colored marbles are used for the spandrel panels beneath second-floor windows, the colonnettes between second-floor windows, and

Physics Building (Herzstein Hall)

inset plaques and discs, most flamboyantly in the vertical fields of purple Breccia marble beneath the Venetian pinnacles. Marble is used to emphasize the perceptual layering of horizontal and vertical. It even articulates interior spatial organization. Note how the panels of dark Negallo marble beneath the second-floor windows graduate in height as the window sills step up. This change indicates the presence of lecture halls on the second floor containing stepped seating platforms. The windows get smaller as the platforms step up but, thanks to the marble insets, the aperture remains the same size, preserving the rhythmic uniformity of the facade. Cram, Goodhue & Ferguson integrated practicality and historical decoration with equal ingenuity: the Venetian pinnacles originally contained the extract registers through which the laboratories were ventilated.

    The cloister of the Physics Building feels different than the Administration Building's cloister. The arched cloister bays are fourteen feet long but each bay is only nine feet, four inches wide. They are narrower and more vertically elongated. Moreover, the ceilings are not vaulted. Instead, they reveal the underside of the concrete-cased, steel-framed second-floor structure. Through changes of proportion and material, and by revealing constructional surfaces, Cram, Goodhue & Ferguson articulated the subordination of the Physics Building to the Administration Building. Three entrances to the building open from the cloister. At the west end, where the cloister terminates in a delicately detailed, wall-mounted limestone drinking fountain, the floor of the cloister steps up to a secondary entrance.

    The principal entrance is set in an alcove, several steps above the partially exposed basement. A rotated square panel of Verde Antico marble

Detail, Physics Building (Herzstein Hall)

in the brick paving of the cloister walk marks this bay. The entrance alcove is framed with an arch and ceiling vault. Above the arch is a marvelous field of glazed tile, executed by Mary Chase Perry and the Pewabic Pottery Company of Detroit. With Henry Chapman Mercer of the Moravian Pottery and Tile Works, Perry ranked as one of the foremost American tile artists of the early twentieth century. To either side of the principal entry doors are a pair of apsidal niches let into the brick walls of the alcove. People standing in each niche, with faces to the wall, can communicate in whispers, since acoustic properties facilitate the transmission of sound inaudible to those standing in front of the doors. Here again, Cram, Goodhue & Ferguson built-in a ritual action that, through repetition, constructs a "tradition" passed on from class to class during freshman "O-Week" orientation.

Opening the paneled oak doors of the principal entrance (the door pulls are scaly dragons), visitors enter a vestibule and stair hall. The vestibule is ceiled with a Guastavino tile vault. Here, unlike the Administration Building, the cohesive tiles are exposed. Mary Chase Perry executed the polychrome tile roundels embedded in the ceiling. At the Physics Building, the iconography refers to the physical sciences—a practice that initiated an iconographic program developed in subsequent buildings, especially those for scientific disciplines, in which the decorative detail is keyed to the discipline. The main stair is set into a triple arched aperture. The design of the vertically elongated stilted arches appears to have been derived from one of the buildings at the medieval monastery of St. Luke of Stiris. The bronze lamps illuminating the stair feature bronze owls.

The lateral corridor to the right of the stair indicates, with its very plain finishes, the architectural character of Cram, Goodhue & Ferguson's interiors. Despite their buildings' rhetorical architecture, their interiors were economical and austere. Note the glass transom panels above interior doors. These could be opened to facilitate airflow when the door was closed. Where the lateral corridor intersects another corridor, turn left and exit through the double wood doors to enter a rear cloister ceiled with Guastavino tile vaults.

This cloister was originally called the "museum cloister" because it is aligned alongside a one-story segment of the Physics Building originally designated as an apparatus museum. The Physics Building breaks apart here into three separate blocks. Cram, Goodhue & Ferguson subdivided most of their Rice buildings into long, narrow rectangular bars to ensure good ventilation. The museum cloister links the portion of the Physics Building facing the Academic Court to its two-story rear wing, which contains the 400-seat physics amphitheater.

The architects detailed the physics amphitheater wing less richly than the Academic Court front of the building. Brick predominates and the building stone is limestone rather than marble. However, the limestone sculptural decoration (especially the carved owls in the upper reaches of the gabled east face of the amphitheater block) emphasizes the special status of this portion of the Physics Building. For several decades the physics amphitheater was the institute's largest assembly hall and thus a space of campus- and community-wide significance. The amphitheater interior is one of the most significant historical spaces on campus. It is a classic academic lecture hall, with tier upon tier of seats rising up beneath the exposed pine roof trusses.

The north side of the amphitheater contains a separate entrance portal, accessible from the campus loop street. The portal is marked by a carved stone pediment and pairs of sculptural relief plaques flanking the doors (note that mayhem is transpiring in one, while in another a wise old sage wags his finger at a student who seems to be dozing off over his reading assignment). To the left of the entrance bay are the high-set arched windows of the amphitheater, capped by a parapet that masks the tile roof. To the right of the entrance bay, there are windows at the first and second floor levels, the parapet is dispensed with and the eaves of the tile roof overhang the wall. Cram, Goodhue & Ferguson make differences in the interior spatial organization of this portion of the building the basis for their architecture. They construct a spatial narrative that registers nuances in use and volumetric configuration. The building seems to be telling a story about itself and the activities that transpire within. Even an outside entrance to the basement, on the west side of the one-story museum wing, occasions an architectural flourish: an arched bridge spanning the basement stair well. What is impressive about this technique is the tectonic discipline with which the architects controlled their narrative. Their vignettes, often tied to ordinary circumstances of use, never seem cloying or meretricious.

Moving past the amphitheater along the campus street, the difference in treatment between the back of the physics amphitheater and the back of the main block of the Physics Building is evident. So is the fact that, architecturally, these are the "backs" of both portions of the building. Cram, Goodhue & Ferguson constructed this aspect of the Physics Building to identify it with an intermediate group of science buildings, to be developed where the cross-axis from Entrance Three intersects the campus loop street behind the Physics Building. In the General Plan, the double rows of live oak trees that line this street stop three trees beyond the west end of the amphitheater (as they do on the ground). The trees were then to have made right angle turns and outline a rectangle of open space centered on the intersection of the cross-axis and the street. The back of the Physics Building outlines the southeast corner of this intended cross court, the Chemistry Building, diagonally across the street from the Physics Building, bounds the northwest corner, and Anderson Hall the southwest corner.

The back elevation of the Physics Building was accorded the least ornament, in order to make the transition from the Academic Court to this cross court. However, to distinguish ever finer degrees of transition, Cram, Goodhue & Ferguson wrapped the Academic Court façade around the narrow west end of the Physics Building's main block and continued it on the three westernmost bays of the "back" of the building, facing the never-developed cross court. Here, where the landscape has not been systematically integrated with building shape, the clarity of external space begins

Rear elevation, Physics Building (Herzstein Hall)

to dissipate. In the late 1950s, and again in the 1990s, trees were planted along the street to continue the Cram firm's oak allée, bisecting the center of the cross court. Lost is the degree of surprise and complexity—such as the transformation of an allée into an open space, and the front/back reversals—Cram, Goodhue & Ferguson were capable of constructing.

The Physics Building demonstrates the conceptual rigor of Cram, Goodhue & Ferguson's dialectical approach to architectural design as well as their extraordinary ingenuity. Its ability to embody contradictory conditions (such as a facade that is symmetrical *and* asymmetrical) and perform multiple identities without sacrificing coherence is remarkable. The Physics Building is simple and straightforward where such attributes were wanted (such as its flexible internal organization; it still houses the department of physics and space physics and has never been added onto) but complex where complexity was required: socially constructing a university.

The Physics Building was planned in consultation with President Lovett's star faculty recruit, Harold A. Wilson, a British physicist. Wilson had been a professor of physics at McGill University in Montreal when Lovett lured him to Houston. In 1924 Wilson left Rice to become Kelvin Professor of Physics at the University of Glasgow. The next year he returned and he taught at Rice until his retirement in 1947.

In 1998 the Physics Building was named Herzstein Hall in honor of Ethel A. and Albert H. Herzstein. Herzstein, a Houston investor, was an officer of the Big Three Welding Equipment Company.

6. Sewall Hall *Lloyd, Morgan & Jones, 1971*

Sewall Hall

Blanche Harding Sewall (class of 1917) was a Houston matron who studied art in the architecture department at Rice. An artist and a supporter of Houston artists, Blanche Sewall was so beguiled by Cram's architecture that she and her husband, the wholesale grocer Cleveland Sewall, commissioned Cram & Ferguson to design their Spanish-style house in River Oaks, completed in 1926. Near the end of her life Mrs. Sewall, by then a widow, provided the funds to build Sewall Hall as a memorial to her husband. She stipulated that the building complete the east end of the Academic Court and that it match the Physics Building. The Houston architects Lloyd, Morgan & Jones rose to this challenge. Although at the time it was completed Sewall Hall was perhaps more respected than admired, it vindicates Mrs. Sewall's wisdom in maintaining the integrity of Cram's architectural vision and the tact and skill of Herman Lloyd (Class of 1931) and Arthur E. Jones (Class of 1947). The architects showed great tact and skill in maintaining Cram's constructional and material standards while incorporating programmatic requirements quite different from those of the Physics Building. The 117,000 square-foot, concrete-framed building contains the departments of art and art history, anthropology, Asian studies, and psychology in the schools of humanities and social sciences.

In 1929 Cram & Ferguson had prepared preliminary sketches for a three-story classroom building on this site, which repeated the spatial rhythms of the Physics Building but took considerable liberty with the disposition of openings within its bays. Unlike the 1929 Cram design, the north-facing Academic Court front of Sewall Hall virtually duplicates the front elevation of the Physics Building. Lloyd, Morgan & Jones did not attempt to repeat Cram, Goodhue & Ferguson's nuances and idiosyncrasies, or invent new ones. They substituted limestone for Tennessee marble as the building stone, there is less decorative marble work on Sewall Hall, and the range of colored marbles is not as extensive. However, the architectural sculptor Ross M. Correll reproduced the relief discs of paired peacocks on the piers of the cloister connecting Sewall Hall to the Administration Building, the carved frieze above the arches of this cloister, the pierced marble screen inset into the arches of the endmost cloister bays, and even the Venetian Gothic pinnacles.

Lloyd, Morgan & Jones deftly planned the building's interiors, minimizing conflicts between 1970s' requirements and the thin, pre-

Sewall Hall

air-conditioning floor plates of the 1910 era. Mirroring the location of the ex-apparatus museum in the Physics Building is the Rice University Art Gallery in Sewall Hall, which opens onto a stone paved courtyard alongside the Administration Building.

What is not apparent from the Academic Court is that Sewall Hall has two underground floors. At the time it was planned, the board of governors thought it prudent to build densely at the center of the campus without exceeding the height limits established by Cram's buildings. At the southwest corner of Sewall Hall, in the rectangular space created by the building's L-shaped plan, is a basement-level courtyard. This is accessible from outside stairs that lead down to the art department's sculpture and printmaking studios.

The back wing of Sewall Hall (the counterpart of the physics amphitheater) is five stories high: three above ground and two below. Containing faculty offices and seminar rooms, it exhibits a sense of dignity and decorum that did not always prevail in the era of 1990s neo-traditionalism. Sewall Hall defers to the narratives Cram, Goodhue & Ferguson constructed sixty years before it was designed. It fulfills Cram's conviction that future generations would adhere to the General Plan if it was sufficiently compelling. Sewall Hall's success derives not from its stylistic conformity, but from Lloyd, Morgan & Jones's ability to produce a generously proportioned, well planned building within the framework Cram devised.

7. Founder's Memorial

John Angel, sculptor; Cram & Ferguson, architects of the base, 1930

The Founder's Memorial is William M. Rice's tomb. His ashes are deposited in the base of pink Llano granite. Designed by Cram & Ferguson, the base rises from a low plinth and is encircled by a seating bench. Cram prevailed upon President Lovett and the trustees to commission the British-born sculptor, John Angel, to model the seated bronze statue of Rice in 1927. Angel was chief sculptor at the Cathedral of St. John The Divine in New York, for which Cram had been consulting architect since 1911.

Founder's Memorial

The 2,000-pound statue depicts Rice draped in a great coat and seated on a Greek *klismos*-type chair. The statue's right arm is thrust forward holding an open book. The left arm hangs over the side of the chair, the left hand grasping an unfurled scroll containing a relief map of the General Plan. The four faces of the base contain relief carvings of the Seal of Rice University, flanked by torches of knowledge, and the seals of the states of Massachusetts, Texas, and New York, where Rice lived. Cram & Ferguson detailed the granite base structure with understated authority. The proportioning of the planes and profiles, the incision of the corners, and the subtlety with which the upper part of the base is battered inward contribute to its sense of dignity. The density of the granite offsets the patinated depth and folded surfaces of Angel's statue.

The Founder's Memorial was one of the few structures that the architects permitted to straddle the main axis, underscoring its exceptional status. Astride the organizing axis of the campus, it gives physical form to what anthropologists would describe as Rice University's foundation myth. In tersely coded symbols, it narrates William M. Rice's personal story (the state shields), his intentions (the open book), and the shape in which his intentions took form (the General Plan). That Cram, Goodhue & Ferguson's master plan should be the icon of Rice University underscores the ideological significance Lovett and Cram assigned architecture in constructing an identity for the university. William M. Rice is presented as a benevolent patriarch dispensing knowledge, not a nineteenth-century Yankee entrepreneur. The monument's appeal is mythical not discursive; its purpose is not to present history but to construct identity.

Ritual use "naturalizes" these mythical associations by absorbing the statue into the actions and stories of Rice. It is not the ceremonial laying of wreaths at Homecoming that accomplishes this operation but spontaneous student actions, such as crowning "Willie's Statue" with pumpkins, shaving cream, T-shirts, and hats. In April 1988, a group of students, using portable technology, pivoted the statue during early morning hours. When students, staff, and faculty arrived for the first classes of the day, the Founder was looking toward Fondren Library, for the first time in 58 years. The administration was not amused, but the story is still told.

The General Plan proposed numerous sites for sculpture, most of them punctuating prospects along axes. Yet the Founder's Memorial was the only work of heroic figural sculpture installed on campus. It was one of only two such statues, typical of the progressive era, to be erected in Houston—the other being Enrico Cerracchio's bronze equestrian statue of Sam Houston at the entrance to Hermann Park. The communal act of remembering—and the construction of communal identity that this presupposes—did not appeal in Houston. By the time Rice University embarked on its post-World War II building boom, the civic art style of the progressive era had lost its momentum. The impulse to conserve, memorialize, and mythify seemed out of step with the optimism that characterized postwar expansion. The Academic Court displays the repercussions of this change in attitude in the most radical and controversial departure that the university made from the General Plan.

8.   Fondren Library

Staub & Rather, William Ward Watkin, consulting architect, 1949;
Staub, Rather & Howze, 1968

The General Plan failed to provide space for a university library. President Lovett directed the architects not to affix labels to the buildings shown on the General Plan drawing, and therefore it is not clear which building facing the Great Square was to have been the library. The drawing shows the buildings aligned at the west end of the square as long, thin bars with centered cloister bays. In 1927 Cram & Ferguson prepared a schematic plan for a library building, of which only a perspective drawing of the exterior survives. The front of this building could have fit the Great Square site. But a five-story book stack wing, projecting from its rear, would seem to stretch too far back to have fit the shallow site alongside the Great Square.

In 1932 Cram & Ferguson completed the Edward L. Doheny, Jr., Memorial Library at the University of Southern California in Los Angeles. So closely did it resemble Rice's Administration Building that the Doheny Library could well be the Cram library building Rice never received. Since the "temporary" library space in the Administration Building had been

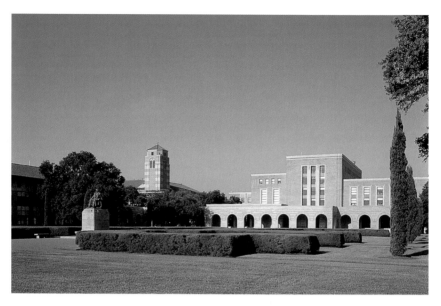

Fondren Library

judged inadequate as early as 1921, the need for a purpose-built library was acute by 1940, when President Lovett and the trustees consulted Cram & Ferguson and William Ward Watkin about a library building. By this time a new site for the library had been chosen, near the head of the second cross-axis, where George R. Brown Hall was built in the 1990s. Cram & Ferguson prepared at least a site plan for a building at this location. Watkin, however, was authorized by the board of trustees to make schematic plans for a library at this site, an expansive two-story building symmetrically configured in a U-plan around a forecourt.

Between 1941 and 1945 James A. Baker, chairman of the board of trustees since 1891, died, as did two other trustees and Ralph Adams Cram. President Lovett, who tried to retire in 1941, succeeded in doing so in 1946. At the same time several elderly members of the board of trustees retired. Therefore by the beginning of 1946 Rice was guided not only by a new president, William V. Houston, but trustees representing a new generation of Houston's business elite.

In late 1944 Rice participated with eleven other American universities in a joint committee to plan new libraries. The chair of the committee, John E. Burchard, librarian of the Massachusetts Institute of Technology and an architect, was the author of a special report prepared for Rice. Burchard forcefully argued for constructing Rice's new library on the site of the Fondren Library and belittled the notion of designing a symmetrically composed building that conformed stylistically to the Administration and Physics Buildings (the only two buildings then facing the Academic Court). Burchard's recommendation reflected a consensus among Rice faculty that the library should not be built at what seemed an unreasonable distance from other academic buildings. William Ward Watkin seems to have been isolated in his advocacy of the cross-axial site. It is tempting to read into this controversy a rejection by the younger generation of Rice faculty of the proprietary attitudes of the old guard. Watkin was designated consulting architect for the Fondren Library and two other postwar academic buildings. His involvement in their design, however, was minimal.

John F. Staub, Houston's great eclectic architect, designed the Fondren Library. Staub had been a student of Cram's at MIT in the early 1910s during the period in which Cram, Goodhue & Ferguson were designing the early buildings at Rice. Staub made his reputation as an architect of houses and had designed the houses of two of the new trustees. The Fondren Library was the most significant of four buildings Staub and his partner, John Thomas Rather, Jr. (class of 1919), produced at Rice in the postwar period. It exhibits what Staub described as "balanced asymmetry" in its exterior composition, his response to Burchard's admonition against "warping the functioning of the plan" to produce external symmetry. Staub & Rather used a combination of brick (slightly more tawny than the Buffalo Bayou brick Cram used, but close in tone) and Tennessee marble to face the exterior of the reinforced concrete-framed building and the adjoining M. D. Anderson Hall.

The library was configured as a block rather than as the elongated bar shape Cram, Goodhue & Ferguson favored. This shift in form reflected the fact that the library was the first building at Rice to be built with central air-conditioning. The narrow, five-story central block of the Fondren Library is fixed on the main axis. To its right is a three-story wing that is five bays long. To its left is a four-story wing, only two bays long, with a tall first-floor reading room shifted forward of the rest of the wing. Until the south-side cloister was added to connect the Fondren Library to Rayzor Hall on the left, the windows of this reading room looked directly out to the Academic Court. The relief plaques depicting the invention of writing, by sculptor Herring Coe of Beaumont, Texas, were originally installed above these windows. When the cloister extension was built, four of the reliefs were reinstalled over the cloister's entrance arches; the fifth wound up around the corner. The cloister extension masks the exercise in projection/recession Staub engaged in, and leaves the front of the library, as the urban designer Drexel Turner observed, looking like it had been "'warped' to produce an asymmetrical result."

The Fondren Library symbolized the authority of knowledge and of the university as a community of learning. The displacement of emphasis from the Administration Building to the library this entailed mirrored the redistribution of what had been presidential authority among the trustees and the faculty after President Lovett's retirement. Yet it is hard not to compare the Fondren Library unfavorably to the Administration Building. The library lacks the complexity of the latter (and of Staub's houses of the 1920s and 1930s). Staub established his compositional theme with building mass, layering the edges of the central block as though it were built up of overlapping planes. The Fondren Library made no use of voids or shadow to elaborate this theme volumetrically. The face brick is laid up with some ornamental bonding patterns, but the wall surfaces are not animated like Cram's. The nuances of proportion and composition that allow the Administration Building to work at a multitude of scales are also missing. This is especially noticeable inside the cloister. Although the library cloister is bigger in size than that of the Administration Building, it is spatially inert, merely a passage to walk through. It does, however, frame a vista of the Chemistry Lecture Hall to the north, constructing a connection not anticipated in the General Plan.

In terms of its architectural conception, the Fondren Library was reactionary. It did not construct a postwar vision of what Rice was to become. The narrative it did construct was a reaction against what Rice had been. Architects of Staub's and Rather's generation, trained in the 1910s and extremely skillful at adapting historical models for contemporary uses, did not make the transition to postwar modern architecture, with its rejection of historical models, easily. It is instructive to compare the Fondren Library with Staub & Rather's Batts, Benedict, and Mezes Halls at the University of Texas at Austin of 1951. Lining one side of the university's principal axis, the South Mall, they were fit into restrained classical envelopes projected by the Philadelphia architect Paul P. Cret in his 1933 development plan for the university campus. They carry through the spatial and architectural principles of the Cret plan for the University of Texas rather than blunting them.

Cret had designed the Fondren Library in 1938 at Southern Methodist University in Dallas, built with a gift from the Houston oil driller W. W. Fondren, a co-founder of the Humble Oil & Refining Company, and his wife Ella Cochrum Fondren. (It was Mrs. Fondren and her children Susie Fondren Trammell (Class of 1927), Catherine Fondren Underwood (Class of 1928), and Walter W. Fondren, Jr. (Class of 1929), who in 1946 gave Rice one million dollars for construction of the library in memory of W. W. Fondren.) Cret had become a pivotal figure in American architecture in the 1930s because he demonstrated how buildings based on historical models could be simplified and streamlined in ways that, to traditionalist architects, seemed modern. The Fondren Library belongs to this historical episode. It demonstrates, however, that the critical architectural consensus sustaining Cret's program of streamlining traditionalism no longer held sway in the postwar era. It also demonstrates the failure of Rice's faculty and trustees to understand the magnitude and profundity of Lovett's and Cram's ambitions. Construction photographs reveal that the triple rows of live oaks intended to define the Great Square were still so young that they did not yet shape this opening. The university uprooted two of the three rows on the north side of the library site to permit the building's erection. The Fondren Library represented a social vision of Rice that seems, in retrospect, much more cautious, conservative, and conscious of limits than that encoded in the General Plan.

Staub & Rather's interior planning of the 126,000 square-foot building was meticulous. Yet here again, uncertainty at the outset led to problems that plagued the building. Fredericka Meiners reported that the Rice faculty committee in charge of planning the library wanted to preserve the open stack arrangement that Rice's first librarian, Miss Alice Dean, had instituted. However, the committee also wanted the library to be able to be converted to a closed stack arrangement should there be any conflict between public and academic use of the library. Therefore, the bookstack floors are only eight feet high. When, after fifteen years in operation, the Fondren Library needed to be expanded, Staub, Rather & Howze added the 99,000-square-foot Graduate Research addition (1968), carrying the low ceiling height of the 1949 building's stack wing over the center's much larger floor plates. Staub, Rather & Howze's initial drawings of the addition show a passage through the library, with entrances from the Great Square on the west as well as the Academic Court on the east, though this was not carried out because of internal planning conflicts. The Graduate Research addition turned a long expanse of blank brick wall toward the Great Square to prevent the stacks from being flooded with west light. Most significantly, the Graduate Research addition defined the Great Square as the university's back yard, cut off from any sense of spatial connection to the Academic Court. The failure to understand the long-term consequences of building in what the General Plan designated an open space is what makes the postwar rejection of the General Plan so regrettable.

César Pelli's Master Plan for Growth of 1983 renewed the call for a west entrance to the library. By then it was clear that the Fondren Library again required expansion. In 1998 Shepley, Bulfinch, Richardson & Abbott of Boston were commissioned to plan a radical reconstruction of the library. This will entail demolition and replacement of the Graduate Research addition, the construction of a public passageway through the building connecting the Academic Court and the Great Square, and a refacing the 1949 building by Venturi, Scott Brown & Associates of Philadelphia in association with the Shepley firm. Yet unless university officials take account of the fact that the library outgrows its quarters in twenty-year cycles—and that because the back of the Graduate Research addition is already close to the second cross-axis, there will be repeated pressure for the Fondren Library to expand across this axis, disrupting cross-campus movement the way the 1949 building truncated movement and vision along the main axis—the Fondren Library will continue to reproduce the consequences of its initial misplacement.

9. M. D. Anderson Hall

Staub & Rather, William Ward Watkin, consulting architect, 1947;
James Stirling, Michael Wilford & Associates with Ambrose/McEnany, 1981

Anderson Hall, which houses the school of architecture, was Rice's first post-World War II building. Although designed in conjunction with the Fondren Library, it was rushed to completion to provide urgently needed classroom space for the humanities, which were still concentrated in the Administration Building. J. T. Rather, Jr., designed the two-story building. Rather, who served on Rice's board of governors from 1954 until 1957 and on the board's committee on buildings and grounds until his death in 1968, was the first architectural alumnus of Rice to be commissioned to design one of the university's buildings. This practice was to prevail for thirty years. Anderson Hall was built on the site of Tony Martino's rose garden. Salvatore Martino, a Sicilian immigrant, was Rice's head gardener and groundskeeper from 1913 until his retirement in 1949, when he was succeeded by his nephew Anthony G. Martino, who held the position until his retirement in 1974. In the 1920s "Big Tony" began cultivation of a cutting garden here. Martino was notorious for jealously guarding access to his blossoms. Woe to the student whom he caught plucking a flower without permission.

Anderson Hall was named for the Houston cotton exporter Monroe D. Anderson, an executive of Anderson, Clayton & Company. In 1942 the charitable foundation Anderson endowed gave Rice funds which enabled the institute to buy half of the Rincón oil field in Starr County, Texas. The trustees of the M. D. Anderson Foundation stipulated that the institute use

M. D. Anderson Hall

income from the Rincón field to construct a building in Anderson's memory. Tom Rather designed a straightforward two-story classroom building (with a three-story bay at its east end), organized on a double-loaded corridor plan. Faced with the same combination of Tennessee marble and buff brick as the Fondren Library, the concrete-framed building is composed in an L-plan figure with the library, mirroring the relationship of the Administration and Physics Buildings. A tall, arched cloister connects Anderson Hall and the Fondren Library. Anderson's interior finishes were substantial but plain. Rather was responsible for the inset angled doorways to classrooms, still visible in the first-floor corridor of the original section of the building. As with Staub's Fondren Library, Rather's Anderson Hall was architecturally conscientious and respectful. It got the job done under difficult circumstances of postwar material restrictions (the roof trusses are of wood). The detailing of the exterior is self-effacing but assured. There is even a note of Cram's collegiate whimsy at the entrance portal on axis with the Founder's Memorial. Vertical lines of cylindrical fluting, when a finger is drawn rapidly down them, produce a sound that has earned this bit of decoration the name "frog wall." Neither Anderson nor Fondren aspired to be great architecture. Anderson embraced an ethos of living within limits—of getting the job done—that tried the patience of a generation of American modern architects younger than Rather, Staub, or Watkin.

When Anderson Hall opened, the department of architecture, still under the leadership of William Ward Watkin, occupied a portion of the building. During the 1960s, when William W. Caudill was director of what he transformed into the school of architecture, architecture began to claim more space in the building. By the late 1970s it became the sole occupant of Anderson Hall. Rather than sacrifice its Academic Court location for a new building site, the school's faculty and its dean, O. Jack Mitchell, elected in 1979 to remodel and expand Anderson Hall. Mitchell and the faculty prevailed upon the board of governors to commission James Stirling and Michael Wilford of London as architects for the expansion. This set the stage for the university's return to a level of architectural patronage not ventured since President Lovett's retirement.

Stirling & Wilford's Brochstein Wing of Anderson Hall, as well as their remodeling of the 1947 Schnitzer Urban Design Wing, also construed the design problem as one of living within limits. Their results were very different from Staub & Rather's. In historical perspective Staub & Rather's work represents the end of an era, while Stirling & Wilford's represents the beginning of a postmodern reassessment of non-modernist architecture. Stirling & Wilford brought a degree of architectural invention and imagination that equaled Cram, Goodhue & Ferguson's to the task of adding to and expanding Anderson Hall, even though their material resources were more akin to those of Staub & Rather's.

Michael Wilford taught at Rice as a visiting professor from 1978 to 1988, which gave him first-hand knowledge of Anderson Hall and the campus. Wilford and Stirling's interest in architecture as urban design and their commitment to understanding buildings in relation to the architectural history of their sites led them to engage Anderson Hall rather than dismiss it. They critically examined Cram's General Plan and developed the Brochstein Wing to shape exterior space as called for in the General Plan. They keyed the bay dimensions of the Brochstein Wing to the bays of the library cloister, which enabled them to develop through-building vistas that systematically integrate buildings and site in a way that Staub & Rather did only perfunctorily. The exteriors of the Brochstein Wing dialectically invert Rather's compositional scheme: where Rather set flat-headed windows in shallow recessed bays, Stirling & Wilford set arched windows in shallow projecting bays. Because Stirling & Wilford don't call attention to such reversals, their dialectics don't seem contrived. Indeed, their achievement at Anderson Hall was to add to the existing building with such understatement that it is not always clear where the 1940s end and the 1980s begin.

Two interior conditions register externally. One, visible from the west alongside the Fondren Library, is the circular second-floor window *not* centered beneath the peak of the gabled end wall. This reflects the fact that the north side of the Brochstein Wing is lined with design studios, which are deeper in plan than the faculty offices they face along double-loaded corridors on both floors. Because of this asymmetry, the central corridor is not centered beneath the gable—therefore, neither is the window that lights this hall. The second condition occasioned Stirling & Wilford's only modification to the Academic Court front of Anderson Hall: the addition of a conical aluminum and glass skylight above the cloister entrance door. This was their salute to the Venetian Gothic pinnacles atop the Physics Building, as they let light in rather than carrying noxious fumes out. The skylight marks one end of a passage Stirling & Wilford cut through Anderson Hall to connect the Academic Court to the north, or street, entrance to the Brochstein Wing, which is marked by a matching skylight. This concourse was designed in section as a modernist insertion complementing two double-volume spaces Stirling & Wilford added to Anderson Hall: the Farish Gallery and the top-lit Jury Room. When the Philadelphia architect Louis I. Kahn lectured at Rice in 1968, he evoked the ideal space of an architecture school as a campus passage overlooking spaces where students could present their design work. Kahn's poetic image was so compelling that it became the basis for Stirling & Wilford's design of the Anderson Hall concourse. Their ingenious, low-tech sliding wall panels enable the Farish Gallery and the Jury Room to be opened to or closed-off from the concourse, which operates very much the way Cram, Goodhue & Ferguson envisioned the cross cloisters as work-

M. D. Anderson Hall

ing in their buildings. Stirling & Wilford's use of interior windows fills the building with light, even though studios, classrooms, and offices are all separately partitioned spaces.

Despite alterations (Stirling & Wilford's abrasive interior colors were browned out the first time repainting occurred and a crude opening has been punched through an upper wall of the Farish Gallery), Anderson Hall resonates with energy. With limited means, Stirling & Wilford demonstrated how new buildings could continue to shape campus space in accordance with the General Plan. In their willingness to develop the potential of what seemed like a hopelessly dull and ordinary building they rose to the challenge of reclaiming the university architecturally. They did not construe Rice's architecture as merely a "past," to be rejected (as Fondren Library seemed to do) or copied (as Sewall Hall did), but a "present" to be analyzed, interpreted, and extrapolated, with wit and imagination. They didn't write off everything after Cram, but sought to make a new whole from existing pieces. M. D. Anderson Hall, in its post-1981 condition, constructs a spatial narrative of recovery. It demonstrated the possibility of constructing campus space with the techniques Cram, Goodhue & Ferguson employed, while continuing to invent architecturally. Modern architecture at Rice had done this since the early 1950s, but what set Stirling & Wilford's work on Anderson Hall apart was their enthusiasm for a larger context and their commitment to shaping interior spaces for learning and work that were designed with as much consideration as exterior surfaces.

Rayzor Hall

10. **Rayzor Hall** *Staub, Rather & Howze, 1962*

Rayzor Hall, named for the Houston admiralty lawyer and marine towing company executive J. Newton Rayzor (Class of 1917), the first Rice alumnus elected to the board of trustees and a generous benefactor of the university, and his wife Eugenia Porter Rayzor, is a three-story classroom building occupied by the language departments of the school of humanities. Designed by Tom Rather, Rayzor Hall fills the site designated for a liberal arts classroom building in the General Plan. Its combination of marble and brick facing, its hipped tile roof, and minimal sculptural decoration make it a decent addition to the Academic Court. Decency appears to have been the limit of Staub, Rather & Howze's ambition; the exteriors and interiors of Rayzor Hall are prosaic.

Rayzor was the first building constructed on the south side of the Academic Court. Its crucial site perhaps explains why, architecturally, it is running on empty. Unlike the modern buildings that George Pierce-Abel B. Pierce and Lloyd & Morgan designed at Rice in the 1950s, Rayzor Hall faces what seems to have been construed as the "traditional" center of the campus. The university entrusted its design to Staub, Rather & Howze, whose firm embodied "tradition" in Houston architecture. The lack of energy evident in Rayzor Hall indicates how defensive veteran eclectic architects had become by the 1950s, when the skills and sensibilities they had refined were held in such low esteem by architectural critics that their buildings were dismissed as not being architecture at all. If, in the understanding of the university's building authorities, "tradition" carried more weight in the Academic Court than architecture, their chosen architects seem to have felt that being inoffensive was less risky than aspiring to greatness.

Rayzor Hall represents a dilemma not restricted to Rice. In the 1950s a strong ideological tension existed on many American university campuses between the affirmation of identity and modern architecture; boards of trustees and university administrators were typically more apt to endorse the identity alternative with weak renditions of their pre-World War II buildings than entrust building commissions to modern architects. In its decency Rayzor Hall suggests how the uncritical affirmation of identity can ideologically exclude a critical consideration of the constituents of identity, which is what Lovett's and Cram's buildings were premised on.

11. Humanities Building   *Alan Greenberg, 2000*

The humanities building is a freestanding, three-story annex to Rayzor Hall. It contains 47,000 square feet of space and is of reinforced concrete-frame construction. The building houses the departments of history, philosophy, and religious studies of the school of humanities, the office of the dean of humanities, and special humanities centers and programs. Like the rear

Humanities Building

wing of Sewall Hall, and César Pelli's Herring Hall to the west, it adheres to the alignment of buildings prescribed in the General Plan. It is thin in plan and mitigates the impact of its thickest portion. Framed between rows of live oak trees, the humanities building steps back from Rayzor Hall to parallel the campus's south loop street. This places it in close proximity to the south side of the Fondren Library and results in the development of a sequence of architecturally defined passages and courtyards.

The Washington, D.C., architect Alan Greenberg orchestrates pedestrian circulation with a "slype" (as Cram, Goodhue & Ferguson labeled the open-air passageways they tunneled through their buildings, through which pedestrians could "slip" from one side to the other) to maintain the cross-campus sidewalk connecting the library cloister to Baker College. Greenberg's commitment to maintaining and enhancing existing patterns of pedestrian circulation is indicative of his effort to reinforce identity with his design of the humanities building. The exterior detailing of the building contributes to an explicit narrative of architectural continuity. Greenberg quotes selectively from some of the Cram buildings (the pinnacles capping the slype bay pay tribute to those atop the Physics Building; the manneristically extruded molding on the east stair tower and the tiled semicircular panels above windows can also be seen across the campus loop street on Cram's East Hall at Baker College). His use of precast concrete as decorative panels and his tiered configuration of arched niches on the east stair tower evoke Cram's British contemporary, Edwin Lutyens, whose reputation Greenberg was instrumental in rehabilitating in the 1960s. Greenberg's tower, rising over the courtyard and highly visible from the Academic Court, gives the humanities building visual prominence despite its background location.

The humanities building develops the narrative of continuity spatially. Its height and contours ensure that it sits comfortably alongside Rayzor and the library. The thin floor plate of its office wing indicates that building programs can be accommodated in plan layouts that don't result in interior spaces without natural light. The slype and the courtyards create a layering of outdoor space that for too long has been ignored at Rice and break down the hard distinction between indoor (air-conditioned) and outdoor (humidity) space typical of Rice buildings since the 1960s.

It is Greenberg's stylistic development of continuity that raises questions. Can tradition at Rice be engaged only with buildings that appear to have been designed in the 1920s or 1930s? Do scientific disciplines at Rice merit modern buildings while the humanities and social sciences are compelled to freeze in time architecturally? Greenberg produced an intelligent, responsible, and, on its own terms, inventive design. Yet the humanities building fails to problematize identity as Pierce-Pierce, Lloyd & Morgan,

Stirling & Wilford, Pelli, and Predock do in their Rice buildings. Instead it assumes that identity can be affirmed while pragmatically accommodating the practical issues of building in the twenty-first century, a proposition that many of the scholars who inhabit this building would challenge.

Like Rayzor Hall, the humanities building represents Rice as valuing "tradition" more than critical exploration. Cram's buildings planted the seeds of this dilemma, and even when they were new they were criticized for the fictitiousness of Cram's premises. As the architects who have confronted this problem at Rice demonstrate, it is the quest for greatness, rather than decency, that leads to buildings that explore, criticize, and invent, thereby contributing to making tradition at Rice.

Court of Engineering

Framing Space

The Court of Engineering, at the head of the second cross-axis, is focused on the Mechanical Laboratory and Power House and its architectural symbol, the Campanile. This court was designed to establish the pattern for constructing a similarly conceived court at the head of the second cross-axis, to the west. The spatial contractions and releases that distinguished the first cross-axis from the staged, ever-widening space of the main axis demonstrates the sophistication of Cram, Goodhue & Ferguson's techniques for shaping space on the Rice campus. They associated different sectors of the campus with different spatial rhythms. The episodic spatiality of the first cross-axis was intended to reflect its progress from Entrance Three northward through the Residence Group, the Academic Court, and a cross-court before culminating in the Court of Engineering. Cram, Goodhue & Ferguson designed the Mechanical Laboratory and the future buildings of the Court of Engineering in their "basic" Rice style. The buildings of the Academic Court were more elaborate versions of this type, while the buildings of the Residential Group were the simplest and most "domestic" of Rice's buildings. At the Mechanical Laboratory and Power House one can see how this logic was developed to regulate the design of different sectors of this single, but functionally composite, building. The phenomenon of systematic integration is made evident in Cram, Goodhue & Ferguson's effort to construct continuity by articulating difference.

The generations of architects and landscape architects that followed Cram, Goodhue & Ferguson erased many of the landscape and infrastructural elements that gave the court its sense of strongly defined space. The failure of buildings from the 1940s through the 1990s to shape space in the complex, layered way envisioned in the General Plan was amplified by the removal of Cram's landscape improvements in the early 1960s. The result is suburbanized space: broad, flat lawns; wide, straight sidewalks; freestanding trees of different species; no hedges; no cars. Michael Heizer's epic *45 Degrees, 90 Degrees, 180 Degrees* does not reverse this suburbanizing devaluation of space. Rather, it punctuates it with a late twentieth-century sense of critical monumentality, constituting "an awesome physical presence that creates its own space," as William A. Camfield, Mullen Professor of Art and Art History, has observed.

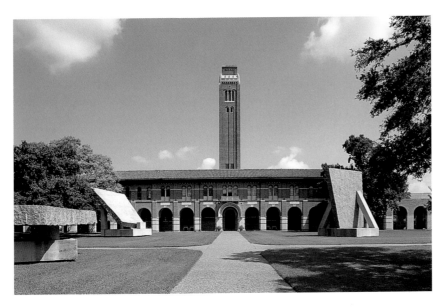

Mechanical Laboratory and Power House

12.　**Mechanical Laboratory and Power House**

Cram, Goodhue & Ferguson, 1912

The Mechanical Laboratory and Power House was one of Rice's four original buildings. The three-part complex is a composite building that serves varied and unrelated purposes. Characteristic of Cram, Goodhue & Ferguson's approach, it projects an image of unity that, on examination, reveals its layered organization.

　　The Mechanical Laboratory is a two-story building that accommodated all the scientific disciplines at Rice until the Physics Building was completed in 1914. It was home to the architecture department until 1925. Behind the Mechanical Laboratory and structurally continuous with it is the Power House, where Rice generated electricity, steam, and refrigeration and distributed these to other campus sites. Today the Power House remains in use as Rice's energy distribution center, although local utility companies supply power. Rising above the Power House is the Campanile, the third component of this group. The Campanile's incongruous mixture of modern industrial function (it was the smoke stack for the Power House) and symbolic image (evinced by its romantic Italian name, although it has never been a bell tower) epitomizes Cram, Goodhue & Ferguson's method for constructing meaning at Rice. They fabricated a narrative of architectural inclusion that assimilated historical typological fragments (such as the medieval Italian *campanile* and the cloister) to modern spatial and servicing requirements. They integrated unrelated uses (such as academic laboratories and power generating and distribution facilities) by developing hierarchies of decorative ornament and figural spaces, which, through graded application, coded the relative standing of each portion within a building complex—as honorific (high status) or servile (low status). They inscribed these hierarchies onto the landscape by aligning building groups on the axes and cross-axes governing the campus's organization. Adhering consistently and imaginatively to these practices, Cram, Goodhue & Ferguson systematically constructed a conservative vision of organic order that used modernity to energize tradition and construct unity while accommodating diversity.

Within the architectural hierarchy implicit in their campus buildings, the Mechanical Laboratory represents the Cram firm's basic Rice style. In contrast to the high style buildings of the Academic Court, the Mechanical Lab is predominantly brick. The piers and walls rise from blocks of Ozark marble set atop a granite base course. Columns and panels of Verona red and Cippolino marble appear, and there is a second-story horizontal belt course of Ozark marble, but sumptuary display is minimal. The lab's south-facing front is composed of brick piers framing arcaded cloister bays. Horizontality is emphasized, rather than balanced by assertions of verticality. The stone belt course is the horizontal datum that regulates continuity within the complex. The low-pitched hipped roof, surfaced with red clay tiles, reinforces this horizontal extension with its continuous, overhanging eaves. The Campanile is the countervailing vertical element, but it is at a remove since it lies behind the Mechanical Laboratory.

The General Plan called for the Mechanical Laboratory to be bracketed by similarly proportioned buildings framing a quadrangular courtyard into which the cross-axis emanating from Entrance Three terminates. As with the Administration Building, the Mechanical Laboratory was designed to work architecturally at a variety of scales. The Campanile operates at the scale of the landscape, projecting the axial, tree-framed approach skyward. The front of the building was intended to control the width of the Court of Engineering; its regulating authority is visible in the subtle gradations by which its centrality and symmetry are unemphatically articulated. There is a balcony above the central cloister bay, on axis with the recessed entrance portal and the Campanile behind, and the bay is framed with freestanding columns and projecting marble bands. A distinction is made between the cloister bays flanking the entrance and the end bays: the center bays receive marble encrustation while the end bays are recessed an extra brick width. Notice how the piers of the central seven-bay register die into corbel tables, the line of decorative arches that runs just below the eaves of the roof in the central bays and contains ceramic tile roundels. (Compensating for their lack of marble, the end bays are treated with exuberant displays of decorative tile work, executed by Mary Chase Perry and the Pewabic Pottery Company.) The dialectics of subtle distinction are brought into play to tone down the Mechanical Laboratory, in comparison to the Administration and Physics Buildings, yet impart an internal architectural mechanism that systematically integrates the Mechanical Laboratory into a larger architectural whole and a unified spatial organization, the everything-in-its-place-and-a-place-for-everything frame of mind that consistently informed Cram's approach to design. As the exemplar of the basic Rice style, the Mechanical Laboratory is the conceptual foundation on which Cram erected the idea of a Rice architecture.

The way in which Cram used likeness and difference to construct a spatial dialectics of meaning can be experienced in the cloister of the Mechanical Laboratory. The proportions of the Mechanical Laboratory's cloister are tall and narrow, as in the Physics Building. But the cloister bays are vaulted, like the Administration Building. One becomes aware here, after visiting the other two buildings, the manner in which Cram, Goodhue & Ferguson associated the idea of vaulted cloisters, through repetition, with Rice, yet gave each building's cloister a distinct feeling. The line of vaults at the Mechanical Lab produces a strongly directed space along the length of the cloister. This space (amplified now by adjoining cloister runs) is intense enough to engage the flat lawn of the Court of Engineering. The lawn is framed between the cloister piers, which must have begun to impose a sense of measure on the campus landscape in the institute's early years. As in Gothic architecture, the piers are stepped in plan, constructing staged layers of depth while declaring the task that each layer performs as it rises to support or to enclose. Behind the screen of piers and arches, the ground floor façade of the Mechanical Lab verges on the picturesque. An episodic array of window and door openings articulates the building's internal layout. To the left of the deep-set, vaulted entrance alcove is a pair of French doors, railed with a shallow wrought-iron balcony that projects into the cloister. To the right is an even more deeply recessed secondary entrance alcove, centered on a wall-mounted drinking fountain set in a vaulted niche. The incorporation of a raised basement means that the interior ground-floor level is several feet above the cloister paving. Therefore, the low basement windows and high-set sills of the ground-floor windows introduce additional levels of scale variation within the Mechanical Laboratory cloister. The layered piers, the depth of openings, and the use of vaulting energize the open-air portions of this flat, planar building, creating perceptible and inhabitable layers that systematically construct ever finer degrees of spatial differentiation in what was, naturally, a flat, treeless landscape. Yet because Cram, Goodhue & Ferguson integrated their production of spatial differentiation as systematically as they integrated their production of surface ornamentation, one's overriding impression of the Mechanical Laboratory is of repetition, continuity, unity, and simplicity.

In plan the building is an oblong rectangle, 200 feet long and forty feet wide. The interior planning is very straightforward. The front doors open into a small vaulted vestibule that is square in plan. The floor is paved with polished tile and the walls are faced with brick. The groin-vaulted ceiling creates arched heads at the tops of the walls. Each arched wall face is decorated with a tile roundel. A pair of arches subdivides three of the four wall faces. In the side walls, one arched bay contains an opening into a cross corridor. Facing the incoming visitor is a brick screen, with the balustrade of the lateral stair expressed as a diagonal that slices through one of the two arched bays. The other arch contains the stair landing. The stair leads up to a cross corridor on the second floor. In the corridor one sees interior windows that once facilitated through ventilation (the back wall of the stair well has blocked-in windows that opened to the out-of-doors before a second-story extension cut off exterior access; these windows provided the only source of exterior light for the first-floor vestibule, which is why it is now lit with fluorescent fixtures). The second-story ceiling of the stairwell is the exposed, gridded frame of the structural concrete slab above, as in the cloister of the Physics Building. Most interior spaces have been repartitioned; the Mechanical Laboratory awaits interior rehabilitation.

A walk around the exterior of the Mechanical Laboratory and Power House explains the joint titular designation and yields demonstrates how the Cram firm constructed meaning through continuity and contrast. Moving around the east side of the building (to the right of the entrance, at the Abercrombie Laboratory end of the building), the narrowness of the Mechanical Lab is evident. The back (north) of the Mechanical Lab contains five bays centered on a back door accessible from an elegantly finished, granite-edged stair. Aligned on the central axis of the Mechanical Lab is the Machine Shop, which originally contained spaces associated with the front (academic) part of the building. The Machine Shop's academic identity was signaled with arched openings and a gorgeous green and gold tile roundel. The pair of stilted arches flanking the central arched portal pays explicit homage to medieval Byzantine architecture. The Machine Shop links the Mechanical Laboratory structurally to the flat-roofed Power House, the industrial part of the complex. Through each of these stages, the continuous stone belt course beneath the second-story windows of the Mechanical Lab maintains a sense of unity.

The east elevation of the Power House (the west elevation is obscured by an addition of 1967) consists of four arched windows set between piers. Random courses of Ozark marble blocks support the lower walls. The only decoration consists of big-scaled tile squares above the window openings. The back (north) face of the Power House is a three-bay enclosure. The center bay, originally the boiler house, is taller than the side bays. Indicative of its non-honorific, industrial identity, the back of the

Power House has no decoration whatsoever. At the lower corners of the walls, only the thickness of the marble blocks facing east and west is exposed. Arched windows (the original, multi-paned, steel-sash awning windows have been replaced with fixed glass in aluminum frames) reveal the servicing technology inside the Power House and its skylit, steel-framed roof structure. The servicing infrastructure of the campus, which otherwise was not given architectural expression, Cram, Goodhue & Ferguson made visible here. Each successive face of the Mechanical Laboratory and Power House displays its position within the hierarchy of honor and service that Cram constructed to give the architecture, and the institution, coherence.

The Campanile is the most ambiguous component in this complex, because it has no visible base. It is always seen from a distance. Since it was built as a smoke stack, it rose from the machine shop, where it could connect to the Power House's central boiler house bay. This distancing per-haps assisted its ideological role, as a symbol of university. In the architects' earliest conversations with President Lovett, they urged that a tower be built to store water, until Frank Ferguson determined that an underground tank was more economical. So captivated were the architects and Lovett with the idea of a tower that Cram, Goodhue & Ferguson earned consider-able good will by finding a practical function that would justify one. Early published descriptions describe the tower as campanile-like. In 1916, when the first Rice Institute student yearbook was published, it was called the *Campanile.* The smokestack's name was typographically upgraded to a cap-ital "C." Like the Sallyport, it found its place as a mythic symbol of Rice.

The Campanile is 140 feet tall. Square in plan, it is sixteen feet, six inches wide, the width of the central bay of the Mechanical Laboratory cloister. Where the tower is set back near the top, a hipped tile hood was originally stationed. This was removed in 1930 when Cram & Ferguson designed the present setback transi-tion, which enhances the tower's verti-cality. Cram, Goodhue & Ferguson accentuated verticality in the way that they incised planes into the wall sur-faces of the Campanile. Shallow inset planes are sunk in two stages into the face plane. Each plane returns in a layer of arches near the summit with an incisive economy that is quite com-pelling visually.

Campanile, Mechanical Laboratory and Power House

The Mechanical Laboratory is of load-bearing brick construction with reinforced concrete floor and roof slabs. The Power House is a steel-framed building. The Campanile is also steel framed; the chimney at its core is of radial brick construction. The Mechanical Laboratory houses the George R. Brown School of Engineering's department of Environmental Science and Engineering and related institutes. The Power House contains the university's central plant.

13. Court of Engineering and *45 Degrees, 90 Degrees, 180 Degrees*   *Michael Heizer, sculptor, 1984*

The Court of Engineering is the quadrangle in which the first cross-axis, which begins at Entrance Three, terminates. The General Plan showed this court bracketed by two U-plan buildings, where the Abercrombie Engineering Laboratory and the Mechanical Engineering Building were eventually built. Each of the U-plan buildings was to be linked by cloisters to the cloister of the Mechanical Laboratory and Power House. As was characteristic of the courts into which the cross-axes terminated, the Court of Engineering was envisioned as being defined by buildings, more so than the Academic Court. The Court of Engineering was not intended to be planted with trees. The cedar elm trees lining the cross-axis stop, as planned, at the point where the cross-axis expands into the court. A street perpendicular to the cross-axis (which survives as the oak tree-lined service alley behind the Chemistry Building) would have marked this point of transition.

Court of Engineering and 45 Degrees, 90 Degrees, 180 Degrees

The Court of Engineering underwent drastic change in 1959. The university replaced the cross-axial street with a wide sidewalk paved with exposed aggregate concrete—an act that eliminated the oval turn-around in front of the Mechanical Laboratory. Hedge rows framing walks on either side of this street and the turn-around were also uprooted. These landscape features had followed the pattern Cram, Goodhue & Ferguson established in the Academic Court by inscribing the flat landscape with redundant lines. The hedges translated lines of movement into volumetric layers, stratifying the site with a secondary horizon. It is indicative of the post-Cram under-standing of campus space as fluid, neutral, and lacking the potential to shape and inform—shared alike by university authorities, architects, and landscape architects—that the Court of Engineering feels as open and unbounded today as it looks in photographs of 1912, despite being enclosed with buildings on three sides.

Arrayed in front of the Mechanical Laboratory are three colossal sculptures by the New York artist Michael Heizer. The Brown Foundation, a Houston philanthropic foundation whose founders included George R. Brown, a trustee emeritus, and his wife Alice Pratt Brown, commissioned these sculptures. Each is a slab of pink Llano granite, the Texas granite Cram, Goodhue & Ferguson incorporated in their buildings. These were quarried from a single exfoliation so that only the edges, not the surfaces, required machine tooling. Heizer's laconic geometric title describes the incli-nations of the slabs, which are supported on reinforced concrete bases and held in place with concrete piers and props. It is not unusual to see classes convened on *180 Degrees* or climbers rappelling down *45 Degrees*.

Heizer's sculptures represent a very different sensibility than Cram's. Yet Heizer engaged the setting materially and thematically. He responded to the recommendation of Alice Pratt Brown that the pieces acknowledge their location in the court dedicated to engineering. Heizer countered Cram's eclecticism with a meditation on materiality, gravity, tech-nics, and the elusive phenomenon of "presence." Although these are phe-nomena that Cram's architecture also engaged, what distinguishes Heizer from Cram is Heizer's lack of interest in figuration, symmetry, and system-atic integration. Heizer did not reject historical association. But he evoked historical resonances with ancient monuments and did not seek to quote specific historical models.

The juxtaposition of granite and concrete emphasizes the natural condition of the granite slabs and the engineered construction of the con-crete bases and props. Like the vanished hedges of the Court of Engineering, *45 Degrees, 90 Degrees, 180 Degrees* translates flatness from the horizontal plane to the vertical plane. These pieces do not seek to restore spatial coherence but to engage the court in a narrative of (dis)conti-nuity, calling Cram's architecture into question. *45 Degrees, 90 Degrees,*

180 Degrees is challenging rather than reassuring. It demonstrates the distance artistic culture traveled in the twentieth century in that its powerful, moving, even disturbing presence exposes the fictitiousness of Cram's architecture and spatial constructions without condemning it.

14.   Abercrombie Engineering Laboratory

Staub & Rather, William Ward Watkin, consulting architect, 1948

Built at the same time as Anderson Hall and the Fondren Library, the Abercrombie Engineering Library is the most assured of Staub & Rather's academic buildings at Rice. It was built with a gift from Lillie Frank and J. S. Abercrombie and their daughter, Josephine E. Abercrombie (Class of 1946). J. S. Abercrombie was a Houston oil drilling contractor and president of Cameron Iron Works, a specialized oil drilling equipment manufacturer and defense contractor. In his design J. T. Rather, Jr., respected the architectural premises of the Mechanical Laboratory and Power House, which Abercrombie flanks. Yet he flattened and linearized the west-facing front of Abercrombie Lab, which has none of the layered depth and narrative subtlety of the Mechanical Lab. He streamlined and exaggerated the horizontality of the Mechanical Lab in Abercrombie's long, flat front. Its unbroken file of square second-story windows and the equally insistent overhanging eave of the low-pitched hipped roof are as redolent of Frank Lloyd Wright's Prairie houses of the 1900s and 1910s as of Cram's Rice buildings. One senses that Rather, though a traditionalist, felt compelled to modernize. Frank Lloyd Wright was at the peak of his popularity in the postwar 1940s. It perhaps speaks to Rather's sense of modernity that the Wrightian architecture he chose to emulate was the body of work Wright produced when Cram's buildings at Rice were new, not the work Wright was doing after World War II.

Rather asserted continuity with Cram, Goodhue & Ferguson's architecture with far fewer reservations than Staub & Rather's Anderson Hall and Fondren Library. The streamlining impulse of American architecture of the 1930s is evident in the reduction of Abercrombie's exterior facing to limestone, up to the level of the first floor window heads, and a horizontal brick band above, abstracting the stratification of stone and brick of the cloister piers of the Mechanical Lab. The arches of the cloister that connect Abercrombie to the Mechanical Laboratory are elegantly proportioned but attenuated. The building's base course of granite, especially the granite terrace at the long, recessed, glass-faced entrance portal with its broad, shallow steps, measures up to Cram, Goodhue & Ferguson's tectonic detailing. The external surfaces are a veneer; the two-story portions of the building

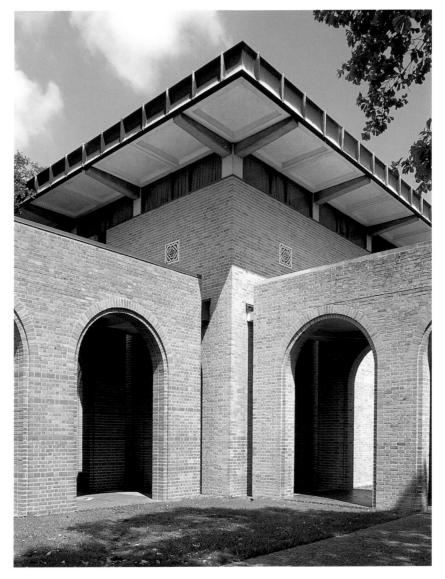

Detail, Ryon Engineering Laboratory

modern architecture of the 1960s but alien to Cram's integrationist ideal. The consequences are spatial laxity, loss of depth, an indifference to tectonic resolution, and the reduction of style to thematic patterning. In the 1960s the American architectural historian Vincent Scully described this reductive process as "packaging." The experiential flatness of Ryon Lab's cloister—evident in the detailing of the piers, the ceiling panels, and the glass curtain wall—is keenly felt when walking into it from the Mechanical Lab's cloister. The building's perfunctory relationship to adjacent outdoor spaces, especially the vehicular service alley on the west between Ryon and the Seeley G. Mudd Building, and the undesigned terrain in front of Ryon, display a lack of foresight on the effects of the lab's siting.

The shortcomings of Ryon were magnified twenty years later in the Mechanical Engineering Building of 1985, a bulky, two-story office and classroom building constructed on a high berm on the west side of the Court of Engineering for the department of mechanical engineering and materials science. This was built with a gift from John L. Cox (Class of 1945), an independent oil operator from Midland, Texas, and a Rice trustee, and his wife Maureen. A neo-traditional style design, the Mechanical Engineering Building lacks Ryon's grace in its composition, proportion, and detail, especially internally where it feels like a speculative office building. Only its east-facing front elevation acknowledges adjacent campus space. Cesar Pelli & Associates addressed the important issue of how this building should be shaped in plan in their Master Plan for Growth of 1983. They recommended that the Mechanical Engineering Building be configured in a T-plan, its back wing aligned with Herman Brown Hall and outfitted with a cloister in order to shape a coherent figural greenspace—which would tie the back of the Mechanical Engineering Building, Ryon Lab, Herman Brown Hall, and the Seeley G. Mudd Building into a new whole. As built, the Mechanical Engineering Building ignored Pelli's recommendation.

This pair of buildings demonstrates that narrowly defining the purview of architecture as providing certain kinds of spaces for certain uses is inadequate. Building blocks that do not engage their surroundings or develop the implications of their sites at a variety of scales are inert. When architecture is treated merely as formal imagery, and when the process of building becomes an assembly of engineered systems that does not require tectonic resolution, what results is the construction of social space where no one seems to be in charge and no one takes responsibility.

16. Chemistry Building (W. M. Keck Hall)

Cram & Ferguson and William Ward Watkin, 1925

The Chemistry Building was the first Rice building for which Cram & Ferguson shared design responsibility with William Ward Watkin. Evidence suggests that Watkin was responsible for the preliminary plans and elevations, which he worked out in 1922 with Harry B. Weiser, professor of chemistry. Watkin's correspondence with President Lovett indicates that Cram & Ferguson made revisions to these preliminaries. Comparing Cram & Ferguson's drawings with those prepared by Watkin, it seems that Watkin re-revised the Cram office's drawings; Watkin's architectural office in Houston prepared the construction documents for the Chemistry Building and administered construction. Watkin's leading role in the design of the Chemistry Building mirrors his professional ascendance in Houston in the 1920s. Watkin collaborated with Cram & Ferguson on the design of Trinity

Chemistry Building (W. M. Keck Hall)

Church on Main Boulevard (1919) and the Houston Public Library in the Civic Center in downtown Houston (1926). He also designed the Museum of Fine Arts, Houston, (1924) and the master plan and initial buildings for what is now Texas Tech University in Lubbock, Texas (1924–26,with Sanguinet, Staats & Hedrick). Watkin's hand is visible in the picturesque profiles of the Chemistry Building, its functionally responsive ground plan, and its stylistic conventionality.

Early published accounts of the Rice Institute's architecture diverge in describing the historic sources for Cram, Goodhue & Ferguson's designs. Cram, Goodhue & Ferguson emphasized Greek Byzantine sources in their accounts, while Watkin favored the Romanesque architecture of northern Italy. The Chemistry Building reflects what seems to have been Watkin's long-standing admiration for medieval Italian architecture. This genre was quite popular among American architects in the 1920s, when it was known as the Lombard Romanesque. In conforming to the Lombard Romanesque style, the Chemistry Building represented a move away from Cram's singular eclecticism toward what perhaps seemed a more up-to-date interpretation of his historical sources during the interwar period.

According to Watkin, the program for the Chemistry Building required much more space than anticipated in 1910, when the General Plan had called for the ground plan of the Physics Building to be mirrored in the other three quadrants of the cross-court centered on the cross-axis that begins at Entrance Three. Instead of the Physics Building's thin parallel bars, Watkin planned the Chemistry Building in a modified E-shape, with the Chemistry Lecture Hall advanced forward of the other two wings to frame the outer edge of the cross-court. Watkin filled the other two wings with stacked pairs of laboratories that face into the prevailing southeast breeze. He skillfully balanced the architectural preference for solid wall planes with the need for maximum ventilation, providing for the latter with bifold steel casement windows in the laboratory wings. As at the Mechanical Laboratory and Physics Building, the tile-roofed tower originally housed a mechanical system for venting the laboratories.

Watkin adhered to the material and ornamental conventions established by Cram, although the exterior of the steel-framed building is more ornate than the back elevation of the Physics Building. The base course and first floor are faced with limestone blocks laid up between courses of oversized brick. From the sill line of the second-floor windows up, the walls are faced with brick laid up in Flemish bond and trimmed with limestone. The Chemistry Building seems to have been the last campus building faced with Buffalo Bayou brick. Watkin and the general contractor, Tom Tellepsen, located the retired foreman of the defunct Sherman Brady Brick Company, who specified the type of clay and firing process used to make bricks for Rice's pre-war buildings. Colonnettes of Verona red, white Brocadillo, and gold-veined Portoro marble are stationed at various points between window openings on all three floors. Watkin liberally used ceramic tile and carved limestone roundels and plaques. The inscriptions and symbols on the tiles iconographically underscored the building's association with chemistry and alchemy, providing a mythico-historical narrative of the sort Cram delighted in. Tile friezes in the portions of the building flanking the tower reproduce the brilliant color combination of turquoise and malachite visible on the Administration Building.

The Chemistry Lecture Hall is more architecturally extroverted than the physics amphitheater. Students enter from the street front of the stepped auditorium. Double stairs lead them up from the street to the brick-vaulted entrance portico in several stages. Watkin, an alumnus of the University of Pennsylvania, evoked the similarly configured entrance to the university museum at Penn of 1893, designed by the Philadelphia architect Wilson Eyre, Jr. Given the Princeton connections of Lovett and Cram, it is tempting to suspect that Watkin took this occasion to pay a sly architectural tribute to his own alma mater.

As at the Administration and Physics Buildings, sculpture was employed to introduce a note of collegiate humor. The cloister alongside the Chemistry Lecture Hall contains a band of reliefs in the capitals of the arch piers. James Chillman, Jr., professor of architecture, art historian, and artist, prepared the cartoons for these reliefs, which were executed by Oswald Lassig. The street-facing arch has the "three fates"—philosophy professor and chair of the committee on examinations and standings Radoslav

A. Tsanoff, dean Robert G. Caldwell, and registrar S. G. McCann—determining the fates of students. (Professor Tsanoff got cut out due to an error in centering the arch.) The companion capital contains a freshman struggling with a dragon labeled "100" representing Chemistry 100. On the side-facing arch, prostrate students pay obeisance to William Ward Watkin on one capital, while on the opposite capital Professor Weiser is depicted as a winged monster crushing a hapless student. Today these icons of academic terror oversee a ritual student gathering unimaginable in the 1920s: the Friday afternoon beer bust at Valhalla, the graduate student pub housed in the undercroft of the Lecture Hall, a tradition since the mid-1970s.

The Chemistry Building represents an intermediate stage in Rice's architectural history, one that never developed fully. Limits in the 1920s and '30s on the expansion of what had seemed to be Rice's enormous endowment meant that the Chemistry Building was the only permanent academic building constructed during the interwar period. To what extent it might have portended a shift in Rice's architecture remains uncertain, since Cram & Ferguson did continue to produce preliminary designs for buildings after the Chemistry Hall was built. In its orientation toward the north campus loop street rather than the axes and cross-axes of the General Plan, it established a precedent followed after World War II. The failure to develop the ring of live oak trees defining the cross-court prescribed in the General Plan made the Chemistry Building's frontality and street orientation more emphatic, an emphasis reinforced by the planting of non-conforming overcup oak trees in a row along the street in front of the building in 1959. Watkin's eclecticism was more relaxed, less intense, and less inventive than Cram's. Because his planning and compositional conventions grew out of the architectural culture that produced the Cram buildings, Watkin's digression was not disruptive. But the Chemistry Building lacks systematic integration with the General Plan. Its spaces are not authoritatively shaped, like those of the Mechanical Laboratory or the Physics Building. Its surfaces lack the dialectical complexity and subtlety of Cram's buildings. The Chemistry Building reveals that Cram's architecture at Rice is not simply about style. It was about constructing an identity grounded in spatial experiences that resonated through a hierarchy of scales.

In 1997 the chemistry department moved out of the Chemistry Building. Between 1998 and 2000 its interior (with the exception of the Chemistry Lecture Hall) was reconstructed to become laboratories for the department of biochemistry and cell biology and the department of bioengineering (Falick Klein Partnership, architects for exterior restoration and interior reconstruction). Reconstruction and restoration were financed with a grant from the William Myron Keck Foundation for Biomedicine and Biosciences.

Anne and Charles Duncan Hall

17. Anne and Charles Duncan Hall

John Outram Associates and Kendall/Heaton Associates, 1996

Duncan Hall is shocking. Its architect, John Outram of London, aspired to
no less. Obsessive syncopated rhythms of black and white glazed brick
mark the building's faces like totemic scarring. These patterns participate in
a complex narrative that Outram developed, based in part on a highly
original reading of Cram's General Plan. His purpose was to construct
what he called a "mythic landscape." Outram confounds expectations. He
is passionately engaged with history, myth, and symbolism, but he is not a
traditionalist architect. Outram's project was to invent iconography that
was thematically and formally consistent with a modern building housing
one of the most advanced scientific fields at the turn of the twenty-first
century, computational engineering research, yet link this iconography to
what he considers to be archetypal mythic narratives. Outram uses architecture to connect the routines of daily life in an academic building containing the departments of computational and applied mathematics, computer
science, and statistics; the Centers for Multimedia Communications, and
Research on Parallel Computation; the Institutes of Computer and Information Technology, and Rice Engineering and Design; and the office of the
George R. Brown School of Engineering to spaces, shapes, figures, and
symbols resonant with ancient, cosmic associations. Duncan Hall is named
for Anne Smith and Charles W. Duncan, Jr. (Class of 1947). Duncan was
president, successively, of Duncan Foods Company and the Coca-Cola

Company. Secretary of Energy during the administration of President Jimmy Carter, he was chairman of the board of governors of Rice from 1982 to 1996.

The three- and four-story, 112,000-square-foot building is shaped in plan like a squat H. Its entrance is aligned on the cloister of the Administration Building. A double-height cloister of deeply embrasured arches faces the campus loop street. The huge, tile-clad hipped roof covering Duncan Hall emphasizes the building's horizontality and weightiness. Outram acknowledged the pier and bay system of Cram's basic Rice style with thick piers and rotund columns spanned by heavy concrete sills and lintels. The exaggerated girth of the piers and columns is meant to indicate their status as hollow mechanical chases, containing the advanced servicing that "supports" the endeavors housed inside Duncan Hall, alongside the building's reinforced-concrete structural frame. Outram designates these columns and piers as his "robot order," fulfilling their service function invisibly and silently inside their striped brick shells.

The black and white glazed brick patterning that stands out on each elevation of Duncan Hall represents four symbols of mythic significance—water, earth, sky, fire—stacked atop each other. The patterning of the south-facing street elevation evokes Mayan symbols; the west elevation, facing the Chemistry Building, Greek symbols; the north elevation, facing the parking lot behind Abercrombie, Renaissance Neoplatonism; and the east elevation, Indian, Iranian, and Islamic symbols. Outram's decoration images the transmission of ideas derived by many cultures from the observation of natural phenomena.

The piers and columns rise to support pairs of projecting precast concrete cylinders that are blue with white swirls and above the cylinders, green precast concrete molding profiles. Outram explicates these elements with respect to the etymological resonance of the words "rafter," "entablature," and "pyre." The rafters supporting the roof structure evoke the image of a raft, for Outram the mythic figure of a water-borne vessel on which settlers arrive in a new found land. The blue cylinders are the substructure of the raft; the green represents its surface decking. Together, these components form the raft/rafter-like boards comprising an architectural table—an entablature—on which the pyramidal hipped roof, its shape and red color evoking a pyre of flames which the settlers bring with them to light the first fire, rises. In Outram's narrative, the raft has been grounded atop a mountain supported by the structural and servicing columns. The raft was propelled onto the mountain top by a flood that has receded, hollowing out the interior of the mountain into the channels of the four-story high collective spaces that bisect Duncan Hall. Outram interprets the stair hall as a cascade, starting from the west side of the building (the end nearest the Chemistry Building). The floor of the long west concourse, surfaced with patterned terrazzo, is a river that courses eastward into Martel Hall, where it breaks into a wide, Y-shaped delta, the customary location of trading cities that historically are centers of diversity and exchange. Outram deduced this Y figure as latent in Cram's General Plan, and here he internalizes it.

Outram superimposes a secondary mythic construct on this geological narrative: the long concourse is a hypostyle hall—a hall framed by giant columns—which opens into the "crossing" of Martel Hall. This vaguely ecclesiastical spatial arrangement led Outram to designate these spaces as an "occluded temple," a sacred space embedded in the workaday world of Duncan Hall. The columns of the hypostyle hall are dramatic, especially the free-standing columns with flaring black caps that rise from four-point supports, so that corridors can penetrate the column line. The prospect of the hypostyle hall from the second or third-floor landings at Duncan Hall's west end, backlit by the west windows, which frame a view of the tower of the Chemistry Building, is highly theatrical, evoking the splendor of an *Aida*-style stage set (Outram's preferred term is "operatic").

Martel Hall, the four-story high interior court entered from the front and back doors, is activated by diagonally rotated stairs and projecting upper balconies. The robot order columns anchor a vaulted ceiling with a computer-enlarged color sketch by Outram, imprinted on sheets of vinyl, which he calls "The Birth of Consciousness." This reiterates the patterns, coloration, and thematic images found elsewhere in the architecture.

Although Outram's ideas on constructing a mythical landscape are provocative, his effort to develop this landscape as architecture at Duncan Hall recalls Susan Sontag's definition of kitsch as "failed seriousness." It is comparison with Cram's buildings, which stylistically are as eccentric as Duncan Hall, which demonstrates what is flawed about the architecture of the computational engineering building. Composition, proportion, and tectonics are divorced from iconography and the meanings it is intended to represent.

Duncan Hall exemplifies a building type characteristic of American architecture of the 1990s, the big box. It substitutes a pair of interior courts (the hypostyle hall and Martel Hall) for the exterior courts and courtyards of Cram, Goodhue & Ferguson's thin, linear buildings. Outram aligned Duncan Hall with respect to the Administration Building and the Chemistry Building. However, he emulated the frontality of the Chemistry Building rather than configuring the street front of Duncan Hall to complete the cross-court framed by Physics, Anderson, and Chemistry. From inside the Court of Engineering, unshielded by live oak trees, Duncan Hall is an overwhelming presence.

In terms of scale, proportion, and tectonics, Duncan Hall is monotonous and blunt. Despite the contrasts embodied in its two-story high cloisters, it lacks scale variation. The insistence of the protruding horizontal sills, which become more emphatic as the building rises, override efforts to introduce scale variation, impressing Duncan Hall with a relentless feeling of heaviness amplified by blind attic-level panels that are nearly a full story high. Monotony of scale translates into sluggish proportions that do not enliven one's experience of the building. Cesar Pelli and Antoine Predock tectonically articulated the composite construction of the Rice buildings they designed, Herring and Butcher Halls, while Outram and his associates simply accepted the masking techniques common to American construction of the 1980s and 1990s. Duncan Hall derives little benefit architecturally from its construction or materials.

Duncan Hall emphasizes shape making and decoration at the expense of other architectural considerations. This is most evident inside. The spectacular voids of the occluded temple contrast with the back corridors that occupants of Duncan Hall must navigate to reach their destinations. These corridors appear to comply to the letter with Houston building and safety codes defining minimum widths and maximum lengths for dead-end passages. Ceiling-less office cubicles contribute to the dramatic, canyon-like section of the hypostyle hall. But the sacrifice of acoustic privacy and access to exterior views in these offices makes the volume of space expended on the interior courts seem a disproportionate indulgence. In contrast, Stirling & Wilford, in their alterations and additions to Anderson Hall, provided work spaces that are generous, light-filled, and invite inhabitation—with far fewer resources.

Duncan Hall poses the problem of how Rice's postmodern architecture of the 1990s constructed continuity. Although it is more effusive than the original Anderson Hall or Rayzor Hall, it is as perfunctory as they are in its reduction of continuity to axial conformity and striated brick courses. The iconography of Duncan Hall is detached from the narratives that earlier Rice buildings developed. Since Outram had thoroughly rehearsed these in his slightly earlier Judge Institute for Management Studies Building at the University of Cambridge in England, particularities of program and site seem to have been, at most, secondary architectural determinants in the design of Duncan Hall.

Duncan Hall represents an odd marriage of the prosaic and the bizarre. It seems to be about the construction of Rice identity, but ultimately it reflects the obsessions of its architect—to the exclusion of any broader consensus on how architecture might embody cultural meanings. Outram's obsessions are not without interest, but Duncan Hall, with its big floor-plates, thematic styling, and oppressive sense of space, acquiesced to rather than challenged American architectural culture of the 1990s.

Court of Science

The Court of Science, at the head of the second cross-axis, represents an effort to construct a court in the post-Cram era. It consists of two spatial overlays: the first of the 1950s and the second of the 1980s. In the 1950s the Rice campus was divided into traditionalist and modernist zones. Lying outside the centers of tradition—the Cram sectors of the campus—the Court of Engineering was shaped by its location at the head of the second cross-axis and by the imperative the Houston architects George Pierce-Abel B. Pierce felt to produce modern architecture. Pierce-Pierce's buildings embraced the spatial ideal of the open city characteristic of modern architecture in Texas in the 1950s. Yet they planned their modern buildings in accord with Cram's typologies. Organizing them to configure outdoor space in a loosely linked sequence of quadrangles, they invented modernist analogues to Cram's architectural details in order to identify their buildings with Rice.

The 1980s architecture engages in a postmodern critique of such buildings as those designed by Pierce-Pierce. The postmodern buildings employed symmetrical plan configurations and shapes and details borrowed from the campus's pre-modernist buildings. These succeed to the extent that they shape space, reinforce place identity, and respond to adjoining buildings. Because their formal references are to Rice's pre-modernist buildings, however, they are weakest at engaging the buildings that they adjoin.

The last twentieth-century addition to the Court of Engineering, Butcher Hall, by Antoine Predock, acknowledges its surroundings. As different as it is from the buildings of Cram, Goodhue & Ferguson, it exhibits a sense of authority akin to theirs.

18.   George R. Brown Hall

Cambridge Seven Associates and RWS Architects, 1991

George R. Brown Hall, designed by Cambridge Seven Associates of Cambridge, Massachusetts, and RWS Architects of Houston (with Earl Wall Associates of San Diego, California, as laboratory design consultants), houses the department of biochemistry and cell biology of the Wiess School of Natural Science and the department of Bioengineering of the George R. Brown School of Engineering. It also contains the Institute of Biosciences and Bioengineering and the John W. Cox Laboratory for Biomedical Engineering. George Brown Hall was built to provide space for new types of interdisciplinary research drawing on chemistry, biology, and engineering. Chosen because it lay between the chemistry and biology buildings, the site straddles the campus's second cross-axis. The presence of this cross-axis enabled the design architects, Cambridge Seven

George R. Brown Hall

Associates, to conclude a process begun in the 1950s with the design of
the neighboring Earth Sciences buildings, Anderson and Keith-Wiess
Laboratories, and Hamman Hall: building out the Graduate Court called for
in the General Plan as a Court of Science. George R. Brown Hall constructs
continuity by layering paths of movement and deferring to the north-south
cross-axis. It seeks, in a way characteristic of enlightened postmodern architecture of the 1980s, to make a whole that balances internal practical
requirements with the affirmation of historical identities.

Charles Redmon, Cambridge Seven's design principal (Class of
1964), and his associate Dana Miller Baker (Class of 1979) took note of the
fact that the General Plan called for a thin, rectangular, two-story building to
be built across the cross-axis. This building was to be penetrated by a central, open-air passage, so that pedestrians could walk through the center of
the building into the graduate court, a two-staged quadrangle. This was
also the site for which Cram & Ferguson and William Ward Watkin separately planned new library buildings in 1941. When George Pierce-Abel B.
Pierce planned Anderson and Keith-Wiess Laboratories and Hamman Hall in
the mid-1950s, they respected the intention of the General Plan that the
cross-axis terminate in this court. However, they altered the scale of the
General Plan by spacing their buildings at much wider distances than the
General Plan called for. The scale of the Pierce-Pierce buildings was not as
monumental as those by Cram, Goodhue & Ferguson, and they lacked the
facility to control the new Court of Science in front of Hamman Hall with the
spatial authority that Cram had. When César Pelli & Associates prepared
their Master Plan for Growth in 1983, they proposed filling in this green
space with a pair of buildings symmetrically configured to frame the cross-
axis as it approached Hamman Hall.

George R. Brown Hall

Cambridge Seven inserted George Brown Hall into the Pierce-Pierce quadrangle. At three stories and 107,000 square feet in area, it is much larger than the building proposed in the General Plan. But by adopting a U-shaped plan, with faculty offices in the south wings facing the campus loop street and laboratories in the long, two-story rear wings stretching toward Hamman Hall, Cambridge Seven minimized the bulk of Brown Hall and kept the building in conformance with the thin floor plates and spatially responsive plan shapes characteristic of the Rice campus. George Brown Hall constructs figural space in deference to the cross-axis. To make this work, Cambridge Seven gave George Brown Hall its own sallyport, an arched central passage that repeats in height and width the dimensions of the Administration Building's Sallyport. The sallyport of George Brown Hall preserves long-distance views of Hamman Hall and imposes measure and rhythm on the cross-axial approach, dispelling the monotony that was characteristic of the quadrangle before Brown Hall's construction. Cambridge Seven also integrated George Brown Hall into the Earth Sciences group by George Pierce-Abel B. Pierce. A cross cloister tunneled through George Brown parallel to the campus loop street connects an existing walkway next to the Chemistry Building with the system of cloister walks incorporated in the Pierce-Pierce buildings. The rear wings of Brown Hall are stopped by the projection of a walk between the cloister of the geology building and Herman Brown Hall. Cambridge Seven asserted the primacy of George Brown Hall on its cross-axial site while aligning it with existing buildings and circulation routes.

Using a technique characteristic of postmodernism, which aimed to contextualize new buildings with respect to their architectural settings, Cambridge Seven designed the exteriors of George Brown Hall as a collage of elements visible on other Rice buildings. Rather than the linearity of Pierce-Pierce's M. D. Anderson Labs, they chose the frontality and figuration of Watkin's Chemistry Building as a model. Flat wall planes, the telescoping section of the advancing wings framing the sallyport on the street front of Brown Hall, and the emphatic gables that cap these wings are attributes borrowed from the Chemistry Building. They also borrowed from the Chemistry Building the practice of decorating the building with glazed tile medallions bearing scientific symbols. The brick-banded limestone frames around the ground-floor cloister arches are like those of Stirling & Wilford's nearby Anderson Hall addition. The banded walls of St. Joe brick are similar, in their detailing as a veneer, to the system developed by Cesar Pelli for Herring Hall. In order not to appear too fixated on the past, Cambridge Seven used the vent stacks needed to service the labs in Brown Hall to assert the modernity of the building and the scientific research pursued inside. The twin stack houses are thirty feet high and clad in stainless steel. They too participate in the postmodern exercise of seeking out precedents in their obvious kinship to the vent towers of the Chemistry and Physics Buildings and the light cones of Anderson Hall.

Brown Hall is a very responsible building. Yet it lacks the energy and invention of its immediate Rice predecessors, Stirling & Wilford's Anderson Hall additions and Pelli's Herring Hall. The flush detailing of exterior surfaces, a characteristic of Cambridge Seven's work and used very effectively on their modern buildings in Cambridge, Massachusetts, to contrast with older surrounding buildings, makes the walls of Brown Hall feel thin and immaterial rather than layered and modern. Treating the exterior as a compilation of quotations makes Brown Hall feel more like an academic exercise in postmodern contextualism than adventurous exploration; one already knows the answers. In light of subsequent examples of postmodern traditionalism at Rice, George Brown Hall's sense of responsibility should not be undervalued. Yet in architecture as in science, new exploration, new discovery, and new insights are what excite and inspire. Cambridge Seven, in a building that is very different from the modern architecture with which they made their reputation in the 1970s, did not push hard enough to derive something new from something that already existed.

George R. Brown Hall was named for George R. Brown, the first Rice alumnus to become chairman of the board of governors, a position he held from 1950 until 1967. An engineer by training, Brown was an executive of Brown & Root, a Houston-based engineering and construction corporation founded by his brother, Herman Brown. He and his brother were also co-founders of Texas Eastern Transmission Corporation, a natural gas transmission operation. The Brown brothers were especially identified with the rise of Lyndon B. Johnson to political prominence. In 1951 George Brown and his wife Alice Pratt Brown, and Herman Brown and his wife Margarett Root Brown, organized the Brown Foundation, a major benefactor of Rice University during the second half of the twentieth century.

19. Herman Brown Hall for Mathematical Sciences and Seeley G. Mudd Computer Science Laboratory

Herman Brown Hall for Mathematical Sciences *George Pierce–Abel B. Pierce, 1968*
Seeley G. Mudd Computer Science Laboratory
   Charles Tapley Associates and Hugh E. Gragg, 1983

The eastern edge of the Court of Science has a somewhat haphazard feel. During the 1960s, 1970s, and 1980s architects tried to insert new buildings to compensate for departures from the General Plan. In such an ordered campus setting, departures from the norm can be invigorating; here, though, little benefit is derived from the myriad adjustments made to preserve the semblance of order.

Between George R. Brown Hall and the Chemistry Building stands an allée of mature live oak trees that once framed a service road. This road originally paralleled the west side of the Chemistry Building, then made a right angle turn to parallel the rear of the Chemistry Building. The portion of this allée nearest the campus loop street was redeveloped with a seating

Herman Brown Hall for Mathematical Sciences

area and diagonal walkway by Robert F. White & Associates in 1960, while the portion behind the Chemistry Building continued in service as an alley, which was awkwardly extended to provide a truck dock and service court for George Brown Hall in the 1990s, cutting unavoidably into the space of the allée.

Herman Brown Hall, built with a gift from the Brown Foundation and named for George Brown's elder brother and business partner, is a four-story, 57,000-square-foot office and classroom building. It is aligned behind the allée of live oak trees and mirrors the siting of the Keith-Wiess Geological Laboratories on the west edge of the Court of Science. In addition to the department of mathematics of the Wiess School of Natural Sciences, for which Herman Brown Hall was built, it houses offices of the department of education of the school of humanities, the department of physics and space physics of the Wiess School of Natural Sciences, the center for education, the center for the study of science and technology, the computational mathematics laboratory, the Rice University Commission on Women, and the T. W. Bonner Nuclear Laboratory.

The Houston architectural firm George Pierce-Abel B. Pierce designed Herman Brown as a companion to their Earth and Space Sciences building group and Hamman Hall. They aligned it along the east edge of the Court of Science in its pre-George Brown Hall configuration. There was not as much room, however, for buildings to stretch out on this edge of the Science Court as on its west edge. As buildings were constructed beside and behind Herman Brown, the ambivalence involved in its siting has become more apparent. The mathematics department rejected the layout of Pierce-Pierce's earlier buildings, with their open-air access galleries and stairs, in favor of a double-loaded corridor plan served by an elevator and stair core; therefore, Herman Brown does not open out to and architecturally define adjoining outdoor spaces as do the Earth and Space Sciences buildings.

Like other campus buildings of the 1960s, Herman Brown balances an affirmation of Rice identity (embodied in the banded brick walls and panels of Verde Antico marble Pierce-Pierce had used in their earlier Rice buildings) with an expression of modernity—in this case through the exposure of its reinforced concrete structural columns at the first floor level and precast-concrete window panels on the second and third stories. Its heavy lidded fourth floor recalls the roof treatment of Ryon Lab. Herman Brown lacks the crisp, decisive composition and articulation of Pierce-Pierce's 1950s buildings. Its modern tectonic attributes, the precast panels, are so routine that they give the building the appearance of a Houston speculative office building of the 1960s. With the rejection of the linear building typology of the 1950s for a compact block—arguably a more rational configuration for an air-conditioned building—the relationship between building shape and the shaping of outdoor space, critical to Cram, Goodhue & Ferguson's

Seeley G. Mudd Computer Science Laboratory

buildings, was lost. George Pierce-Abel B. Pierce tried to compensate by providing two "slype" spaces on the ground floor, one completely open-air, the other an air-conditioned pass-through lobby. The open-air slype, which intersects a route leading from parking lots behind Hamman Hall to Fondren Library, is aligned on the allée of live oak trees. Thus it connects, at least visually (there is no paved walkway through this allée), with the historic landscape. The lobby passage falls into alignment with an arcaded cloister bay of the Seeley G. Mudd Computer Science Laboratory to the north, which established a visual connection between these buildings.

The 1960s and 1970s represented a period in the design of American universities when bulky buildings with aggressive exteriors defied the scale and organization of established campus plans. Rice was fortunate that such architects as George Pierce-Abel B. Pierce exercised restraint. Their efforts to conserve continuity by integrating buildings that may not have been of individual distinction into the spatial order of the campus saved Rice at a time when other American campuses were not so lucky. The 1980s represented the swing of the pendulum in the opposite direction. This change in attitude (which affected university administrators as powerfully as architects) is represented by the Seeley G. Mudd Computer Science Laboratory of 1983. The Mudd Building, constructed with a gift from the Seeley G. Mudd Fund, was built for the Institute for Computer Services and Applications. It now houses the university's Information Technology Division.

The Houston architect Charles R. Tapley (Class of 1954) and his associate Dean A. Johns, with Hugh E. Gragg (Class of 1941) as associated architect, designed the 28,000-square-foot Mudd Building to be widely used forward plane is of concrete panels striated with courses of brick and pierced to accept the thin steel columns upholding the canopies framing Hamman Hall. The back wall plane is of brick on a granite base course and incorporates raised planting troughs at either end filled with Lady Banksia roses. The screen walls layer space, separating the paved forecourt in front of Hamman Hall from the grass and parking courts behind. They force pedestrians circulating between them to negotiate a series of right angle turns. They divert and slow forward movement and spatially complicate what, otherwise, is a flat, monotonous plain. Pierce-Pierce repeated this use of pierced walls in back of Hamman Hall to screen the stage service dock and imply more spatial layers than in fact exist.

To the east of Hamman Hall, behind the screen wall, is an auto drop-off court—accessible from the service road behind the Mechanical Laboratory and Ryon Lab. Hamman Hall and the Earth Sciences group were the first buildings at Rice to integrate car parking into the initial site planning. North of Hamman Hall and Space Science lies an extensive perimeter parking lot, bracketed by Entrances Thirteen and Fourteen. These parking lots contribute little in the way of designed space to the Rice campus, but they are significant for being intrinsic to the Court of Science, a rare instance of coordinating parking lot location and design with new building design.

Hamman Hall demonstrates the possibility of affirming Rice identity with modern architecture. Like the Earth and Space Sciences buildings and Herman Brown Hall, Hamman Hall is implicated in the suburban spatiality that overtook Houston in the 1950s and 1960s. Robert White's landscaping reinforced this suburbanized environment, with loblolly pine trees, the iconic suburban tree of Houston in the 1960s. The building's lightness and thinness mean that it does not have the monumental presence of Cram's buildings, a trait that modern architects of the 1950s would likely have rejected anyway. Pierce-Pierce did not accurately gauge the ability of their buildings to control the distances interposed between them. Although they adhered to the patterns embodied in the General Plan, they would have done better to approximate the plan's more compact intervals. Consequently, they do not always avoid the problem of spatial monotony latent at Rice because of its flat terrain. Planting, including hedges, tended to be kept low. White's choice and arrangement of plants did not introduce stepped horizons or construct redundant alignments, as Cram, Goodhue & Ferguson did to fill the void and project architecture into the landscape. The Pierce-Pierce buildings lack the complex nuances of rhythm, measure, and framing as well as the authoritative proportions of the Cram, Goodhue & Ferguson buildings.

Their virtue is Pierce-Pierce's lack of prejudice. The firm's commitment to a rational, modernist resolution of the "problems" the commission entailed did not exclude the problem of designing new buildings that needed to relate to an existing architectural complex. By making this condition more problematic (rather than simply decorating functional dia-grams with historical details) Pierce-Pierce reinvigorated architecture at Rice in the 1950s, as did Lloyd & Morgan with their Mary Gibbs Jones College of 1957. It is even possible to discern in the exterior detailing of Hamman Hall some of the lessons Cesar Pelli and his associates absorbed as they were preparing to design Herring Hall in the early 1980s.

Hamman Hall was built with a gift from Mary Josephine Milby Hamman in memory of her husband, George Hamman, a Houston banker and sulfur and oil investor.

22.   Dell Butcher Hall

Antoine Predock and Brooks Coronado Associates, 1997

Dell Butcher Hall, which houses the Center for Nanoscale Science and Technology, reinvigorates Rice architectural traditions in unpredictable ways. It is an 83,000-square-foot building that steps up from one to four sto-ries in a tight, irregular U-shaped plan on a left-over site next to Space Science and behind the Keith-Wiess Geological Laboratories. Although its cramped site is back and behind with respect to the Court of Science, Butcher Hall is adjacent to Entrance Thirteen, at Rice Boulevard and Kent Street, one of the principal automobile entrances to the campus. Like Stirling & Wilford and Cesar Pelli, the Albuquerque architect Antoine Predock, working with the Houston architects Brooks Coronado Associates, fundamentally reinterpreted Rice architecture in his design for Butcher Hall by shaping space, constructing a hierarchy of scales, and projecting a mythic landscape. Like Stirling & Wilford and Pelli, he absorbed elements of Rice's architectural patrimony outside the Cram canon into the design of Butcher Hall to signify its Rice identity.

Dell Butcher Hall

In the era of the big box, Butcher Hall demonstrates the continuing relevance of the shallow floor plate. It adheres to the tradition of the double-loaded corridor building at Rice, but manipulates the type to accommodate laboratory spaces of various sizes as well as the central Attwell Courtyard. The shallow floor plate maximizes the number of rooms with exterior views and daylight. The public spaces—the entry lobbies from the north (parking lot) side of Butcher Hall and the east (courtyard) approach—are slype-like: they occupy the thinnest part of Butcher Hall and frame views that go right through the building. The views out from the corridor on the upper floors reinforce Predock's construction of identity by focusing awareness on the Attwell Courtyard as well as on the most unprecedented space in Butcher Hall, the "bleachers"—as Predock calls the stepped Jamail roof terrace above the McMurtry Lecture Hall. The Jamail roof terrace resolves the practical problem of capping the lecture amphitheater—the one space too bulky to work with the double-loaded corridor arrangement—with something other than a flat, gravel-surfaced roof, which all the upper-floor windows have to look down on. It also invents a new kind of elevated outdoor public space at Rice, internalizing and domesticating Rice Stadium, which is visible to the west. Here, with unexpected flair, Predock constructs identity by making a connection to the tradition of modern architecture at Rice as well as to Cram's and Watkin's laboratory buildings, with their spatially distinct lecture amphitheaters.

The raking parapet of the outdoor stair leading from the courtyard up to the roof terrace is skewed in plan, in response to the internal arrangement of the McMurtry Lecture Hall. Predock introduced diagonality into the spatial lexicon of Rice. Heretofore, the diagonal was associated primarily with the paths students cut between sidewalks. At Butcher Hall this alignment becomes a powerful instrument for shaping space, directing movement, and framing vision without resorting to symmetry. This can be seen upon entering the courtyard from the Space Science Building. The south cloister frames a distant view of the entrance to Butcher. The wall of the lecture amphitheater not only angles out, but slopes down, toward the entry to Butcher Hall, pushing into the framed vista. This aggressive gesture spatializes the flatness and minimal greenery of the courtyard, which Predock emphasized by using decomposed granite as a ground cover instead of Asiatic jasmine and positioning shrubs as isolated solids in the landscape. Rather than denying the flatness and heat of Houston, the courtyard intensifies the experience of these phenomena, balancing this by emphasizing the long view through the building's entrance slype to the green sports field to the west.

In the Attwell Courtyard visitors are especially aware of how Butcher Hall complements the alignment and coloration of the Space Science Building, and how the courtyard connection between the two suggests a more intense, energetic approach to landscape architecture than the suburban pastoral mode prevailing in the Earth and Space Sciences group. It would have been easy to ignore the Space Science Building. The skill with which Predock annexed it to this courtyard and made it seem integral to a new and larger whole heightens the presence of Space Science. His free-standing steel-framed canopy, much more assertive than the thin, low canopies of the Earth and Space Sciences group, overlaps the stair tower of the Space Science Building. Like the obtruding diagonal of the amphitheater wall, the new canopy posits overlapping as a technique for constructing continuity outside the spatial lexicon employed by Cram, Goodhue & Ferguson. Predock demonstrates that the construction of continuity is achieved most powerfully by making new wholes.

The ground floor public interior of Butcher Hall consists of a pair of intersecting lobbies—one rectangular in plan and entered from the courtyard, the other a lateral corridor accessible from the north parking lot. The courtyard lobby is a serene room with a stone-paved floor. The lateral corridor, an extended slype, leads visitors alongside an external colonnade of oversized piers framing a parallel exterior cloister. The thickness and close spacing of the piers evoke the experience of a hypostyle. Especially from within the cloister, they frame the sports field to the west, slicing its flat, unbounded expanse into vertical slivers, and impose a tenser, more obviously constructed measure on the landscape than do Cram's cloisters. The lateral corridor is partially obstructed by a ceremonial stair, donated by Sue and Steve Shaper in memory of H. Malcolm Lovett, whose alignment overlaps the axial space of the corridor. The Lovett memorial stair is cantilevered and of cast-in-place concrete. Free-standing, it is walled with panels of obscured glass clipped to black painted steel columns, which give the stair the feeling of an ascending room. Inside the stair, one becomes aware that the glass is etched with what looks like representations of bamboo stalks. These are Carbon 60 nanotubes, known as buckytubes, icons that are a third form of carbon named after visionary engineer R. Buckminster Fuller and discovered by Richard E. Smalley, Hackerman Professor of Chemistry and Physics, and Robert Curl (Class of 1954). This discovery led professors Smalley and Curl to become the first Rice faculty members to win the Nobel Prize, for chemistry, in 1996.

The west and north elevations of Butcher Hall comprise its outer walls, and they differ from the inner walls of the building facing the Attwell Courtyard. The outerwalls are visible at a distance, from Rice Boulevard on the north and from Rice Stadium on the west. Predock takes advantage of the building's location at one edge of the campus to treat it as an anchor in the landscape, stepping up to a five-story tower at its northwest corner that contains a two-story high, pergola-roofed viewing terrace. He uses the building's combination of precast concrete and banded brick to create variations of scale, which operate at the scale of the landscape. He varies the location, head height, and proportions of window openings to animate the planar exterior walls and articulate internal spatial variations. High-set slot windows not only admit light, but focus awareness from outside on the ceiling-level servicing.

At the level of details, Butcher Hall is ingenious. The railings of inset, upper-level balconies are thin, closely spaced, cast-stone cylinders, with no continuous handrails. Vertical control joints in the brick curtain wall are aligned with the edges of window openings, causing the vertical seams to stand out and calling attention to the fact that the brick is panelized cladding rather than load-bearing construction, even though windows are deep set. The wedge-shaped Burns Conference Room, on the second floor, is enveloped in copper, identifying it as a special space. Even paving has been rethought. Interior corridors are paved with polished black vinyl splattered with white, a treatment that becomes almost fluid in the Lovett memorial stair. Exterior sidewalks, rather than composed of big slabs, are separated into concrete tiles framed by concrete runners, the tiles and runners treated with different finishes to distinguish the two texturally.

Butcher looks nothing like the Administration Building. But its construction of a hierarchy of scales—which enables the building to work at the scale of the landscape as well as at the scale of the sidewalk paving, its provision of high-set terraces, and its play with the shapes and sizes of windows in uniform wall planes are like the Administration Building. Its rectangular windows, framed with horizontal muntins like the awning windows of Staub & Rather's buildings, resonate with additional layers of Rice's architectural history. Predock constructed Rice identity by engaging in a dialectical exchange with Cram, Rather, Rice Stadium, and the Pierce-Pierce buildings. Yet the fundamental identity his architecture posits is not founded on engagement with other Rice buildings, but on giving form to the phenomenon of discovery. At Butcher Hall the experience of discovery energizes the mythic landscape Predock evokes. With respect to certain episodes—such as the relationship of the sloping roofs, and the inert precast cladding—Butcher Hall seems to have been conceived pictorially rather than resolved in a rigorous, tectonic way. Despite such lapses, it is a building that gives every indication of having been designed to enhance the experiences of the people who study, teach, and work in it. It is a model of how tradition and continuity can be constructed at Rice as innovation.

Butcher Hall is named for E. Dell Butcher (Class of 1934), a Houstonian who was president of American Commercial Lines and a vice president of the Texas Gas Transmission Company. He was a trustee of Rice and chairman of the board of governors from 1981 to 1982.

Great Square and West Axis

Lost Space

The Great Square is the lost space of the General Plan. It survives, but in a truncated, misshapen, and misunderstood form. The construction of the Fondren Library in the Great Square began the process of losing space. The Rice Memorial Center further diluted the authority of the General Plan by destroying the grove of trees that formed one of the square's defining frames. César Pelli proposed the recovery of the Great Square with his design of Herring Hall, which reinforced the remaining grove of trees framing the Great Square. Furthermore, his office produced a building that offered itself as a model for how architecture in the 1980s could come to terms with the architectural legacy of Cram.

The building-out of the westward extension of the main axis beyond the Great Square, where the General Plan originally proposed extensive Persian Gardens, is where Rice University in the 1990s sought to construct its architectural identity in postmodern terms. Postmodernism is represented in two variants. Alice Pratt Brown Hall, the Shepherd School of Music building by Ricardo Bofill and the Taller de Arquitectura, glosses architectural history by engaging Michelangelo in precast concrete, brick cladding, and insulated solar glass. James A. Baker III Hall by Hammond, Beeby & Babka represents postmodernism in its late, neo-traditional phase. What sets these buildings apart from other campus buildings of the 1990s is their lack of connection to the General Plan. Each relates to the westward projection of the main axis. Neither proceeds beyond the presence of the axis to shape space, although it was Bofill's ambition to do so.

The Landscape Vision for Rice, a landscape master plan produced in 1990 by Sasaki Associates, provides a template for transferring elements of the landscape order of the General Plan to this sector of the campus. Whether Robert A. M. Stern's design for the Jones Graduate School of Management conforms to Sasaki's master plan will test the university's willingness to commit to a master plan, a cultural commitment that for Houstonians in the second half of the twentieth century seemed to provoke profound anxiety. Whether lost space will be recovered with the building-out of the west axis depends on whether the model of the General Plan or the model of Rice Stadium and its parking lot prevails. These two models represent clear alternatives of planned versus unplanned development. Yet in late twentieth-century Houston, the latter was consistently opted for, despite the presence of the former.

The Great Square is a phantom court. It exists as the residue of the arrangement prescribed in the General Plan. One of the triple rows of live oak trees planted to bound two sides of the square still lines the south edge, backed by Herring Hall. On cue, as called for in the General Plan, the trees make a right angle turn to frame the westward progress of the main axis. Today, this turn gives the appearance of a misunderstanding in planting. In 1957–58 the Rice Memorial Center was built *in* the triple row of live oak trees outlining the north edge of the square. A pair of live oaks survives to mark the corresponding north edge of the frame. But their role as a landscape bracket is no longer clear. In 1958 a line of deciduous willow oak trees was planted in accordance with Robert White's design, in what was originally intended to have been the open center of the square, further confusing the definition of the Great Square's north boundary. The same year, the street along the right-of-way of the second cross-axis, installed when the Fondren Library was built, was taken out and replaced with a sidewalk. At about the same time, the parallel street that marked the west edge of the Great Square was moved farther west, throwing off the proportioned spatial intervals of the General Plan. Piece by piece, the infrastructural elements Cram, Goodhue & Ferguson used to organize the landscape of the Great Square were eliminated or altered.

The Great Square displays the consequences of omitting the redundant alignments of parallel tree lines, hedgerow, streets, and sidewalks that Cram, Goodhue & Ferguson installed to construct the landscapes of the Academic Court and the Court of Engineering. Without the parallel alignments of hedgerows, sidewalks, and streets, the monotonous flatness of the landscape asserts itself. The General Plan drawing suggests that Cram, Goodhue & Ferguson were prepared to treat the entire expanse of the Great Square (which included the site of Fondren Library) as an open, non-grassed plane, either paved or surfaced with decomposed granite. Had this design been carried out, it might have proved too extreme, too exposed, and too liable to unwanted water retention to have justified the stunning visual contrast between the emptiness of the Great Square and the surrounding volume of black shade and dark evergreen tree canopies the live oaks provide.

The reconstruction of Fondren Library in the early 2000s with a passage to connect the Great Square and the Academic Court provides an opportunity to reassess the landscape architecture of the Great Square. While the library building will remain an obstacle to the realization of Cram's bold vision of space orchestrated on a Texan scale, its reconstruction makes possible the design of a new court that doesn't seem like a soggy backyard.

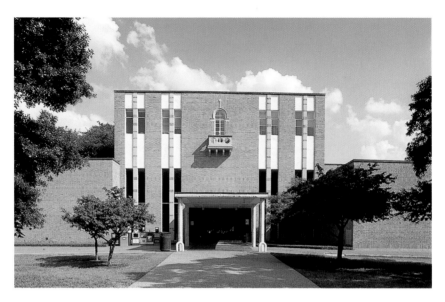

Rice Memorial Center

24. Rice Memorial Center, Robert H. Ray Memorial Courtyard, and Ley Student Center

Rice Memorial Center *Harvin C. Moore, 1958*
Robert H. Ray Memorial Courtyard *White, Klatt & Porcher, 1969*
Ley Student Center *César Pelli & Associates, 1986*

The Rice Memorial Center is the university's student center. It contains a large reception room, the Great Hall; Sammy's cafeteria; Willie's Pub; the Rice Campus Store; and the offices of the student, graduate student, and alumni associations, the student yearbook, the *Campanile*, the student newspaper, the *Rice Thresher*, and Rice Radio KTRU-FM. The Rice Memorial Chapel and the cloister offices are part of the original complex. Two additions to the center are the Robert H. Ray Memorial Courtyard (1969) and the Ley Student Center (1986). The Rice Memorial Center was the first permanent student center on campus. From 1921 until 1949 Rice's de-facto student center was Autry House, across Main Boulevard from Entrance Three. From 1949 until 1959 the Fondren Library housed a student snack bar, the Roost, in its basement. Fredericka Meiners, in her history of Rice, identifies the trustee J. Newton Rayzor as the principal advocate of constructing a student center and chapel during the postwar period. Rayzor and his wife were the donors of the chapel and the primary contributors to the construction of the memorial center, honoring Rice students and alumni who died in military service.

Harvin C. Moore (Class of 1927), a Houston architect who designed Mr. and Mrs. Rayzor's ranch house, designed the 56,000-square-foot center and chapel for the site Cram, Goodhue & Ferguson designated in the General Plan as a students' clubhouse (where Allen Center is located, although the center would have faced toward Baker College). In 1955–56 the university was in the course of planning the transformation of the dormitories, which the student clubhouse was supposed to complement, into residential colleges. Fear that a student center would compete with the commons of the new colleges led to the decision to transfer the Rice Memorial Center—which Moore had already designed—to its present location on the north side of the Great Square in mid-1957. As a result of this decision, it was built at the center of the campus rather than at one edge, But it was aligned with Anderson Hall rather than in the setback prescribed in the General Plan (which would have pushed it north, up against the campus loop street). This resulted in the center being built *in* the triple row of live oak trees bounding the north edge of the Great Square. The live oaks between Fondren Library and the apse of the chapel, and in the Ray Memorial Courtyard, are the remnants of this grove. The decision to truncate the main axis by building the Fondren Library across it was compounded here. The destruction of this grove of trees demonstrated an unimaginable lack of understanding—or willful disregard—of the precepts of the General Plan. The main axis was reinterpreted as a linear file of buildings that faced the campus loop street and abutted the Great Square, confirming the square's post-Fondren identity as a backyard.

The suburbanism latent in this reversal of spatial priorities is reflected in the scale of the center. The chapel and its campanile are based

Rice Memorial Center Chapel and Campanile

on the design of the Early Christian Basilica of St. John Lateran in Rome, but carried out, along with the cloister that links them to the rest of the center, at an almost dollhouse-like scale. The rest of the building consists of a series of separately roofed, steel-framed boxes containing the main program elements. This is the modern segment of the center, its modernity signified by flat roofs and vertical strip windows. Moore's choice and detailing of materials were assured. The Llano granite base courses, banded brick and limestone walls, brick and marble cloister paving, and polished travertine paving in the chapel and the lobbies of the Rice Memorial Center give the complex a feeling of substance. The decorative

Rice Memorial Chapel

frieze on the east, north, and south walls of the chapel, a meander composed of ceramic rosettes, tiles of Verde Antico marble, and panels of inlaid
brick, is especially striking. In adjusting his earlier design to this site, Moore
aligned the center's street-facing entrance portals with those of the Anderson
and Keith-Wiess labs. This constructed an extended framed perspective, in
the tradition of Cram, Goodhue & Ferguson's organization of spaces,
although the intervening distances are longer and the scale of the architectural components smaller. The suburban scale of the Rice Memorial Center
reflects insecurity about the propriety of using historical detail in the 1950s.

   The sense of trying to elide what the architect knew to be ideologically unacceptable is especially strong in the design of the chapel. Despite
its "traditional" exteriors, the chapel has a glass-walled nave, disguised
from outside by brick-walled garden courtyards. The interior of the chapel
features copious use of gold mosaic tile; the entire apse wall is sheathed in
gold mosaic. While this could be interpreted as invoking Cram's Byzantine
sources, it also seems related to the use of gold mosaic tile in a much-
published modern chapel by the architect Eero Saarinen, completed at the
Massachusetts Institute of Technology in 1955, the year Moore received the
Rice commission. The abstract composition of stained glass windows (by
the Los Angeles stained glass designer Roger Darricarrere) and the case
design of a seventeen-rank, 1,120-pipe Baroque organ produced by the
Andover Organ Company underscored the modern sub-theme. Because
William M. Rice's charter specified that the institute have no religious affilia-
tion, the chapel was not designed for denominational worship. In place of

an altar, Moore installed a polished marble cylinder in the apse. Serving as a pedestal for heroic floral arrangements, this non-altar epitomizes the ambivalence that prevails in the chapel. Striving for tradition is insistent. Yet it is pursued so apologetically and with so many crypto-modernist reservations that the chapel has a slightly science fiction feel to it, as though its normality were meant to provoke disbelief.

The chapel is used for the weddings of students and alumni, and memorials for Rice faculty and staff members. In the chapel narthex is an Eero Saarinen-designed pedestal table, a classic of American modern design of the 1950s. Houston's great modernist interior designer Sally Walsh and her partner Jack W. Evans served as interior designers for the Rice Memorial Center. They furnished Sammy's cafeteria with Saarinen pedestal tables and pedestal chairs, and the lobbies with upholstered pieces by Florence Knoll. This table is the only survivor.

The cloister linking the chapel with the rest of the Rice Memorial Center, and the Ray Memorial Courtyard, which the cloister encloses, are the most satisfying elements of the design. The stage-set scale of the chapel front and its campanile, the repeating arches of the cloister, and the remnant live oaks of the north grove of the Great Square shape one of the most thoughtfully designed exterior spaces at Rice. Yet it was not installed until eleven years after the Rice Memorial Center was built. Robert White and his partners Fred Klatt, Jr., and George S. Porcher created low, stepped, brick-framed planting beds around the live oaks, which they filled with a ground cover of liriope. Their simple grid of planting beds surrounds a central square paved with exposed aggregate concrete.

Rice Memorial Center, cloister

Ley Student Center

The entrance lobby of the Rice Memorial Center contains the Rice Trophy Cabinet (Cram & Ferguson, 1916), an extravagant, outrageous, effusively gilded Venetian Gothic vitrine, which aspires to the status of architecture. A framed resolution from the board of trustees, dated January 1916 and posted on a wall of the lobby, thanks the donor, William M. Rice, Jr., for the cabinet, built "in the most seasoned of durable materials, without bolt or binding joint, its carving still further protected by overlays of gold leaf and enamel." Missing from the lobby are a pair of marvelous glass "curtains" installed by Sally Walsh, one where the trophy cabinet now stands, the other symmetrically mirroring its locations. These were "roundelay" curtains, composed of discs of fused, colored glass clipped together with metal fasteners and suspended from the ceiling, the work of art glass makers Frances Stewart and Michael Higgins of the Dearborn Glass Company.

The lobby between Sammy's and the Campus Store turns into a tile-paved concourse, with the Kelley Lounge on one side and the Brown Garden, a second landscaped courtyard, on the other. These spaces are part of the Ley Student Center, a 20,700-square-foot addition to the Rice Memorial Center by César Pelli & Associates. For the design of this extension, Pelli's office adapted the architectural vocabulary it devised for Herring Hall. It also installed the postmodern interiors (the original color scheme in the Kelley Lounge has been changed from an exuberant rose to Rice's colors, drab blue and gray). The Brown Garden, designed by Pelli's partner, landscape architect Diana Balmori, lacks the tree cover of the Ray Courtyard. Its circular paving and planting themes compete with the wall banding and the configuration of the Ley Center's most singular piece, the octagonally planned, conically roofed Farnsworth Pavilion, a small lecture and reception hall. Pelli treated the figural Farnsworth Pavilion as a pendant to the O'Connor Center for Business Information, the library of his firm's Herring Hall on the other side of the Great Square. The final component of the Ley Student Center is the two-story, gable-roofed office wing. In expiation for the Rice Memorial Center's past transgressions, Pelli aligned this wing with the rear wings of Anderson Hall and the Physics Building, as called for in the General Plan.

The center constructs the Rice identity as conflicted. The effort to adhere to traditional stylistic models yet simultaneously be modern, as though these were not contradictory impulses (and in terms of 1950s architecture they were, without question), expresses a longing to transcend the modern-traditional dialectic that can also be deduced from Cram's architecture and planning. The construction of continuity, which George Pierce-Abel B. Pierce pursued at the same time in their Earth Sciences group across the campus loop street, escaped this dilemma by extrapolating Rice architectural traditions into modernist analogues. The ideological distinction between "tradition" and "continuity" visible in the Rice Memorial Center and the Earth Sciences group was critical in terms of constructing competing models of Rice identity in the 1950s. Continuity authorized spatial and tectonic exploration, while tradition meant conformance to formula. The construction of tradition as stylistic formula was so ideologically potent that it absolved architects from pursuing continuity. Thus the apparent lack of consciousness of the violence the Rice Memorial Center inflicted on the grove of trees and the spatial commitment to the General Plan the grove represented. The provision of a green suburban lawn facing the loop street exercised a stronger claim than the trees. The lawn completed an ideal ideological image of suburban propriety, an image implicit in the program of a chapel for a university that had once been so determinedly non-religious that the original president and trustees refused Ralph Adams Cram the opportunity to design one. The landscape of suburban Houston in the postwar period was characterized by modern building types that adopted "traditional" stylistic codes as part of a strategy to escape responsibility for shaping civic space. The Rice Memorial Center participated, in ways that its authors and patrons may not have clearly grasped, in this suburbanizing strategy of dissolving spatial coherence and displacing it with linear repetition.

Pelli's postmodern addition does not escape the conflicts of its host building. The ideal of continuity, which postmodernism exalted, is performed in the Ley Student Center through its plan diagram, which transformed an existing lobby into the backbone of the Ley addition. Pelli's decision to formally inflect the Ley Center toward the architecture of Herring Hall represented an effort to construct continuity at the scale of the landscape by making architectural connections between the two sides of the Great Square. This necessitated abandoning the architecture of the Rice Memorial Center. Despite the smooth confluence of new and old in plan, the Ley Center additions fail to transform the Rice Memorial Center. Pelli doesn't offer a new interpretation of its spatial organization and architectural detail—one that would lead to a reevaluation of the original, as Stirling & Wilford achieved with their additions and alterations to Anderson Hall. The Rice Memorial Center and its additions demonstrate that adhering to tradition and confirming identity are problematic actions. They cannot be accomplished automatically or partially.

The Ley Student Center was built in part with gifts from Judy Ley Allen (Class of 1961), Robert M. Ley, Stephen W. Ley, and Mr. and Mrs. Anthony Espinoza in honor of Audrey Moody Ley (Class of 1935) and Wendel D. Ley (Class of 1932).

25. **Robert R. Herring Hall** *César Pelli & Associates, 1984*

Herring Hall, a two- and three-story building containing 48,350 square feet, was built to house the Jesse H. Jones Graduate School of Administration, Rice's business school, which was organized in 1975. The building is named for Robert R. Herring, who was chairman of the board of directors, chief executive officer, and president of Houston Natural Gas Corporation, and chairman of Rice's board of governors from 1979 until his death in 1981.

Robert R. Herring Hall

César Pelli, the Argentine-born architect and dean of the school of architecture at Yale University from 1977 to 1984, was selected to design Herring Hall in 1982. In 1979 the NewHaven-based Pelli had designed a mixed-use complex in Houston, which was not built, for Josephine E. Abercrombie, then a member of the board of directors of the J. S. Abercrombie Mineral Company and Cameron Iron Works. Mrs. Abercrombie was a trustee of Rice; from 1979 until 1994 she chaired the board of governors' building and grounds committee. Her rapport with Pelli led to the university's decision to commission a second Rice building from an architect who was not a Rice alumnus. Like Stirling & Wilford's additions to Anderson Hall, Herring Hall won widespread critical recognition, including an honor award from the American Institute of Architects in 1986—precipitating the practice of hiring nationally known architects at Rice. Pelli and his associates Kevin E. Hart and William Butler (Class of 1979) demonstrated that new architecture could recover the historic spatial order of the General Plan. They also demonstrated that new architecture could be integrated with existing buildings. This operation did not entail reproducing identity but problematizing it architecturally. Pelli's firm pursued a more rigorous, if less lyrical, approach to generating a postmodern Rice architecture at Herring Hall than had Stirling & Wilford at Anderson Hall. They sought a systematic synthesis of identity and modernity.

Pelli persuaded the board of governors to let him site the building where the General Plan had called for one to go—slotted between the triple row of live oaks on the south edge of the Great Square and a double row of live oaks lining the campus loop street. In configuring the building's ground plan, Pelli and his associates systematically integrated it with the Rice Memorial Center and the Earth Sciences buildings. Herring Hall repeated a Cram-like building form: a long, slender, three-story bar, parallel to the street, and a pair of two-story extensions facing the Great Square grove. In plan it is shaped like a long, shallow, irregular U. The center of the U-shape, between the two-story

Entrance, Robert R. Herring Hall

wings, is the Douglass Courtyard. The courtyard is aligned with and is the same width as the Rice Memorial Center's Ray Memorial Courtyard. The two principal street entrances to Herring Hall align with the axes of

Robert R. Herring Hall

movement and view that penetrate the Memorial Center and the Earth Sciences buildings. Pelli grounded Herring Hall in the typological order established by Cram, Goodhue & Ferguson and in the spatial order of the Great Square and the Court of Science to the north. He demonstrated the feasibility of piecing the frayed fabric of the General Plan back together not by ignoring the offending parties but by systematically reintegrating them.

Pelli's office cited the Physics Building as its general model for the architectural language it developed at Herring Hall. However, the exteriors of Herring Hall display the architects' awareness of Rice's full architectural heritage. The south-facing street front of Herring Hall can be seen as Pelli's tribute to his patron, Josephine Abercrombie. It is not formally dependent on the Abercrombie Engineering Laboratory but it repeats the compositional strategies J. T. Rather pursued in the design of Abercrombie, especially Abercrombie's insistent horizontality, the arrangement of square-sectioned first-floor windows set on a limestone base course, a continuous band of top floor windows beneath a continuous eaves line, and the practice of stopping the protruding entrance bays short of the eaves line. The stepped wall planes framing the axial, north-facing window in the O'Connor Center for Business Information (one of the two-story wings) recall a similar compositional device John Staub used on the front of Fondren Library. These construct, in Rice terms, the center's institutional identity as a specialized branch of the Fondren Library, just as the references to Abercrombie Lab construct a narrative of Abercrombie family philanthropy and patronage spanning two generations.

Pelli's primary architectural narrative focuses on the construction of Rice identity. The architectural "tradition" he felt compelled to respond to was the economical construction system Rice mandated for Herring Hall: a light steel structural frame, steel studs, and an external sheathing of brick.

While taking Cram, Goodhue & Ferguson's articulation of construction in their masonry bearing wall buildings as his model, Pelli sought to formulate an architectural language based on the use of composite construction systems, much like George Pierce-Abel B. Pierce did in their buildings of the 1950s. Pelli's office devised a material code extrapolated from Cram, Goodhue & Ferguson's detailing of materials. This code externalizes the tectonics of the veneered frame with flush surfaces—the thin curtain wall admits no material depth—and explicit control joints; these joints accommodate the expansion and contraction of the brick and stone curtain wall, which occur at a different rate than the expansion and contraction of the underlying steel structure. It also involves such elements as the cloister columns, with their surprising combination of thick, stone-and-brick outer shells and thin, steel-cased inner shells, and the panels and fields of glazed burgundy-colored brick, which Pelli used where carved stone might have been incorporated in a Cram, Goodhue & Ferguson building.

Pelli's architectural code narrates the internal organization of Herring Hall. On the long north and south sides of the building, horizontal banding emphasizes the line of case rooms on the first floor, departmental offices on the second, and faculty offices on the third floors. On the narrow east and west end walls, the division of the building into a tall, thin, case room and office wing and two, lower, specialized wings is made visible. The tall, thin wing has a gabled roof with a pointed bay window centered beneath it. The Avery Lecture Hall on the east is identified by a protruding rounded wall, and the O'Connor Center on the west by a truncated vault.

Pelli and his associates sought inventive ways to make architecture out of expressing the obvious. Their treatment of the narrow east and west ends of Herring Hall offers several examples. Bold criss-cross patterns (a type of brick bonding pattern called diapering) code the brick wall surfaces as non-load bearing. The material thinness of the long north and south walls is evident along the edges of the narrow end walls, identifying all the walls as weightless planes that slip past each other at corners, the place in a bearing wall structure where structural continuity is most critical. Even the coloration of the brick changes between the long walls and the end walls, constructing subtle dialectical relationships that animate the exteriors of Herring Hall.

Pelli's effort to be explicit about how the building is made (even though the steel structural frame is covered up) and how it is organized represent his commitment to a modernist architectural ethos. His foray into architectural coding represents a postmodern enthusiasm for integrating modern architecture with its historic setting. Cram's methodology of systematic integration provided Pelli with the rationalist means to construct the elaborate, coded surfaces of Herring Hall and ground them in the site planning and typological practices of the Rice campus. The diligence with which Pelli's firm pursued integration is attested by their use of decomposed granite as the gravel for flat, built-up roof surfaces visible from third-floor windows.

The interiors of Herring Hall reflect Pelli's ethical commitment to designing amenable spaces for learning and work. Within the three-story wing, the first and second floors are organized with single-loaded corridors. The corridors overlook the Douglass Courtyard; the second-floor concourse is especially notable for its generous width. The building's two sets of fire stairs are also generously dimensioned and detailed with wit, using patterned glazed tile block and articulated stair handrails to give these usually undesigned spaces a sense of place. The third-floor corridor, a double loaded corridor, is extremely long and narrow. Pelli's office accentuated this characteristic—but rather than feeling oppressive, the corridor has a playful quality to it, which extends to the pointed bay windows at either end. Since they are cantilevered, they project the viewer out into space.

The O'Connor Center interior is a postmodern evocation of a nineteenth-century library, with the central well of the reading room encircled by galleries. The proportions of this space are subtly diminutive, giving the library a sense of intimacy unexpected in an institutional building. Pelli's office even lowered the sill lines of the windows to the eye-level of a seated reader. Pelli's office was in charge of the interior design and landscape design of Herring Hall. It is responsible for the interior detailing, although the display of national flags commemorates the use of the O'Connor Center as a conference room for foreign ministers during the 1990 Economic Summit. A nine-square display of national stones and a dedicatory table also commemorate the summit in the Douglass Courtyard. These were installed by the landscape architects Sasaki Associates.

Herring Hall constructs Rice identity as complex and layered. It fuses awareness of Rice's architectural history with a determination to acknowledge that the conditions under which architecture was produced in the 1910s were not those of the 1980s. Pelli constructs postmodern historicism as a principled engagement with historical architecture. This engagement is based on materialist analysis rather than formal quotation. His practice of investing 1980s composite construction with the tectonic intricacy of 1910s monolithic construction enabled him to suggest that identity is neither static nor formulaic. It stakes a claim to authenticity by rigorously questioning received traditions rather than reproducing them. Herring Hall further suggests that this critical process must be renewed with each successive architectural undertaking and that, as the Ley Student Center and Cambridge Seven's George R. Brown Hall imply, it loses its momentum when reduced to a stylistic formula.

Herring Hall proved to be an important model for postmodern institutional and commercial architecture in Houston of the late 1980s and early 1990s. Ben Taub General Hospital in the Texas Medical Center (CRS Sirrine and Llewelyn-Davies Sahni, 1989) and the Shepherd Square shopping center at Westheimer and South Shepherd (Watkins Carter Hamilton, 1990) exhibit the impact that its vibrant brick banding had on local architecture.

In 1997 a new dean, Gilbert Whitaker (Class of 1953), reorganized
the Jones Graduate School of Administration as the Jesse H. Jones
Graduate School of Management. The reorganization entailed expansion of
the student body, the faculty, and the school's educational programs. In
1999 it was decided that a new building would be constructed for the Jones
School rather than an addition to Herring Hall. After the Jones School occupies its new building, the English and linguistics departments of the school
of humanities will occupy Herring Hall.

26. Lee and Joe Jamail Plaza *Sasaki Associates, 1998*

Lee and Joe Jamail Plaza introduced a new kind of designed open space to
the Rice campus. Constructed in conjunction with James A. Baker III Hall,
the dark brick and granite-paved square, flanked by four garden parterres, is
centered on a low, domed fountain from which five jets of water emanate.
Embedded in the paving on the cardinal points are relief plaques of birds by
Farley Tobin, a ceramic artist who teaches at the Rhode Island School of
Design. The plaques include an eagle (the United States), a mocking bird
(Texas), doves of peace, and an owl (Rice). The fountain lies astride the
main axis. Sasaki Associates of Boston, Rice's landscape architectural consultants since 1990, planned the plaza so that it could also be used as a
motor court for dignitaries arriving at the Baker Institute.

The plaza occupies a problematic site along the axis. In 1990
Sasaki Associates prepared a landscape master plan, called a Landscape
Vision, for the campus. They proposed reconciling the willow oaks that
Robert White installed in the Great Square next to the Rice Memorial Center
by using them to define a narrower channel along the main axis, which
would widen as the axis continued west beyond the site of the plaza to

Lee and Joe Jamail Plaza

recover its 300-foot width. To this end Sasaki Associates proposed that two buildings, facing each other, be pulled forward toward the center line of the axis at this point. Sasaki's recommendation resulted in the siting of Baker Hall to the south, and the new Jones School building to the north of Jamail Plaza, facing Baker Hall.

In the General Plan the line-up of academic buildings was to end where the cross street between Jamail Plaza and Herring Hall now passes. The main axis was then to traverse the Persian Gardens that stretched as far west as the site of Alice Pratt Brown Hall. Sasaki had to deal with the west-ward migration of academic buildings in the 1980s into the never-cultivated Persian Gardens and fill the void that extended from the Rice Memorial Center and Herring Hall all the way to Alice Pratt Brown Hall. They also had to deal with the consequences of moving the cross-axial street in 1959, which threw off the alignment of the third cross-axial proposed in the General Plan. The extension of M.D. Anderson Biological Laboratories in 1967 froze the cross street in place, creating the awkward half-site depth vis-ible between the cross street and the west end of Herring Hall (the depth within which Predock's Butcher Hall was built).

Jamail Plaza is where Rice begins its second century. Sasaki's corporate aesthetic and the formulaic spatiality and plant palette of their garden parterres give this space a feeling of anonymity, which may dimin-ish once the plants and the live oaks mature. The westward prospect, toward the still-distant Alice Pratt Brown Hall, Rice Stadium, and the east stadium parking lot, is a reminder of the landscape conditions Cram, Goodhue & Ferguson confronted when they came to Houston in 1909. Sasaki's landscape vision suggests a pleasant academic mall leading to Alice Pratt Brown Hall. Sasaki tried to resolve the contradictions created when the 1950s landscape order was superimposed on that of the General Plan by returning to Cram's practice of shaping a sequence of strongly defined figural spaces. How this accommodates cross axes with links to other parts of the campus; how adjoining building groups relate to each other; and what the measure, rhythm, and proportion of this new landscape order will be are not yet clear, as the university has not authorized Sasaki Associates to proceed with anything approaching the magnitude of Cram's Academic Court or the planting of live oak trees that defined the Great Square. The decision not to obscure the front of Baker Hall with new trees suggests that Sasaki's academic mall plan may clash with a desire for archi-tectural visibility. The university's reluctance to construct campus space on the grand scale that Cram and Lovett did is typical of post-Progressive Houston. The Jamail Plaza unwittingly problematizes Rice identity by virtue of the open-ended yet non-committal prospect it constructs.

Jamail Plaza was a gift to the university from Lee Hage Jamail, a trustee and member of the committee on buildings and grounds, and her husband Joseph D. Jamail, a Houston lawyer.

James A. Baker III Hall

27.   James A. Baker III Hall

Hammond Beeby & Babka and Morris Architects, 1997

Baker Hall houses an institute of international public policy and diplomacy. Its dedication honors James A. Baker III, grandson of the first chairman of Rice's board of trustees. Baker, a Houston lawyer, was chief of staff during the first term of President Ronald Reagan and Secretary of the Treasury during Reagan's second term. He was Secretary of State during the administration of President George Bush. James Baker is honorary chairman of the Baker Institute and a trustee of Rice University. The James A. Baker III Institute of Public Policy shares Baker Hall with the department of social sciences. Richard J. Stoll, professor of political science, proposed the organization of the institute in 1992. Two former presidents, George Bush and Gerald Ford, attended the groundbreaking for the building in 1994; three former secretaries of state, Henry A. Kissinger, Cyrus R. Vance, and Warren Christopher, as well as former Soviet president Mikhail Gorbachev participated in the dedication in 1997.

Baker Hall is two stories high, with a third story incorporated in its attic. It contains 64,100 square feet. The exterior is faced with St. Joe brick and precast concrete and roofed with red clay tile. The building is square in plan and is organized around a central, top-lit court, the William J. Doré Commons. Opening off the Doré Commons is the Kelly International Conference Facility, a plushly appointed auditorium seating 138 people. The commons and the conference auditorium were designed and engineered so that events there could be broadcast using real-time audiovisual links. The offices of the Baker Institute are on the east side of the commons, those of the school of social sciences on the west. The second floor contains the offices of fellows, faculty, and staff. Loggias surround the court on the upper floors; these double as seating loges for events in the common.

Baker Hall is curious. Thomas H. Beeby, the Chicago architect who designed it, did what César Pelli had assumed to be inconceivable when he designed Herring Hall in the early 1980s: Beeby produced a building whose façade might have come from the drafting boards of Cram & Ferguson's office in the 1930s. Beeby and his associates Dennis Rupert, Gary Ainge, Kirsten Beeby, and Frank DeSantis were extremely conscientious in their efforts to compose and detail the surfaces of Baker Hall. They gave the building a provocative Islamic subtext, which resonates with the observation of the architectural critic Montgomery Schuyler in 1910 that Bertram Goodhue's hypothetical design for the Rice Institute of 1909 was "Saracenic," and memorializes what was to have been the Persian Gardens. It resonates as well with James Baker's tenure as U. S. secretary of state during the Persian Gulf War of 1991.

Beeby sited Baker Hall to conform to Sasaki Associates' Landscape Vision for Rice. Rather than being built against the south sidewalk in alignment with Herring Hall, it is advanced forward, toward the centerline of the main axis. Because it was built in a part of the campus where there was no mature tree growth, Baker Hall stands out, as does the residual space between its south-facing rear elevation and the campus loop street. Beeby's analysis of the planning requirements for Baker Hall resulted in its organization as a thick block rather than as thin parallel slabs. Thus it has more in common with the big box typology that came to be a feature of Rice's architecture in the 1990s than with Cram's buildings. It forms reciprocal relationships with the landscape only in its frontal orientation toward Jamail Plaza.

The north-facing front elevation of Baker Hall is crisply detailed. Beeby sought to give it some of the scale complexity of Cram's buildings by recessing the entrance doors and the second-story windows above them in two-and-a-half-story high arched portals and by banding second-story windows with molded belt courses. Beeby, who was dean of the school of architecture at Yale University from 1985 to 1991, collaborated with Kent Bloomer, professor of architecture at Yale, on the iconographic detail. Bloomer, known for his interest in architectural ornament, was responsible for the design of the limestone column capitals. Those framing the triple entrance portals exhibit figures representing students (center portal), scholarship (right portal), and diplomacy (left portal). Bloomer designed the wall-mounted sculptural light fixtures flanking the entrance portals, which evoke the outspread wings of an owl. Plaques exhibiting an array of iconographic images are the work of ceramic artists Farley Tobin, who also executed the Venetian glass mosaic wall panels, displaying excerpts from James Baker's speeches.

Baker Hall's public spaces are spare, reflecting the austerity of Cram, Goodhue & Ferguson's interiors at Rice. The floor of the entrance vestibule, the Grand Hall (a gift of the Sultanate of Oman), is polished concrete. An intermediate lobby between the Grand Hall and the Doré Commons displays tile and marble paving, inspired by examples in the Administration and Physics Buildings, inlaid in the concrete. The Doré Commons is restrained. Bloomer's *trompe-l'oeil* "tiles" in the spandrels beneath the second- and third-floor loge openings are a clever touch. These are acoustically absorbent fabric panels onto which tile patterns have been stenciled. The highlight of the Doré Commons is the extraordinary Bin Hamoodah chandelier, its design based on those of the Sultan Ahmet Mosque in Istanbul. Light diffusers are attached to three concentric rings suspended from a central chord with radial cables. The scale of the chandelier is awesome, yet it is light and modern rather than neo-historical in design. Currents of air-conditioning cause the rings to rotate slowly; the effect is subtle and hypnotic.

The Bin Hammodah chandelier radiates what Baker Hall otherwise lacks: energy. Beeby and his associates are profoundly earnest. But their good intentions—even their "Orientalist" subtext—do not animate the architecture. The public spaces are dull, in part because they receive so little daylight, in part because of the lackluster finish of the woodwork. The Doré Commons is a peculiar combination of a middle eastern domestic courtyard and nineteenth-century provincial opera house, its heavily draped boxes inadvertently suggesting that the state events below are merely a kind of theater. Looking up from the commons, visitors are all too aware of the suspended acoustical tile ceilings in upstairs offices. The failure to integrate modern building systems with thematic styling reinforces the stage-set feel of the interior architecture.

Using a figure of speech Beeby excerpted from one of James Baker's speeches, Baker Hall was conceived as bridging architecturally from the world inside the hedges to a global context. Yet it is an inward turning building, insulated from its setting. Beeby and his associates seemed to sense that performing historical revivalism was inadequate. Architecture that aspires to parity with Cram's buildings has to be as bold and original, even if, like Cram's, it is based on historical models. Their building lacks boldness. It presents itself as a lesson in how to combine shapes and materials to reproduce a desired image, not as a startling synthesis of the familiar and the unimagined. It constructs Rice identity as already determined. The architecture's most tantalizing characteristic, its Islamic orientation, is evasive and unresolved. Like Rice identity, it is treated as unproblematic rather than as a medium for representing Houston's connection, via its energy economy and politics, to conflicts that played a major role in James Baker's diplomatic career and continue to affect domestic and international policy.

28. Jesse H. Jones Graduate School of Management Building

Robert A. M. Stern Architects and Morris Architects, to be completed in 2002

In 1999 Rice University retained the New York architect Robert A. M. Stern, dean of architecture at Yale University, to design a building in association with Morris Architects of Houston for the Jones School of Management. Stern's three-story building complex will completely fill the north side of the axis extending from Jamail Plaza westward to Alice Pratt Brown Hall. A two-story pavilion, centered on an arched loggia will confront Baker Hall from the north side of the Jamail Plaza. A deep indentation of the Jones School's north face will separate this pavilion from its west wing. Along the campus loop street to the north, the building is treated as a continuous expanse of banded brick wall, penetrated by paired, arched windows and a pair of gabled entrance pavilions. It will be, by far, the biggest of the big box buildings constructed at Rice since the mid-1990s.

The Jones School design appears to be even more detached and space-neutral than Baker Hall. It dispenses with the fine-grained, north-south, cross-axial landscape connections that César Pelli's Master Plan for Growth proposed for this sector of the campus in 1983, as well as the less nuanced recommendations of the Sasaki Landscape Vision. Stern's Jones School design threatens to reduce the west axis to a monotonous linear mall in which landscape is totally subordinated to buildings. By cutting off cross-campus connections to the tract north of the campus loop street, the design could well exercise the same deadening effect on this presently undeveloped meadow that the Fondren Library did on the development of the Great Square.

The exterior elevations of the Jones School complex are florid effusions of neo-Rice styling. They mask the dearth of commitment to constructing a systematically integrated landscape order that expands the campus tradition of spatial continuity, an essential element of Rice's historic architectural identity. The Jones building will introduce a new feature connected to the conservation of campus open space, the first underground parking garage at Rice.

29. Alice Pratt Brown Hall

Ricardo Bofill and the Taller de Arquitectura and Kendall/Heaton Associates, 1991

Alice Pratt Brown Hall, named for the wife of the Rice trustee George R. Brown, a philanthropist and art patron, houses the Shepherd School of Music. Sallie Shepherd Perkins provided Rice with an endowment to fund a music department in 1950 as a memorial to her grandfather, the nineteenth-century Houston banker Benjamin A. Shepherd, a contemporary of William

Alice Pratt Brown Hall

M. Rice. The Philadelphia architect W. Pope Barney prepared a schematic
design for a music building in 1953, based on the neoclassical Parris House
of 1811 in Richmond, Virginia, where Mrs. Perkins lived. Although income
from the endowment was used to fund a music program, it was not until
1975 that the Shepherd School of Music came into being as a full-fledged
academic department.

In 1986 when the composer, conductor, physiologist, and philoso-
pher Michael P. Hammond began his tenure as dean, the Shepherd School
did not have permanent facilities for instruction, practice, or performance.
Hammond had been dean of music at the State University of New York
(SUNY) at Purchase and then president of the university during the 1960s
and 1970s. He participated in the design and construction of SUNY's campus, planned by the New York architect Edward Larrabee Barnes and completed while Hammond was president. Frustrations involved in the SUNY
experience and his conviction that an exemplary music school building had
yet to be built caused Hammond to pursue the design of the Shepherd
School with exceptional ambition. That his stepfather had been an architect
increased his appreciation for what could be achieved.

Hammond was instrumental in convincing the university to retain
the Barcelona architect Ricardo Bofill, whose son was a Rice architecture
alumnus, in 1987. Bofill's firm, the Taller de Arquitectura, impressed
Hammond because of the bold scale of the buildings it had produced in
Spain and France. Bofill and the Taller designed an immense building of
127,000 square feet—465 feet long and 240 feet wide—composed as two
parallel slabs. The two-story academic wing terminates the main axis. It contains teaching studios, practice rooms, faculty offices, two long cross corridors, and two open-air internal courtyards. Parallel to it is the performance

wing, which faces west toward Rice Stadium and its surface parking lot. The performance wing contains the 1,000-seat Stude Concert Hall, the 236-seat Duncan Recital Hall, the Wortham Opera Theater studio, and the 200-seat Old Recital Hall and Grand Organ. The Old Grand Organ (1996) was built by Manuel Rosales of Los Angeles and C. B. Fisk of Gloucester, Massachusetts. It is a seventy-five-stop, 4,493-pipe mechanical tracker organ and reflects French organ building tradition. R. Lawrence Kirkegaard & Associates were acoustical consultants for Brown Hall and S. Leonard Auerbach & Associates were theatrical consultants. Sasaki Associates were landscape architects for the two interior courtyards, the Lummis Courtyard and the Wintermann Courtyard. Alice Pratt Brown Hall is of steel-framed construction. It is faced with St. Joe brick and precast concrete.

Bofill rewarded Dean Hammond's confidence by producing a big building. Brown Hall terminates Cram's main axis just before it dissolves into the stadium parking lot. Despite its isolated location, the site made sense for the music school's performance spaces because of proximity to the 4,685-car east stadium parking lot. Isolation gave Bofill the ability to work at the scale of the landscape. He also responded to Hammond's concept of the Shepherd School as a monastery where students proceed from the cells for individual practice, to the common spaces of instruction, to the public "chapels" and "abbey" of the performance spaces.

Bofill sought to engage the landscape with his design. The long, low, east-facing academic wing is gently bowed in plan, so that it seems to absorb the impact of the axis as it sweeps across the flat site. The west-facing performance wing has a variegated skyline, which expresses the volumes of the Stude Concert Hall and Old Recital Hall. The performance

Alice Pratt Brown Hall

wing has a Michelangelo-esque aspect; a struggle for exterior expression seems to be ensuing between the various halls. Bofill's overlay of emphatic horizontals, imposed by continuous belt courses, accentuates rather than resolves the sense of conflict on the west face of the school. On the east face, which is considerably lower than the west side of the building, horizontality dominates. As built the curvature of the east elevation was so flattened that it is almost imperceptible.

Alice Pratt Brown Hall is a relentlessly schematic design. It is intriguing that Bofill, a European architect (like John Outram at Duncan Hall), appears to have been unmoved by postmodern contextualism as interpreted by American-based architects working at Rice in the 1980s and 1990s. Beyond the use of St. Joe brick laid up in Flemish bond, he made no effort to confirm Rice identity with architectural references. His design involved a response to the landscape that was Cram-like in its magnitude. But despite its size, Alice Pratt Brown Hall doesn't absorb the landscape and reinterpret it in a new or compelling way. Bofill proposed to do this by producing a heroic landscape plan, which included a semicircular reflecting basin (whose convex thrust would counter the concave recession of the east front), a virtual forest of potted trees along the stripes of the east stadium lot, and a new entrance drive from University Boulevard aligned with the main axis and integrated with the south plaza of Rice Stadium. This drive would have reproduced the spatial choreography of Entrance One. Such improvements were not part of the budget for the Shepherd School. While they would have made more sense of some of the building's compositional gestures, they would not have compensated for its architectural underdevelopment.

The interior spaces of Alice Pratt Brown Hall are generous in scale. The lateral corridors in the academic wing, because of their 450-foot length, are imposing but not oppressive. Natural light, which enters these corridors from each end as well as from the open-air courtyards along their length, animates them. Lack of architectural detail makes the interiors seem unpretentious and emphasizes the building's academic purpose. The central lobby serving the two large performance halls (which memorializes Houston architect Ralph A. Anderson, Jr., Class of 1943) repeats the exterior columnar theme in drywall. It is the scale, openness, and infusion of natural light that rescue the lobby from pretentiousness. The organization of the Stude Concert Hall was based on the Musikverein in Vienna. African sapele wood, used to panel its interior, contributes to its acoustical quality. The most striking interior is that of the 78-foot high Old Organ Recital Hall. Confronting the enormous 49-foot, six-inch high case of Honduran mahogany, designed by Charles Nazarian and studded with symmetrically arrayed pipes, is a bit like opening the door to a closet and finding a skyscraper inside.

The architecture of Alice Pratt Brown Hall disappoints because it was begun with such ambition. Bofill's landscape design displayed his capacity to work at the scale of the landscape and recover the coherence of Cram's General Plan. His difficulty conforming to the constraints of American institutional patronage, with its diffusion of authority and insistence on economy and efficiency, resulted in a building with no tectonic depth. Alice Pratt Brown Hall is redeemed by the quality of it ordinary spaces. More so than its bombastic but inert exteriors, these reflect the commitment to vocation embodied in Michael Hammond's monastic metaphor for a community of learning.

Frequent public performances by faculty, students, the Shepherd School Symphony Orchestra, the Shepherd Chamber Orchestra, the Shepherd Contemporary Ensemble, the Rice Chorale, SYZYGY—New Music at Rice, the Campanile Orchestra, the Rice Symphonic Band, and visiting artists occur in Alice Pratt Brown Hall.

The Residential Group

The southern sector of the campus was designated in the General Plan as the Residential Group for Men. It was to include not only four men's dormitory groups, which President Lovett hoped to convert to residential colleges, but a student union and the institute's gymnasium and stadium. Cram, Goodhue & Ferguson locked these components together in a generously scaled site plan, which provided space for casual sports with a 300-foot wide secondary axis framed by rows of live oak trees (perhaps with some insight into potential rivalries among the colleges, the width of the axis kept them at a safe distance from each other). The three dormitory buildings that the Cram firm designed conformed to their preferred building shape: the long, thin bar. This configuration was optimal in Houston's hot, humid climate because it opened the maximum amount of frontage to the prevailing southeast breeze. The typological repetition of the dormitories was qualified by the addition of such elements as towers with terrace decks—which were intended to provide high-set common rooms where students could study on sultry nights—and cloistered passages providing sheltered outdoor spaces for casual socializing.

The intentions of the General Plan have been preserved in the Residential Group, although site planning configurations changed. Wiess College, Rice's first postwar dormitory, was designed by Staub & Rather. It exhibits the same purposeful break with Cram's architecture that the Staub firm's other Rice buildings did. The residential college additions to the Cram dormitories of 1957, by Wilson, Morris, Crain & Anderson, are not architecturally distinctive, but they reinforced the broad patterns of the General Plan. The residential college additions changed the scale of outdoor spaces, however, and partitioned what were to have been Cram's colleges into separate new colleges.

The pair of colleges planned in the 1960s, Lovett and Richardson, fit less securely into the spatial order of the Residential Group, in part because the residential college additions of 1957 afforded no obvious place for subsequent colleges to be built. During the 1960s, a non-residential building, Allen Center, the university's administrative office building, was constructed in the Residential Group where the student union was to have gone in the General Plan. A replacement for Wiess College, designed by Machado, Silvetti & Associates, breaks new ground by being built outside the quadrants of Cram, Goodhue & Ferguson's Residential Group. It reaffirms President Lovett's vision of collegiate quadrangles while interacting poetically with the campus landscape.

Cohen House, the faculty club of Rice University, was foreseen in the General Plan. It was built in the Residential Group as the institutional equivalent of the faculty's house. The failure of Cram, Goodhue & Ferguson in 1910 to predict the impact of the automobile on a university campus is evident in the Residential Group. Although there is not enough space for all the students living in colleges to park adjacent to each college, surface parking lots nonetheless consume a very visible amount of territory. College parking lots have been concentrated along Main Boulevard, along with the servicing docks for many of the colleges. This creates an unfortunate layer between the university and the city, in contrast to the park-like landscapes along Main Boulevard north of Entrance Three and south of Entrance Four.

30. Residential Group Axis

Cram, Goodhue & Ferguson designated the portion of the campus between Main Boulevard and the Academic Court and Great Square as the men's dormitory sector. In *The Book of the Opening*, President Lovett spoke of his goal of creating a system of residential colleges at Rice. Consequently, the men's dormitories were grouped into four quadrangles aligned on a secondary axis, 1,200 feet long and 300 feet wide, parallel to the main axis. At the east end of the axis, its edges defined by double rows of live oak trees, was to be the student union. At the west end was a gymnasium fronting one end of a stadium whose bleachers returned in a half-circle at the far end, so that it figured like a Roman *circus* in the General Plan. The intersection of the Residential Group axis and the second cross-axis created four

Residential Group

Residential Group Axis

quadrants, each occupied by a college. Between Main Boulevard and the secondary axis, the cross-axis was outlined with double rows of live oak trees. North of this intersection, it was outlined with an allée of cedar elm trees. Aligned on the cross-axis was a street, which stopped at the south campus loop street until it was extended northward in conjunction with construction of the Fondren Library. The street was flanked by sidewalks and hedges to shape space, direct movement, and frame vistas on the flat, treeless plain.

Between 1912 and 1916 three dormitories and the Institute Commons were constructed, filling out the northeast quadrant with South Hall and East Hall (now part of Will Rice and Baker Colleges) and commencing the northwest quadrant with West Hall (now Hanszen College). Not until the postwar period was the next increment, Wiess Hall (now Wiess College) built. This filled out the northwest quadrant, but made no effort to connect to West Hall. The Rice Gymnasium and Autry Court was built at the same time, but it was constructed in isolation, far to the west, disconnected from the Residential Group.

Between 1955 and 1956, the university made the decision to institute the residential college system Lovett had wanted. In 1956–57, additions were made to the Cram dormitories to transform them into colleges. In order to ensure that each of the colleges would have an "old" portion, the northeast quadrant was partitioned. The Commons and East Hall became part of Baker College, and South Hall became part of Will Rice College. New residential wings were added to the three older dormitory buildings and new commons buildings were added to Will Rice, Hanszen, and Wiess. Each of the four colleges received a master's house, where the college master (a faculty member) and his family lived. The Houston architects Wilson, Morris, Crain & Anderson adhered in principle to the residential group axis prescribed in the General Plan. They configured the Will Rice additions to South Hall and the Hanszen additions to West Hall with reflective symmetry to outline an axis, aligned on the single rank of live oak trees that had been planted. However, they reduced the width of the residential group axis to one-third its intended dimension. They located the commons of Will Rice and Hanszen astride the axis, blocking any future extension. In conjunction with the construction of the colleges, the street along the cross-axis was eliminated. The creation of the college system led to the decision not to build the Rice Memorial Center at the east end of the Residential Group axis.

Subsequent college construction has filled in the blank spaces left over from 1957. Lovett College was constructed in 1969 astride the width of the Cram, Goodhue & Ferguson residential group axis. Since it lay behind Will Rice College, though, it did not participate in the larger organization of the landscape. Sid W. Richardson College was constructed to one side of the second cross-axis, cutting it off from Main Boulevard, in 1971. Both were elevator-buildings: Lovett was a slab and Sid Rich a tower, so that they did not shape exterior space in the way that prior residential buildings had. In the late 1990s the university decided to build a new undergraduate college in the Residential Group to replace Wiess College. The Boston architects Machado & Silvetti Associates seek with their design for a new Wiess College to claim expanded terrain for the Residential Group outside the parameters of the General Plan. Between the 1960s and the 1990s a fundamental change occurred in Rice colleges; notably, between 1973 and 1987 each of the colleges changed from single-sex to coeducational membership.

31. Institute Commons, East Hall, and Baker College

Institute Commons   *Cram, Goodhue & Ferguson, 1912*
East Hall   *Cram, Goodhue & Ferguson, 1915*
Baker College and Baker House   *Wilson, Morris, Crain & Anderson, 1957*

Baker College, named in memory of James A. Baker, William M. Rice's lawyer and chairman of the board of trustees from 1891 until 1941, comprises two Cram, Goodhue & Ferguson wings as well as the 1957 college addition and master's house. South Hall, now part of Will Rice College, was originally part of what was called Residential Group Number One.

Cram, Goodhue & Ferguson marked the Residential Group as domestic to distinguish them stylistically from the buildings of the Academic Court and the Court of Engineering. These building constitute a third subset of Cram's Rice style, or meta-style, since it dispensed variations conditioned by situation and use. They demonstrate how consistently, rigorously, and imaginatively Cram, Goodhue & Ferguson constructed a mythic landscape of organic order at Rice, using composition, materials, and site configurations as components of a spatial narrative that "naturalized" variation in the context of a larger order. President Lovett in *The Book of the Opening* described the architecture of the Residential Group as "characteristically Venetian"; William Ward Watkin described it as "a distinctly domestic type of Italian architecture," and in a memoir written about 1950 he evoked the vernacular domestic architecture of Genoa that "preceded the extreme regularity which came with the Renaissance."

The architects' penchant for adducing dialectical distinctions based on hierarchies, and making architecture out of these distinctions, is evident here. They surfaced the residential buildings with brick and stucco rather than a Byzantine combination of brick and stone. Brick was concentrated on the lower floor of each building; the upper floors were finished with gray stucco. Pitched roofs with overhanging eaves were not suppressed behind parapets. The architects varied the treatment of these elements on each building, so that individual identity could be asserted within the Residential Group.

The Institute Commons originally contained the dining hall (now Baker College Commons), a kitchen and staff apartment, a commons room (now the college library), and dormitory rooms and studies for graduate fellows and unmarried faculty in the five-story faculty tower. East Hall contained bedrooms organized around three separate entries, each with its

East Hall, right; *Baker College*, left

own set of stairs. Each building is a long, thin slab shape. Neither is symmetrically composed. Oriented toward the south, each building contains a five-story tower at one end. The Institute Commons, although it now has a north-facing entry aligned with the Humanities Building and Fondren Library (which is considered its front door), was originally entered from the south, through the cloister that connects it to South Hall. The cloister at the base of East Hall faces south, as do the cloisters of South and West Halls. Cram, Goodhue & Ferguson constructed a domestic identity by emphasizing circumstance, avoiding symmetry, and by facing the buildings southward, which entailed turning their backs toward the campus loop street.

Institute Commons, faculty tower

The layout of the commons can be read in the massing of the building. The kitchen was virtually a separate structure, although connected to the dining room. The dining room—a double-volume hall rising up beneath exposed pine roof trusses and the most "collegiate" interior at Rice—is expressed externally by tall, high-set, arched windows grouped in pairs between piers. The faculty tower reads as a separate element, as does the two-story west end block containing the college library.

Cram, Goodhue & Ferguson extended their narrative by transforming functional differentiation into architectural incident. From the southwest corner of the Institute Commons, nearest the cross-axis, they distinguished between the stucco-faced brick piers of the free-standing cloister, which cuts through the quadrangle to connect to South Hall, and the arched bay where the cloister returns against the south face of the commons, inserting a colonnette to divide one arched bay into two. To articulate the presence of the commons room next to this columniated bay, they cased pairs of French doors with brick surrounds, inserting tile borders and marble spandrels to frame the pointed-arched transoms surmounting the French doors. The walls of the Institute Commons are finished with stucco and banded with brick.

The first floor walls of East Hall are brick, and the second- and third-floor walls are surfaced with stucco—except on the tower, where brick encompasses the second floor level as well. On the north side of East Hall, facing the campus loop street, the arrangement of windows and doors communicates the presence of interior stairs. Note that tile panels in the arched heads above doors and the arched moldings with pinnacle-like caps above windows reappear on Alan Greenberg's Humanities Building across the street. Interlining the brick courses of East Hall are decorative tile courses executed by the Enfield Pottery and Tile Company of Enfield, Pennsylvania. Enfield was also responsible for the tile and brick frieze belting the tower at the level of the fifth-floor windows. A distinctive feature of East Hall is its projecting wooden bay windows. With the shallow pitched hipped roof of the tower and the tile frieze, these windows were inspired by the vernacular architecture of the Himalayan kingdom of Bhutan, a source even more exotic than Venice. The journalistic account of Bhutan cited by Cram's associate Alexander E. Hoyle as a design source also inspired the design of the original buildings at the Texas College of Mines and Metallurgy (now the University of Texas at El Paso) in 1917.

The cloisters of East Hall and the other residential halls were places for casual socializing. Perhaps to restrain to the exuberance of Texan students, the column capitals of East Hall's cloister were carved with passages invoking wisdom, from *Proverbs* and the *Wisdom of Solomon,* which can be read sequentially.

The Institute Commons has two notable interiors (which are not always publicly accessible). One is the library. The other is the dining hall, which can be entered from the north-facing cloister. In 1938 William Ward Watkin expanded the dining hall (which is why the commons now collides with East Hall) and paneled the lower reaches of its walls. In tribute to this collegiate interior, Baker College stages an annual Shakespeare festival. Double doors underneath a musicians' gallery at the west end of the dining hall lead on axis to the college library (the former commons), which retains its Cram, Goodhue & Ferguson mantelpieces.

When the architectural firm composed of F. Talbott Wilson (Class of 1934), S. I. Morris, Jr. (Class of 1935), B. W. Crain, Jr., and Ralph A. Anderson, Jr. (Class of 1943) designed the college additions, they produced thin, two-story-and-basement dormitories that are one-room deep and entered from separate entries with exterior stairways. Bedrooms are paired with a bathroom. The reinforced concrete-framed, brick-faced dormitories are arranged in an L-plan configuration to shape quadrangular spaces. Vertical concrete fins stationed between windows counter the horizontality of the continuous eaves. Pitched roofs are surfaced with red clay shingle tiles. At the re-entrant angle of the L is a three-story block. Beneath the windows are decorative panels of mosaic tile graduated in color as they rise, designed by James Chillman, Jr., professor of architecture and art history.

Talbott Wilson's design is a bit evasive, as it tries to be responsive to the Cram buildings while preserving a modern identity. It is tempting to discern the influence of the British townscape movement or Italian neo-realism of the early 1950s, because of Wilson, Morris, Crain & Anderson's quixotic effort to embrace familiarity and newness without acknowledging that these were contradictory positions. The diminutive scale of Wilson, Morris, Crain & Anderson's college addition makes it unlike the older buildings. As at the Rice Memorial Chapel, reduced scale seems to have represented an appeal for inoffensiveness that, in the polemically-charged 1950s, was not apt to be honored.

Facing the second cross-axis, where it intersects the campus loop street, is Baker House, the master's house, also by Wilson, Morris, Crain & Anderson. This is an innocuous two-story house with a pitched roof. It is fronted by a high brick wall enclosing an entry courtyard and giving the master's family a measure of privacy. Baker House and its twin, Wiess House, face each other at this point, architecturally reinforcing the threshold that occurs here as the cross-axis leaves the Residential Group and enters the Great Square.

32. South Hall and Will Rice College

South Hall *Cram, Goodhue & Ferguson, 1912*
Will Rice College, Will Rice Commons, and Will Rice House
Wilson, Morris, Crain & Anderson, 1957

Will Rice College is named for William M. Rice, Jr., the nephew and name-sake of the founder, a Houston businessman, and trustee of the institute from 1899 until his death in 1944. Rice was chairman of the board of trustees from 1941 until 1944. Will Rice College includes South Hall, the first dormitory built at Rice. It was part of Residential Group Number One until this was partitioned when the residential college system was adopted.

South Hall is a three-story building with a central, five-story tower. Dormitory rooms were laid out in a double-loaded corridor arrangement, which meant that nearly half the bedrooms had a north rather than south orientation. In Houston's hot, humid climate this arrangement must have proved unsatisfactory, as East and West halls were subsequently built with separate entries organized around stairwells. South Hall originally

South Hall

housed 200 students. It is linked to the Institute Commons by a 100-foot-long cloister, making it possible for students to walk under cover between the two buildings. The cloister penetrated South Hall as an open-air "slype," which made a right angle turn to become the south-facing cloister of South Hall. Doors were subsequently installed at the entrances to South Hall to enclose the slype.

The first-floor walls of the building are surfaced with brick; the upper stories are finished with stucco. The arches of the south-facing cloister spring from low columns. The columns are faceted, of layered brick and stone construction, with luxuriantly carved stone capitals. Some second-floor rooms have wrought iron balconies. A colorful tile frieze, fabricated by the Pewabic Pottery Company, belts the top of the tower.

Lined up outside the south front of South Hall are the live oak trees planted under Cram, Goodhue & Ferguson's direction to define the residential group axis. When Wilson, Morris, Crain & Anderson added the new college wing and commons, they mirrored the alignment of South Hall with one arm of the dormitory wing and backed up the second cross-axis with the other. However, they reduced the width of the residential group axis to one-third its intended dimension. In siting Will Rice Commons between South Hall and the new college wing, they terminated Will Rice's quadrangle and foreclosed further extension of the residential group axis to the east. The proportion of the Will Rice quad is more manageable and less grandiose than the residential axis proposed in the General Plan. Yet the seeming exclusion of Lovett College, behind the Will Rice Commons, is attributable to its being cut off from the rest of the Residential Group.

The Will Rice Commons is the only one of the 1957 college commons that remains substantially intact. It contains a lounge at grade level and, a split-level above, the college dining room. The college commons buildings were originally furnished with classic modern furniture from Knoll Incorporated—which has all disappeared. Tile solar screens once shielded the east and west-facing windows (originally outfitted with jalousies, as were all the windows in the Wilson, Morris, Crain & Anderson buildings); these are also gone.

Will Rice Commons

Beneath the west-facing windows looking into the college quadrangle are a series of humorous polychrome terracotta relief panels by William McVey. These illustrate scenes from college life and incorporate personalities and mischievous incidents from McVey's academic career at Rice in the 1920s. When the college additions were built, the dormitories were not air-conditioned, but the commons buildings and the master's houses were.

Will Rice House, at the south end of the second cross-axis next to Sid Richardson College, had its landscaped courtyard planned by Robert F. White & Associates, who were responsible for new landscape installations in the Residential Group. White's Thomas Church-like design, incorporating circular and curvilinear geometries, was the most notable of his master's house gardens.

33.   West Hall and Hanszen College

West Hall   *Cram & Ferguson, 1916*
Hanszen College and Master's House   *Wilson, Morris, Crain & Anderson, 1957*
Hanszen Commons
    William T. Cannady with F. Talbott Wilson, consulting architect, 1976

Hanszen College is named for Harry C. Hanszen, an independent oil operator and chairman of the board of trustees from 1946 to 1950. Hanszen incorporates West Hall, the last of the dormitories by Cram & Ferguson (as the firm name became after Bertram G. Goodhue withdrew at the end of 1914) to be built. It was to be the first increment of Residential Group Number Two. West Hall has a stucco base banded with brick in its cloister range. In place of columns, the cloister arcade is supported on piers. On the north-facing back of the building, two stair bays are marked with brickwork that

West Hall

migrates into the stucco zone. The stair doors and windows are decorated with stone detailing. West Hall is studded with glazed ceramic discs fabricated by the Enfield Pottery and Tile Company.

The college additions and master's house mirror those of Will Rice College across the cross-axis. In 1975 a fire damaged the Hanszen Commons, and it was replaced by a slightly larger building designed by William T. Cannady, professor of architecture. Talbott Wilson, who was then serving on the board of governors, served as consulting architect. In 1998 university authorities decided to demolish the 1976 Hanszen Commons and replace it with a new commons linked to a satellite kitchen. This satellite kitchen will serve Hanszen, the new Wiess replacement college, and the college that will eventually be built on the site of the original Wiess College. The new Hanszen College commons will be designed by Machado & Silvetti Associates of Boston and will incorporate artifacts, such as the William McVey terracotta relief panels, from the first Hanszen Commons.

Hanszen College

Sid W. Richardson College, named for the independent oil operator Sid Richardson, who lived in Fort Worth, Texas, and whose charitable foundation was the major contributor to the construction of the building, is fourteen stories high. Its 153-foot height, unusual for Rice, reflects the concern of the board of governors in the mid-1960s that the campus was filling up. The university commissioned the firm of George Pierce-Abel B. Pierce to make recommendations for management of the campus. The architects proposed that the university consider a new profile for campus buildings:

Sid W. Richardson College

low at the center, in deference to the historic two and three-story skyline, while stepping up toward the perimeter of the campus. Especially along Main Boulevard, adjacent to the Texas Medical Center and away from residential neighborhoods, mid-rise construction was suggested. Brown, Lovett, and Richardson Colleges were planned in accordance with this recommendation.

Richardson was the last residential college established at Rice during the twentieth century. The Houston architects Neuhaus & Taylor produced a tower with an offset one-story base (containing the college commons and the master's house), all raised on a high exposed basement. The building was built astride what had been the right-of-way of the street that formerly traversed the second cross-axis, severing the cross-axis from its point of origin at Entrance Four on Main Boulevard. Because it was thought that a twin tower and commons would join Sid Richardson College, the Richardson commons sits just off-axis, blocking the right-of-way without quite terminating the axis of view. The complex does not interact spatially with its setting.

The tower, housing 220 students, is of reinforced concrete construction. It is faced with a brick curtain wall and precast concrete window bays. Rooms, paired with bathrooms, step out around a central elevator and stair core. Each residential floor is a half level above or below the elevator landing. In its emphasis on technique, Sid Richardson College reflects much American university architecture of the 1960s and 1970s. The building is not offensive. It merely seems disconnected from what goes on around it, not only at the south end of the cross-axis but along Main Boulevard, where frontage is dominated by a surface parking lot. Perfecting the plan diagram (on the tower residential floors if not at the base) and articulating the building's precast concrete components represent the architectural achievements of Richardson College. Given the spatial incoherence that institutional architecture of this period spread across many college campuses, Richardson College is considerate and discreet. It represented the sense that Rice University had excelled in architecture when it needed to, and that such achievements were no longer required.

Richardson College was dedicated on October 16, 1971, by late President and Mrs. Lyndon B. Johnson. Richardson had been a strong political supporter of Johnson's; the research collection wing that is part of the Lyndon Baines Johnson Library and Museum at the University of Texas at Austin (also dedicated in 1971) is called Sid W. Richardson Hall. The University of Texas's Richardson building (by Gordon Bunshaft of Skidmore, Owings & Merrill) is a 1960s building that works with, and at the scale of, the landscape. It demonstrates that even through the 1970s there were mainstream modernist alternatives to the spatial inertia of Rice's Richardson College.

35. Wiess College

Machado & Silvetti Associates and Kirksey & Partners, 2002

Rodolfo Machado and Jorge Silvetti are Argentine-born, Boston-based architects; they teach at the Graduate School of Design at Harvard University, where Jorge Silvetti chairs the architecture department. Machado taught at Rice as a visiting professor in architecture in 1986. Machado & Silvetti's design for a new college complex that will replace Wiess College is planned for a site west of Hanszen College that sits outside the Residential Group precinct prescribed in the General Plan. Machado & Silvetti's design excites because it works at the scale of the landscape. The way that materials are juxtaposed suggests that the three-story building will figure strongly on its flat, open site, especially in the long view from Main Boulevard. The complex features a broad stair that relates to playing fields between the college and the Rice Gymnasium; the stair leads from ground level to a roof terrace atop the satellite kitchen, providing a viewing stand of the athletic domain. The dormitory wing is configured around a spacious inner quadrangle. As at the old Wiess College, the floor plate of the dormitory wing is one-room deep, so that students' rooms look into the quadrangle and out to the campus. Rooms are served by open-air balcony corridors, as at old Wiess. The balconies are to be faced with stainless steel chainlink, which will serve as an armature for vines.

César Pelli's Master Plan for Growth of 1983 proposed the location of the new Wiess College as a site for future residential college expansion. How the edges of this expanded residential precinct are defined—or whether they are defined—and how it is linked to the Residential Group are pertinent issues. The demolition of Hanszen's commons might have led to recovery of the residential group axis. Instead, a new Hanszen commons will be constructed on this site, attached to the satellite kitchen serving new Wiess, Hanszen, and the college to be built where old Wiess now sits. The new Wiess College will contain rooms for 234 students. Kirksey & Partners of Houston are associated architects.

36. Wiess College, Wiess House, and Wiess Commons

Wiess College   *Staub & Rather, 1950*
Wiess Commons   *Staub, Rather & Howze, 1957; Taniguchi Shefelman Vackar Minter, 1975*
Wiess House   *Wilson, Morris, Crain & Anderson, 1957*

Wiess College, originally called Wiess Hall, was named for the Houston oil company executive Harry C. Wiess, a trustee of the institute, and was built with a gift from his widow, Olga Keith Wiess. It will be replaced by the new Wiess College. When the new college is completed in 2002, the present complex will be used as temporary office space for academic departments whose buildings are undergoing rehabilitation. It will then be demolished and, eventually, replaced by a new residential college.

Like Staub & Rather's other postwar buildings, Wiess Hall broke with the General Plan. It was built in what was to have been Residential

Wiess College

Group Number Two and was sited where the commons building for West Hall—Hanszen College—would have gone. Its dedication as a separate dormitory laid the groundwork for the partitioning of the Cram, Goodhue & Ferguson architectural ensembles that occurred six years later when the residential college system was adopted.

J. T. Rather's design was iconoclastic. The spatial organization, scale, proportions, and architectural composition of the E-plan dormitory differed radically from that of West Hall. Rather set the building at grade instead of on a partially raised basement. Its ceiling heights were low in comparison to those of the Cram dormitories. Rooms were laid out in a floor-through organization, accessible from open-air balcony corridors and stairs. Bedrooms were paired with bathrooms rather than having communal bathrooms on each floor. The thin floor plates, balcony corridors, and overhanging eave lines of Wiess give it a motel-like aspect. The building's architectural composition reflected Rather's interest in contemporary trends based on the architecture of Frank Lloyd Wright, although only Wright's penchant for horizontal alignment survived the translation.

Like Fondren Library, Wiess College rejected the architectural conventions of the General Plan and Cram's original buildings. Its architecture reflected a view of Rice in the postwar era as an open city, liberated from the cultural aspirations and architectural rhetoric of the Lovett-Cram period. Yet because Staub & Rather's uninspired version of Wrightian modernism lacked the commitment and energy of MacKie & Kamrath—the Houston modernists who were exponents of Wright's Usonian architecture in the postwar decades—Wiess College, despite its considered planning and

Wiess Commons

sound construction, always seemed marginal to the Residential Group. It lacks the strong space-shaping attributes that rescue the architecturally ambivalent Wilson, Morris, Crain & Anderson college additions of 1957 from anonymity.

Wiess College's architectural highpoint was a remodeling of the commons carried out by the Austin, Texas, architects Taniguchi Shefelman Vackar Minter in the mid-1970s. Alan Y. Taniguchi was director of the school of architecture at Rice; his partner, Walter Vackar, was responsible for the exposed steel pipe joist and butt-jointed glass incursions into Staub, Rather & Howze's very staid commons building of 1957. Vackar replaced the east-facing entrance vestibule with a glass-walled dining and conference room, separated from the college dining hall by a new entrance way that connected one of the college's quadrangles to the campus loop street. He engaged the host building in an energetic dialectic involving transparency and transgression, liberating it from its insularity without demeaning it. Unfortunately, the transgressions didn't stop in 1975. More recent alterations have diluted the impact of Vackar's alterations.

37. Edgar Odell Lovett College

Wilson, Morris, Crain & Anderson, 1968

Lovett College, like Margarett Root Brown College and Sid W. Richardson College, was built to accommodate an increase in undergraduate enrollment, which Rice's third president, Kenneth S. Pitzer, instituted as part of his program to ensure that Rice University remain in the front rank of U.S. research universities. Rice architecture in the 1960s failed, however, to reflect Pitzer's ambitions. Lovett College exemplifies the shortcomings of the campus's modern architecture of the 1960s. These shortcomings reversed the trend of the 1950s, when modern architecture reinvigorated the social construction of a Rice identity.

Edgar Odell Lovett College

Lovett College, named for Rice's first president, was built with a gift from the Brown Foundation. The complex consists of a six-story dormitory block housing 230 students, a one-story college commons, an entrance courtyard, and a two-story master's house integrated in an L-plan configuration. The complex sits at the foot of the first cross-axis just inside the gates of Entrance Three, astride the residential group axis but blocked from it by the commons of Will Rice College. Although its L-plan configuration defines an open quadrangle on the west, and the six-story block backs up the allée of elm trees along the cross-axis on the east, Lovett College stands aloof from its surroundings. The architecture articulates the building's cast-in-place concrete-frame construction, infilled with stucco panels, brick piers, glass window walls, and—enveloping the upper floors of the dormitory block—a concrete and brick solar screen. Student rooms are organized back-to-back and paired with bathrooms. The rooms are accessible from exterior balcony corridors. The only windows in the student rooms are high-set clerestory strips, which provide views of the underside of the balcony floor slabs and the concrete brackets that support them.

In the 1950s, making modern architecture from construction resulted in tectonic articulation and scale gradation. By the 1960s, this approach had become a formula. The small scale characteristic of the 1950s gave way as bigger dimensions and more robust structural members came to be preferred, resulting in an engineering mono-scale that was not qualified by the engineered enclosure systems that enveloped it. The use of a mixed blend of textured St. Joe brick does not compensate for the mechanical repetition of piers and grilles or the unarticulated expanses of blank walls with which Lovett College's concrete frame is in-filled. Modern buildings of the 1950s shaped exterior space in part because they were designed to be environmentally responsive, even when centrally air-conditioned. Lovett College, designed with central air-conditioning, is spatially inert because it no longer indulged in the fiction of environmental responsiveness. The production of space as a byproduct of framing and filling, rather than as a priority of architectural design, meant that the experience of inhabiting a building, externally as well as internally, was subordinate to the organization of space according to the deterministic logic of economics and construction. In the entrance courtyard is *Paul Bunyan's Bouquet II*, a steel sculpture by the Houston artist Jim Love of 1968. It is a gift of the Brown Foundation.

38.   Allen Center for Business Activities

Lloyd, Morgan & Jones, 1967; Lloyd Jones Fillpot Associates, 1988

Allen Center, an office building housing academic and university business offices, was built with a gift from Helen Daniels and Herbert C. Allen. Allen (Class of 1929) was president, then chairman of the board of directors, of Cameron Iron Works. He was chairman of Rice's board of trustees from 1972 to 1976. Allen Center was constructed where Harvin Moore initially

Allen Center for Business Activities

sited the Rice Memorial Chapel; Moore's 1955 Rice Memorial Center design would have had what is now the Ray Memorial Courtyard locked into a reciprocal spatial relationship with the quadrangle of Baker College.

Allen Center was designed to be a background building. It adopted the design formula characteristic of mid-1960s speculative office buildings in Houston, yet this does not detract from its dignity. The generous proportions of its front and rear cloisters and its ground-floor public spaces, its permeability by natural light, and the unpretentious detailing of its curtain wall—a limestone base course striated with brick banding beneath a field of St. Joe brick—enable it to fit into the Residential Group. Klatt & Porcher with Robert F. White designed the landscaped parking lot along the cross-axis behind Allen Center. White's firm installed what are now giant crape myrtle trees along the west side of Allen Center.

Allen Center was originally three stories, but was engineered to accept the addition of a fourth floor. When this was added in 1987–88, Lloyd Jones Fillpot, successors to Lloyd, Morgan & Jones, were directed to incorporate neo-Byzantine colonnettes and arches framing fourth-floor windows and a huge, tile-covered hipped roof enclosing a windowless fifth-floor attic. These attributes foreground Allen Center. Instead of making it fit in, they make the building stand out in away that undermines its original dignity and reserve.

39.   Robert and Agnes Cohen House
William Ward Watkin, Cram & Ferguson, consulting architects, 1927;
Lloyd & Morgan, 1958; Robert F. White & Associates, landscape architects, 1960;
William T. Cannady & Associates and Anderson Todd, 1976

George S. Cohen, the president of Foley Brothers, Houston's major department store, built Cohen House in honor of his parents, Agnes Lord and Robert I. Cohen of Galveston, Texas, as a home for the Rice Institute Faculty Club. George Cohen and his wife Esther Meyer Cohen worked closely with Watkin in planning Cohen House. Mr. and Mrs. Cohen maintained a lifelong interest in the club and its facilities.

Robert and Agnes Cohen House

Watkin planned Cohen House with a lounge, dining room, and meeting and game rooms, as well as rooms for overnight guests of the institute. Although it is not a large building, Watkin imbued it a sense of grandeur. The raised entrance figures as part of a composition involving the stair and the guestroom tower and terrace, which repeat the tower configurations of Cram, Goodhue & Ferguson's dormitories. The entrance bay is framed at a distance in the cloister of the Administration Building. Watkin constructed an identity for Cohen House that allied its massing to the buildings of the Residential Group and its materials to the buildings of the Academic Court. Cohen House is faced with brick laid in Flemish bond with thick mortar joints above a limestone base striated with brick. Watkin used limestone to frame openings on the club house's front elevation. Like the Institute Commons at Baker College, the massing of the faculty club reflects the distribution of interior volumes.

Cohen House had more elaborately finished interiors than did other Rice buildings. Vestiges of its *echt*-1920s style remain in the polished tile floors and in the stenciled, wood-beamed ceiling of the lounge. Its heavily textured plaster walls were originally stenciled with a multicolored pattern imitating tilework. The lounge and dining room of the faculty club opened to a rear, raised terrace paved with flagstone and surrounded by a balustrade of stone piers and wrought-iron railings. The pier caps of a cloister-like loggia between the lounge and the terrace are decorated with sculptural relief portraits of original members of the faculty club. These were detailed by Watkin's former student Edward B. Arrants (Class of 1925) and executed by Oswald Lassig.

By the 1950s Cohen House could no longer accommodate Rice's growing faculty. Mr. and Mrs. Cohen financed a modern, 7,000-square-foot addition by Lloyd & Morgan, which entailed covering the terrace with a flat roof; this roof was extended to enclose a new dining room built at grade level behind the terrace. The south side of the dining room is a wall of glass. Mr. and Mrs. Cohen commissioned Robert F. White to plan a garden enclosed by a faceted brick wall, focused on a large fountain by the Parisian glass sculptor Maurice Max-Ingrand, which the new dining room looks onto. The garden's curvilinear geometries are indebted to the modern design style of Thomas Church. William McVey supplemented the earlier relief portraits of faculty with eighteen terracotta reliefs of the 1960 generation of Rice professors. Subsequent additions to Cohen House by William T. Cannady and Anderson Todd, both professors of architecture at Rice, and an office wing of 1994 had minimal impact on the original club house.

Because the trustees never authorized a house for President Lovett, Cohen House was the closest the institute came to providing spaces for entertaining as well as for daily faculty lunches and meetings. Despite its compact size, Watkin's building feels dense. He built incident into the architecture as Cram & Ferguson did by narrativizing local conditions and making architecture out of these. The turned stair of the main entrance portal is a good example: it compels those entering and leaving to make several right-angle turns, spatially layering the experience of arrival and departure. Local symmetries, the disposition of window openings, and its varied rooflines energize Cohen House. It is this implied activity that gives the building a presence bigger than its size.

Detail, Robert and Agnes Cohen House

In front of the main entrance is a paved plaza installed by Sasaki Associates in 1990 for the Economic Summit. The sundial near the street, a gift of Esther and George Cohen, was installed in a setting designed by Robert F. White & Associates in 1965. White's firm was also responsible for the landscaped parking lot.

East Residential Group

The northeast corner of the campus became the women's residential group in the 1950s. In the General Plan, a faculty residence group was to have been developed here, with professors' houses framing a very grand country house for the president. The President's House was not constructed until the period of postwar expansion. It was joined by Jones College in 1957 and Brown College in 1965, the first two housing complexes built on campus for female students. The General Plan had proposed that a *single* women's college be located to the northeast of the Administration Building, facing the forecourt. The site chosen for Jones College was even farther removed from the men's colleges. It also provided the president's family with quiet, respectful, and sedate student neighbors (this changed after Rice's residential colleges became co-educational between 1973 and 1987).

Although this sector of the campus was developed in the postwar era for different uses than those prescribed in the General Plan, it employed spatial arrangements similar to those in the General Plan to reproduce Rice space. Jones College was the harbinger of this trend. Its architects, Lloyd & Morgan, adopted the forms and organization of the men's Residential Group in configuring the two dormitory wings and the commons building of Jones College. As George Pierce-Abel B. Pierce were to do in the Earth Sciences Group, Lloyd & Jones reinforced Rice identity spatially while venturing a modern architectural interpretation of that identity. Albert E. Sheppard constructed continuity with Jones by adapting its architecture for Brown College, despite the fact that Brown is a midrise building. The Mary Ellen Hale Lovett Memorial Garden by the Houston landscape architects A. Gregory Catlow and Douglas Herbert Pickworth provides a rare instance at Rice of an intensively developed landscape design that shapes outdoor space at an intimate scale.

Michael Graves's Martel College will complete the East Residential Group. It promises to follow the lead of Lloyd & Morgan at Jones College not by reproducing prior Rice residential prototypes but by imaginatively adapting them to the programmatic circumstances of the early twenty-first century.

40. President's House (Ralph S. O'Connor House)
Staub & Rather, 1949

One of the conditions that William V. Houston, professor of physics at the California Institute of Technology, set for becoming the second president of Rice was that a president's house be constructed on campus. In 1912–13, 1916–17, and 1923–24 Cram & Ferguson had prepared designs for a house

President's House (Ralph S. O'Connor House)

for President Lovett and his family. Their designs of the 1910s were typolog-
ically related to the Rice dormitories, with cloisters and towers. Each would
have been among the grandest houses in Houston had it been built. Their
design of 1923–24 was for a house in the Spanish Mediterranean style; it
too was expansive, and expensive. Each of the three houses was designed
to be built in the Faculty Residential Group, a subdivision of twenty house
sites accessible from the secondary gate at Entrance One. President Lovett
seems to have emulated Woodrow Wilson, who built houses for faculty at
Princeton. Given the distance between Houston's South End residential
neighborhoods and the Rice campus in 1909 and 1910, President Lovett perhaps saw such houses as essential for recruiting faculty. By the time Rice
opened in 1912, the gap between Houston and Rice had narrowed. The
Southmore Addition north of Hermann Park had been developed, and it is
here where a number of early faculty members instead built houses.

The President's House was to have terminated the north end of the
diagonal street that leads from the forecourt in front of the Administration
Building toward Jones College. It would have sat where the canopied walkway leading from Jones North to the Jones Commons makes a right-angled
turn, flanked by the faculty houses, most of which would have faced the live
oak-lined axis emanating from the secondary gate at Entrance One. The
grandeur of the designs for President Lovett's house seems to have been the
reason none was built. President and Mrs. Lovett rented houses in the South
End until their children left home. They then lived at the Plaza Apartment
Hotel on Montrose Boulevard, from which the president walked to Rice.

John F. Staub designed the President's House. His preliminary designs show that the house was to have been sited in accordance with the General Plan, although it would have faced Sunset Boulevard rather than backing up to it as Cram & Ferguson's houses did. As built however, the house was reduced in size and relocated to a site between the main entrance drive and the secondary entrance drive, facing the diagonal street. Apart from his choice of brick, Staub made no effort to relate the President's House to Cram's neo-Byzantine architecture. The President's House is a symmetrical two-story block capped by a hipped roof, with a flat-roofed, one-story garage wing framing a rear terrace. The front entrance is in a deep-set alcove. Staub used awning windows, as he and Rather did on their other Rice buildings of the period. As was characteristic of Staub, the principal downstairs rooms are generously proportioned and detailed with refinement. The living and dining rooms overlook the rear garden. In 1970, a cast iron canopy over the front door and a pair of iron canopies over the rear terraces were replaced with a wooden portico and a glass-walled extension to the back of the house. These were designed by the Houston architect Robert F. Lent, a former member of the architecture faculty.

The President's House is consistent with Rice's postwar buildings. It rejected the rhetoric of Cram's architecture yet remained quite conservative. It is quiet and dignified, but possesses none of the narrative liveliness that animates Staub's interwar houses.

The President's House was named O'Connor House in 1987 in honor of Ralph S. O'Connor, a Houston oilman, investor, and former president of Highland Resources, the son-in-law of Alice and George Brown, and president of the Marian Fox and Speros P. Martel Foundation. Ralph O'Connor was a trustee of Rice University from 1976 to 1988.

41.   Mary Gibbs Jones College and Jones House
Lloyd & Morgan, 1957

Jones College was the first housing for women to be built on campus, the first student housing complex to be designed as a residential college, and the first student housing to be centrally air-conditioned. It is an important work of modern architecture because it demonstrated that Cram's architecture could continue to provide models for new development, once architectural style was no longer treated as the sole issue. Lloyd & Morgan constructed a modern identity for Rice liberated from the restrictive, stylistic interpretations of the postwar decade. This identity was based on constructing continuity with the building- and site-planning techniques of the General Plan. It engaged Cram's buildings to elicit a modernist architectural analogue based on the tectonics of cast-in-place concrete-frame construction and curtain wall assemblies. Lloyd & Morgan problematized Rice

Mary Gibbs Jones College and Jones House

identity. They explored, in terms of modern architecture, whether and how continuity might be constructed. Like the buildings of the Earth Sciences group and Hamman Hall by George Pierce-Abel B. Pierce, Jones College asserted architecturally that Rice identity was not static and had to challenge received traditions rather than acquiesce to them or ignore them.

     Jones consists of two four-story slabs, offset in plan so that they slide past each other. Dormitory rooms for 220 students occupy the upper three floors, and commons spaces and other specialized rooms occupy the ground floors. Rooms are arranged along double-loaded corridors. Between the two slabs is a one-story commons containing the college dining hall (altered and expanded in 1979 by Rice architecture faculty members Harry S. Ransom and Dennis Kilper). Jones Commons is connected to the residential buildings by a wide canopy-covered walkway, which frames an edge of the college parking lot.

     In designing the buildings' exterior curtain wall, Lloyd & Jones used a technique often employed in American modern architecture of the early and mid-1950s to indicate that the exterior wall surfaces were not load bearing. The narrow end elevations of the four-story slabs are blind: they contain no window or door openings. At Jones they are surfaced with a one-story base of limestone striated with brick, while the upper floors are faced with banded brick laid in Flemish bond with thick mortar joints. The long elevations are detailed with an open ground floor of glass, recessed behind the exposed columns of the structural frame. The cylindrical columns are faced with pink and white mosaic tiles. On each of the upper floors, a curtain wall of vertical aluminum mullions framing aluminum casement windows is slotted between the exposed concrete floor slabs. Spandrel panels beneath the windows are thin plaques of Georgia Etowah pink marble, a flamboyant gray-veined pink marble that MacKie & Kamrath had used for the surface exteriors of M. D. Anderson Hospital and Tumor Institute in the Texas Medical Center, completed three years earlier. Lloyd & Morgan used pink marble to code Jones as a women's residence.

Jones South is aligned behind the double row of live oak trees that canopy the street and sidewalk along the axis of the secondary drive from Entrance One. It does not terminate the vista along this road so much as it frames it to one side. In typical modernist fashion, it is not the center of the slab that is privileged but the edge. At the base of the building, glass-walled interiors face broad terraces paved with brick. The walled terrace at the east end of Jones South, with its landscape design by Robert F. White & Associates, constructs the romantic indoor-outdoor relationship integral to American modern architecture from the 1930s through the early 1960s. The canopy between Jones Commons and Jones North, consisting of a thin roof slab supported on cruciform columns, brick solar screens, and brick and concrete sidewalk paving invokes Cram's cloisters. It constructs continuity at Rice by making sheltered outdoor passageways that are thoughtfully designed and conscientiously detailed, and that resonate with collective memory not because they imitate other Rice cloisters but because they serve the same purpose and do so with tectonically articulate means. Jones College, like Staub & Rather's Wiess College (and like Pierce-Pierce's Earth Sciences group and Hamman Hall), embraced the Open City concept of modern spatial liberation. It is implicitly suburban, rather than implicitly urban like Cram, Goodhue & Ferguson's buildings. But it engages Rice in a way that Staub & Rather at Wiess College and their other postwar buildings seemed unable to do.

To the east of Jones Commons, facing Sunset Boulevard, is Jones House, the master's house. This is a flat-roofed courtyard house, a type of modern house that appealed strongly to vanguard Houston architects and their clients in the 1950s. It is the only modern house of distinction on the Rice campus. The university plans to demolish Jones House and Jones Commons to build a satellite kitchen serving Jones, Brown, and the new Martel Colleges. Michael Graves, architect for the new kitchen, will also design a new block of rooms that will span between the two slabs of Jones, as well as a new commons and a new master's house.

Jones College is named for Mary Gibbs Jones, wife of the Houston businessman and public figure, Jesse H. Jones. Jesse Jones was Houston's major urban real estate developer during the first half of the twentieth century. He was the publisher of the *Houston Chronicle* and chairman of the board of directors of the National Bank of Commerce. In 1928, he brought the Democratic Party to Houston for its national presidential convention. During the administration of President Franklin D. Roosevelt, Jones was appointed chairman of the Reconstruction Finance Corporation, then Federal Loan Administrator, and then Secretary of Commerce. He was the first Houstonian to serve in a presidential cabinet. In 1937 Mr. and Mrs. Jones established Houston Endowment, a charitable foundation. In 1955 Houston Endowment contributed one million dollars toward the construction of what became Jones College. The next year Houston Endowment supported the construction of Jones Hall at the University of St. Thomas in Houston (1958), designed by Philip Johnson as part of his master plan for the small Roman Catholic university. Jones College is linked by patronage as well as design to the transmission in the 1950s of high style modern architecture to cultural institutions in Houston that had not previously displayed an interest in modernism.

For forty-five years after the institute opened, Rice had no place for female students to live on campus. Women students who were Houstonians were expected to live at home; non-resident female students had to live in boarding houses. From 1951 until Jones opened, Rice provided housing for 110 women students at two apartment complexes, one near the Plaza Hotel in the Turner Addition and one on South MacGregor Way east of Hermann Park.

42. Mary Ellen Hale Lovett Memorial Garden

A. Gregory Catlow, Douglas Herbert Pickworth, Associate, landscape architects; Carl Milles, sculptor, 1970

One of the most serene open spaces on campus is the court containing four low pools with fountains—one of which features a pair of bronze female figures, *The Sisters*, by the twentieth-century Swedish sculptor Carl Milles.

Mary Ellen Hale Lovett Memorial Garden

The Houston landscape architects Gregory Catlow and Douglas Herbert Pickworth installed this fountain court in a quadrangle between Jones Commons and Brown College, defined on two sides by the back fences of Jones House and Brown House. Robert F. White & Associates designed the landscape for the quadrangle in 1966 after the completion of Brown. Catlow inserted the Lovett Garden at the west end of White's quadrangle. Catlow and Pickworth intensified the level of landscape detail, both constructed and planted, with their combination of brick and exposed aggregate concrete paving and their selection of ground covers, especially the contrasting textures, scale, and diversities of green (emphasized by the subsequent planting of ardisia to contrast with Asiatic jasmine). The hedge of Japanese yew that steps down to a hedge of wax leaf ligustrum, and the fence of vertical wood slats behind the ligustrum, on the north edge of the fountain court, are a significant part of the spatial composition. White crape myrtle trees are planted around the perimeter. The evergreen woodland landscape that became the Houston style of domestic landscaping in the 1940s and 1950s is presented here in an especially beguiling form, because of the intimate scale and the density of detail Catlow and Pickworth achieved.

The courtyard, the fountains, and the Milles sculpture were a gift of Ida Kirkland and Joseph Mullen, Martha Wicks and H. Malcolm Lovett, and Adelaide Lovett Baker in memory of Mary Ellen Hale Lovett, wife of Edgar Odell Lovett and mother of Adelaide L. Baker and Malcolm Lovett. This landscape ensemble will be demolished to make way for a new dining hall serving Jones and Brown Colleges. The structural elements of the Catlow-Pickworth design will be reconstructed where the 1957 Jones Commons is located, yet they will be set in a larger space, bounded by buildings rather thin greenery, losing the intimacy that gives this garden its charm.

43.   **Margarett Root Brown College**   *Brown & Root, 1965*

Brown College was named for Margarett Root Brown, the wife of Herman Brown, and was built with a gift from the Brown Foundation. Brown & Root's staff architect Albert E. Sheppard designed Brown College and Brown House. It is intriguing to examine the eight-story slab in which rooms for 176 students are incorporated. Sheppard constructed continuity by simply transposing the curtain wall of Jones College to a taller building, substituting precast concrete mullions for aluminum mullions and spandrel panels of brick laid in a basketweave bond for those of Georgia Etowah pink marble. He even repeated Lloyd & Morgan's cruciform columns and thin concrete canopies. Brown College is not architecturally inspired, but it has aged with dignity. Sheppard used cross-axes to organize the complex. The west garden doors align with the center of the Lovett Memorial Garden, unobtrusively structuring the landscape in relation to the building. Facing Sunset Boulevard, the dormitory slab sits behind walled courtyards; the college parking lot is an unfortunate intrusion of asphalt, which extends to Entrance One.

Margaret Root Brown College

The secondary street emanating from Entrance One (the Main Boulevard gate is always closed) traverses an oak alley between the street front of Brown House and the garden wall and service court of the President's House. This space feels quite different from the formality of the main drive at Entrance One, although both are shaped by allées of live oaks. Here it is the lushness of low plants and ground and wall covers that thrive in shaded environments, the layering of space with walls and courts (even though the courts are driveways), and the spatial intimacy that give this street a domestic, non-official feeling, constructing a buoyant yet relaxed ambiance that has not been achieved elsewhere at Rice.

When a new dining hall for Brown and Jones Colleges is constructed where Jones House and the Lovett Memorial Garden stand, the architects, Michael Graves and Pierce Goodwin Alexander & Linville, will design additional students rooms for Brown College facing Sunset.

44. Martel College

Michael Graves and Pierce Goodwin Alexander & Linville, 2002

In conformance with Cesar Pelli's Master Plan for Growth of 1983, Rice's first new residential college in twenty-five years will be built west of Jones College, filling out the west edge of what was to have been the faculty residence group. Michael Graves, professor of architecture at Princeton University, repeats Jones' thin, slab-shaped form. He adapts the Jones (and Brown) curtain wall, using dark Negallo marble in contrast to the Georgia Etowah pink marble of Jones. With admirable formal economy, Graves demonstrates sympathetic awareness of his neighbors. He tempers his dependence on existing architecture with a concave, one-story kitchen that has the awkward function of connecting the Martel College commons to the new Jones-Brown dining hall. Martel College, which will house 235 students, is named for Marian Fox and Speros P. Martel. Speros Martel was a Houston real estate broker and investor. Mrs. Martel was the granddaughter of the nineteenth-century Houston banker Henry S. Fox, a contemporary of William M. Rice.

Arts, Athletics, and Horticulture at Rice

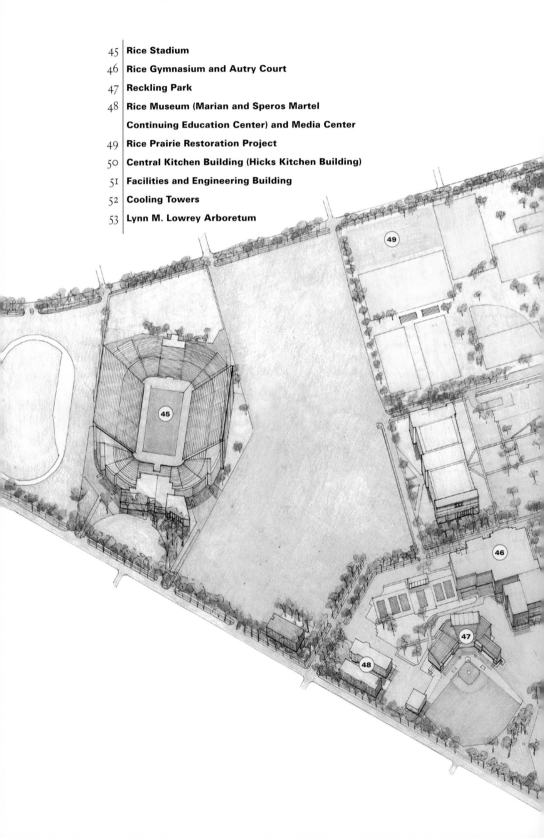

The stadium parking lot serves a wide variety of activities that require flatness, openness, and a hard surface. In addition to hosting special events (many of them independent of the university), it is where generations of young Houstonians have learned to drive. Rice Stadium has acquired opportunistic accretions in the form of shed structures built inside the concourse. The enclosure of a portion of the main concourse on the east side of the stadium for use as long-term storage for the Fondren Library and the conversion of the visitors' lobby into a warehouse compromise the integrity of the stadium's public spaces and should be restored. On the narrow south end of the stadium, behind the score board, the R Room (1973), a club for supporters of the Rice Owls), the Stadium Weight Room (1984), and the John L. Cox Fitness Center (1995) have been attached. Lloyd, Morgan & Jones and its successors and the McGinty Partnership collaborated on these additions.

Because of Lloyd & Morgan's involvement with the design of Rice Stadium, they were commissioned to design the Astrodome in 1960. Milton McGinty was asked to collaborate with them, but declined because of the amount of work in his office at the time; Wilson, Morris, Crain & Anderson instead became the Lloyd firm's associated architects. The first indoor, air-conditioned football and baseball stadium in the world, the Astrodome ranks as Houston's most historically significant stadium. Rice Stadium, however, is the superior work of architecture. Lloyd & Morgan and Milton McGinty resolved the problems of stadium design architecturally at Rice. At the turn of the twenty-first century, when the Astrodome faces an uncertain future because the professional sports teams and other clients who used it have abandoned it, Rice Stadium is as useful and admired as the day it opened.

46.   Rice Gymnasium and the Autry Court

Jessen, Jessen, Millhouse & Greeven, 1951

Rice Gymnasium and the Autry Court (the gym's 5,000-seat basketball arena) were built with a gift from the Houston matron Allie May Autry Kelley (Class of 1925), in memory of her mother Allie Kinsloe Autry, the donor of Autry House. The Rice Gymnasium bore out William Ward Watkin's prediction about the baleful influence that the "chaotic void" of the stadium parking lot would exert on subsequent buildings. Constructed at the same time as Rice Stadium, although not on a fast track construction schedule, the gym exhibited the disturbing tendency of Rice's building authorities to decide, from time to time, that some buildings are not important enough to merit ambitious design. Compounding an obvious lack of concern about the architectural design of the gym was disregard for the consequences of its siting. Rather than locating it with respect to the

Rice Gymnasium

secondary axis that Cram, Goodhue & Ferguson had used to organize the Residential Group, as called for in the General Plan, the gym was built facing an extension of the south loop street, on one edge of the stadium parking lot. Not only did it depart from the General Plan, it precipitated the systematic disintegration of this sector of the campus. By virtue of its scale and singularity, Rice Stadium could claim exceptional status. The Rice Gymnasium could not.

The board of trustees' committee on buildings solicited competitive bids in the spring of 1949 from general contractors, who provided their own architectural designs as part of the bidding process. Frank Lloyd Wright, in Houston in March 1949 to receive the Gold Medal of the American Institute of Architects at its annual meeting there, wrote a terse note on a copy of the bid solicitation—scolding William Ward Watkin for permitting this insult to the architectural profession to happen at Rice. Watkin, of course, was powerless to stop it.

Jessen, Jessen, Millhouse & Greeven, a firm of Austin, Texas, architects who had affiliated with the winning builder, the J. M. Oden Company of Austin, produced a straightforward, late modernistic institutional building. The Autry Court is symmetrically flanked by two lower stories of offices. A lobby faces the street. The students' portion of the field house projects off the southeast rear corner of the central block. The athletes' portion originally projected off the rear southwest corner of the central block. The gymnasium was doubled in size in 1979 with an addition to the rear of the complex (McKittrick, Drennan, Richardson & Wallace, architects). In 1998 the Fox Gymnasium was added to the west side of the Autry Court as a supplemental practice gym (Jackson & Ryan, architects). Not until 1991 was the gym centrally air-conditioned.

The Autry Court is home to the Rice Owls basketball and volleyball teams. It is where Commencement is held when it rains. On October 24,

The Rice Museum and Media Center constructed an identity that Rice University's administration never felt especially comfortable with. The marginalization of the buildings, in the unplanned athletic sector of the campus, represented the official distancing of the Menil enterprise from the rest of the university. It seemed not to matter that the exhibitions organized at the Art Barn traveled to major U.S. and international museums or that the Institute for the Arts sought to involve faculty and students from the humanities and sciences in interdisciplinary projects. By 1973, when John de Menil died, Mr. and Mrs. de Menil had decided not to build a museum for their collection at Rice. At the time of John de Menil's death, Louis I. Kahn had begun plans for a museum complex near the University of St. Thomas—next to the Rothko Chapel, which Barnstone & Aubry designed for Mr. and Mrs. de Menil and which opened in 1971. It was in this area that the Italian architect Renzo Piano would eventually design the Menil Collection art museum and the ancillary Cy Twombly Gallery (1995).

After the opening of the Menil Collection, the Institute for the Arts ceased to exist. The Sewall Gallery in Sewall Hall (now the Rice University Art Gallery), which had opened in 1971 as the art and art history department's teaching gallery, became the university's only gallery. The expanding school of continuing studies took possession of the Art Barn in 1988 and adapted its former gallery, storage, and studio spaces for offices and classrooms. The Media Center continues to function as the art and art history department's center for film and photography. It screens film programs, open to the public throughout the year.

Rice's inability to absorb what Dominique and John de Menil had to offer remains cause for regret (mitigated by the fact that Dominique de Menil kept her collection in Houston and built one of the great art museum buildings of the twentieth century to house it). The Art Barn and Media Center represent the extraordinary sensibility the Menils developed in Houston. It was a sensibility profoundly committed to exploration, criticism, and discovery—and to greatness. Indeed, it was their linkage of critical questioning and unyielding standards of excellence that repeatedly brought them into conflict with the Houston cultural institutions with which they sought affiliation from the 1950s to the 1970s. Their passionate conviction that art and architecture were means of exploration, rather than of institutional legitimization, perhaps made them incomprehensible to other members of Houston's elite, who tended to seek consensus on cultural issues rather than assert intense, singular points of view. With respect to the university's grand spatial narratives, the Art Barn and Media Center construct "otherness." They retain a trace of subversiveness as well as the wit with which Barnstone & Aubry customarily invested their buildings.

49.   Rice Prairie Restoration Project   *1983*

Paul Harcombe, professor of ecology and environmental biology, established the Rice Prairie inside the fenced two-acre site on the east edge of the stadium parking lot at Entrance Twelve, parallel to Rice Boulevard between Wilton and Hazard Streets. It is a teaching landscape where experiments in biology, chemistry, and environmental engineering can be conducted. Harcombe's objective was to reinstate vegetation of the coastal plain as it had existed before Anglo-Americans introduced cultivation in the 1820s. By 1995 the prairie contained 150 species of grasses, broadleaf herbs, and other plant types that thrive in the impervious overbank deposits of Beaumont clay formation, the subsurface soil condition most characteristic of the campus.

50.   Central Kitchen Building (Hicks Kitchen Building)

Wilson, Morris, Crain & Anderson, 1965

The band of territory along Rice Boulevard, north of the Court of Science, developed as an extension of the service sector related to the Power House. This is where much of the reproductive labor that sustains the university is based. The General Plan did not foresee the day-to-day maintenance, repairs, groundskeeping, and housekeeping activities of the university staff. People of color—African-American, Mexican-American, and Mexican immigrant—and women have traditionally performed much of this work; they constituted distinct minorities (if present at all) in the student body, faculty, and staff of

Central Kitchen Building, now Hicks Kitchen Building

the university during most of the twentieth century. (By the end of the century, 35.5 percent of Rice undergraduates were Asian-American, Hispanic, African-American, Native American, or of mixed racial heritage.) This is an "other" Rice, demographically and occupationally. It is an "other" Rice spatially. Unlike the athletic sector of the campus, it is not unplanned. But it is planned as a series of staging grounds for action, rather than ceremonial settings framing and projecting the presence of honorific architecture.

The Central Kitchen, now Hicks Kitchen, replaced the original kitchen of the Institute Commons at what is now Baker College. It is a flat roofed, brick-faced pavilion, raised a half-level above grade over an exposed basement. The rear elevation is the loading dock, where prepared food is dispatched to warming kitchens at each college. In 1999 the building was named for Marion Hicks, director of the university's food and housing department from 1970 to 1999. The basement of the Hicks Building is home to The MOB, Rice's Marching Owl Band.

51. Facilities and Engineering Building
Justin M. Elliott, 1964; Jackson & Ryan, 1999

Tucked inconspicuously back from the rear service street and set just inside the ligustrum hedge outlining the university's Rice Boulevard frontage is the one-story, flat-roofed Facilities and Engineering Building, where the professional staff overseeing the maintenance, remodeling, and construction of the university's infrastructure and buildings is headquartered. Justin Elliott, who had worked for Staub, Rather & Howze, designed the original office building. Jackson & Ryan expanded it with a hipped-roofed, banded, brick-veneered extension that wraps around the central air-conditioning plant.

When construction began on the institute grounds in 1910, a spur line of the San Antonio & Aransas Pass Railway was run from the main line (its right-of-way is where U.S. 59, the Southwest Freeway, was routed) southward to Rice. The spur entered the campus site at the Rice Boulevard-Greenbriar Drive intersection, made a broad curve over Harris Gully, and then headed northeast before aligning with the north property line of the campus to come in behind the Mechanical Laboratory and Power House in a double track configuration. In the early 1920s, in preparation for the development of the Southampton residential neighborhood north of campus, and because the university no longer required the rail line to transport fuel for the Power House, the spur line was taken up.

52. Cooling Tower

Lockwood, Andrews & Newnam, 1991, 1995

Cooling Tower

Central air-conditioning, incorporating humidity control, was introduced to Houston in 1932, although as early as 1911 local buildings had been equipped with mechanical air cooling systems. During the 1930s movie theaters, department stores, and office buildings tended to be the building types where central air-conditioning was first installed in Houston.

Educational institutions did not generally embrace it until the postwar period. The Fondren Library of 1949 was the first building at Rice to be designed with a central air-conditioning system. Only in 1957, with the completion of Jones College and the commons and master's houses of the other colleges, and construction of the Earth Sciences group, Hamman Hall, the Rice Memorial Center, and the additions to Cohen House was there a network of air-conditioned buildings at Rice that justified the construction of a central air-conditioning plant. The 1957 plant was extended ten years later as not only new buildings, but also existing campus buildings, were freed from dependence on Houston's hot, humid, sultry climate. When the cooling tower was reconstructed in 1991, it was cloaked with a screen wall of Rice brick.

53. Lynn M. Lowrey Arboretum

Charles Tapley, landscape architect, 2001

Occupying the abandoned streambed of Harris Gully, the Lynn M. Lowrey Arboretum is named for the twentieth-century Houston horticulturist, nurseryman, plant propagator, and collector who from the 1950s until his death in 1997 advocated the use of native plants as well as imported plants that would thrive in Houston's stressful climate. According to his biographer, Mary Anne Pickens, Lowrey was especially important for introducing many northeastern Mexican plant species that had not been cultivated in Texas.

The eight-acre site of the arboretum will emphasize the three forest zones—Southeastern pine forests, western prairie forests, and the temperate forests of the coastal bayous—which historically merged in the vicinity of Rice and Hermann Park. It will supplement the Rice Prairie as a teaching landscape by highlighting native trees and providing outdoor laboratory conditions for the biological and horticultural study of native trees and plants. The recovery of the former streambed of Harris Gully serves a practical ecological purpose by providing increased storm water detention capacity on campus. Given Houston's propensity for flooding—the city's combination of topographical flatness, impervious soils, and uncontrolled urbanization creates the circumstances in which torrential rains can cause water to "stack up," as local hydrologists describe it, with alarming rapidity—this is a necessity. Charles Tapley, as landscape architect, conceived the Lowery Arboretum as the initial phase of a movement to expand the presence of native plants on the Rice campus. The trees that trace the former course of Harris Gully through the campus from Main Boulevard to the Rice Gymnasium provided the point of departure for the arboretum.

Cram, Goodhue & Ferguson did not address the sector of the campus between Harris Gully and what is now University Boulevard. The earliest departures from the General Plan occurred in this area. An athletic track, grandstands, and a field house designed by William Ward Watkin were installed at what is now the Main Boulevard-University Boulevard intersection in 1921. A double allée of live oaks, perpendicular to Main is aligned with the athletic track and mark one side of the old Field House site. Cram tried to persuade President Lovett not to put up temporary buildings, because of the likelihood they would become permanent. The Field House, although designed in a Mediterranean style to present an appropriate countenance to Main Boulevard, bore out Cram's apprehensions. By the time it was demolished, following completion of the new gym, it was falling apart. From 1924 to 1927 John W. Heisman coached Rice's football team, which played here. Despite Heisman's reputation, the Rice Owls did not have winning seasons and Heisman left the university before his contract expired. During the tenure of football coach Jimmy Kitts (1934–1939), the Rice Owls football team performed so admirably that Houston fans paid for the first Rice Stadium. In 1938 a public subscription supported the construction of a 30,000-seat Rice Stadium. Watkin designed the stadium seating structure, which he wrapped around the still extant track and playing field. This superstructure, with exception of several steel-framed grandstands, was dismantled after the present Rice Stadium was completed.

From the ligustrum hedge-lined sidewalk along Main Boulevard there are long views across the arboretum toward the cluster of skyscrapers in Greenway Plaza and, beyond these, to Philip Johnson's Transco Tower in the Post Oak district. Note that between Gates Three and Four the double row of live oaks on Rice's side of Main Boulevard becomes a single row.

Outside the Hedges

Around Rice

"Outside the hedges" is the coded Rice expression for the rest of Houston. Outside the hedges of wax leaf ligustrum that surround the campus are several distinct worlds, each of which relates in one way or another to Rice.

Main Boulevard is Rice's front door. This is where Houston learned from Rice how to shape itself. The development of the Main Boulevard parkway and Hermann Park converted the territory of suburban dairy farms where Rice was built into the most comprehensively planned and fashionable sector of Houston in the 1920s. The opening of the Museum of Fine Arts in 1924 brought added luster to this cultural arena, and the development of the elite enclave neighborhood of Shadyside between the museum site and the Rice campus confirmed the social prestige of this district. William Ward Watkin played a critical role in maintaining the coherence of the Main Boulevard civic arena in the 1920s. The buildings he designed there constructed a unifying civic style of Mediterranean architecture, derived from Cram's buildings at Rice. This civic style enabled new buildings, as they were constructed, to extend the spatial discourse on harmony, beauty, and order on which the visual singularity of this district depended.

The Main Boulevard Mediterranean style was applied to Hermann Hospital of 1925. When the Texas Medical Center began to be developed around Hermann Hospital in the postwar 1940s, it seemed as though its first buildings might extend this civic style and the commitment to urban order it portended. The Hermann Professional Building, the first skyscraper office building in Houston constructed outside downtown, deferred architecturally to this civic identity. Other buildings in the Texas Medical Center did not. After 1960, new construction associated with the Medical Center abandoned the commitment to urban civility. The present landscape of Main, with massive ranks of parking garages abutting what was to have been a parkway boulevard, represents the fundamental difference in attitude between officials of the Medical Center and Rice University on the virtues of planned architectural and landscape development.

To the north of the Rice campus, along Rice Boulevard, lies the subdivision of Southampton, which was planned by William Ward Watkin. Watkin's extension of the live oak allées united suburban space with Rice space, just as the allées of Main Boulevard and its Mediterranean architecture extended the spatial and architectural discourse of Rice outward into the new city. As an architect and urban planner, Watkin was important for demonstrating how continuity could be constructed by expanding the landscape of Rice to adjacent, newly urbanizing territories. The subdivision of Southgate, along University Boulevard on the south edge of the campus, adhered to these lessons.

In the Village, the suburban shopping district west of the Rice campus, the architectural, landscape, and space planning lessons were not extended. Surrounded by restricted residential neighborhoods—restrictive covenants are the legal instrument used to secure land-use controls in Houston, which has never adopted a zoning code—the Village provides convenience shopping and commercial services. It serves Rice as well, which, because of the insulation that its large tract imposes, feels somewhat isolated despite its location in the center of the city. Rice affects the Village through ownership and control of real estate. Working through an investment builder and property manager, Rice revolutionized retail trading in the Village in the 1990s by replacing a major portion of its urban fabric with a highly capitalized, thematically designed, specialty shopping center.

Rice expanded its hedges farther into Houston than newly arrived undergraduates may sometimes imagine. Occupying one of the largest blocks of land under single ownership in Houston, it is a powerful but quiet presence.

54.   Main Boulevard Parkway

George E. Kessler, landscape architect, 1916

Early in 1915 the City of Houston retained the St. Louis landscape architect and city planner George E. Kessler to transform Main Street Road into Main Boulevard. From McGowen Avenue, in the 2500 block of Main, to Bellaire Boulevard (now Holcombe Boulevard) in the 6900 block, Kessler's new Main Boulevard was laid out in 1916. The portion of the boulevard that was developed most consistently was from the 5600 block to the 6400 block (Binz/Bissonnet avenues, adjacent to The Museum of Fine Arts, to University Boulevard at the south end of Rice's frontage on Main). Double rows of live oak trees were planted in 1916 and 1917 in staggered formation to frame the boulevard and adjacent sidewalks. The improvements to Main Boulevard were planned in conjunction with Kessler's master plan for development of the 410-acre Hermann Park, acquired by the City of Houston between 1914 and 1915 with an initial gift of property from the Houston real estate investor George H. Hermann. The site of Hermann Park lay across Main Street Road from the institute campus and extended east to Brays Bayou. Unlike the Rice campus site, the park possessed substantial tree cover, especially of loblolly pines. Although lying in open countryside that was incorporated into the City of Houston only in 1913, this area became what *The Houston Gargoyle*, Houston's short-lived version of the *The New Yorker*, humorously designated "Houston's Cradle of Culture" by the 1920s.

Here Houston shaped itself in the image of Rice. Cram, Goodhue & Ferguson's General Plan provided a template for constructing the new

Houston of Main Boulevard as a green, garden city. The systematic integration of landscape architecture, city planning, and architecture within an armature of live oak trees imbued the Main Boulevard civic arena with a degree of coherence that was unique in Houston and highlighted the area's superior status in comparison to other parts of the city. As at Rice, this landscape possessed an underlying ideological significance. Comprehensive urban infrastructure and landscape improvements identified the new Houston of the twentieth century as stable, rooted, rational, spacious, and beautiful—all attributes of the good city, which tacitly reinforced the authority of Houston's progressive era elite who brought it into being.

The live oak trees forcefully construct "Southern-ness" here, as they do at Rice. In the geography of the imagination, they link the parkway to similar oak allées in New Orleans, Mobile, and Savannah. They are the infrastructural element used to transmit this spatial identity to the surrounding middle and upper income residential neighborhoods developed in the 1920s. Main Boulevard remains one of the exceptional urban spaces of Houston, despite the cutting back of its central esplanade to a thin sliver in 1940. It is a strong-form power space, constructing images of unity and coherence, framing privileged prospects, and concentrating visitors' awareness on them by editing out all the distracting attributes of Houston that would subvert this carefully orchestrated perception.

In 1996 the concrete sidewalks along the west side of Main Boulevard between the Mecom Fountain and University Boulevard were removed. They were replaced by paths surfaced with decomposed granite, like the original sidewalks of Rice.

55.   Museum of Fine Arts, Houston

Caroline Wiess Law Building   *William Ward Watkin, 1924 and 1926*
Cullinan Hall and the Brown Pavilion   *Ludwig Mies van der Rohe, 1958 and 1974*
Audrey Jones Beck Building and Visitors Center
   Rafael Moneo and Kendall/Heaton Associates, 2000

Where Montrose Boulevard intersects Main Boulevard, George Kessler planted a traffic circle (occupied since 1964 by the Mecom Fountain) that momentarily interrupts the flow of directed movement and views along Main Boulevard. Here Montrose becomes the main entrance to Hermann Park, proceeding south into the park to another traffic circle, where in 1925 a bronze equestrian statue of Sam Houston by the Italian-American sculptor Enrico Cerracchio was installed. The site of the Sam Houston statue is the point of intersection between the Montrose entrance axis to Hermann Park and the main axis of Cram, Goodhue & Ferguson's General Plan, were it to be projected eastward from Entrance One. The distance involved is too far

Museum of Fine Arts, Houston

to make this connection work visually without reinforcement by planting, which did not occur. But Kessler's linking of the two axes demonstrates how the civic arena evolved in the 1910s and 1920s through an elite consensus on the value of constructing coherent urban space in Houston.

The statue of Sam Houston also reflects the process of consensus formation on how Houston was to derive value from coordinated civic improvements. The monument to the mythical hero—Sam Houston was military victor of the Battle of San Jacinto of 1836, at which Texas won independence from Mexico; first president of the Republic of Texas; and the man for whom the city was named—seeks to ground the unfocused history of Houston in a figure, deeds, names, and gestures meant to ensure the reality of city, arrest its cyclical disintegration, and shape a civic consensus on its essential (that is mythical) identity. The live oak matrix along Montrose (installed to Kessler's design) focuses awareness on the monument. As totemic symbols of durability and legitimacy, the live oak trees naturalize this constructed vision of spatial order and mythic history. They root unstable Houston, foreground its history, and civilize it.

The task of civilizing Houston at the turn of the twentieth century, as in other U.S. cities during this period, was of concern to an emerging constituency, elite women who banded together in associations to promote cultural and social welfare activities. The Museum of Fine Arts, Houston, which faces the Mecom Fountain at Main and Montrose, is an outgrowth of the Art League of Houston, a women's organization formed in 1900 to support art education in the public schools. In 1916 The estate of George H. Hermann and Mr. and Mrs. J. S. Cullinan gave the league this triangular two-and-three-quarters-acre site on the condition that it build a museum building there by 1926. The Rice Institute provided the cultural infrastructure that enabled the Art League to undertake this ambitious venture. The first two male presidents of the league were Albert Leon Guerard, professor of French at Rice, and T. Lindsey Blayney, professor of German. Mrs. Edgar Odell Lovett was elected to the league's board of trustees in 1914 and Stockton Axson, professor English (and Woodrow Wilson's brother-in-law) was elected to its advisory board. In 1917, William Ward Watkin was selected as architect (Ralph Adams Cram was designated consulting architect). In 1923, as completion was nearing on the first phase of Watkin's building, James Chillman, Jr., assistant professor of architecture at Rice, was named the first director of the museum, a position he held until 1953. When the museum opened in 1924, it was the first public art museum in Texas.

Watkin's museum building was constructed in two phases. The central screen of limestone Ionic columns facing the Main-Montrose intersection is the original building. The pair of wings that frame it were added in 1926. Watkin planned the museum so that it could be expanded in phases to encircle an open-air central courtyard. This allowed for two floors of galleries (side-lit galleries on the ground floor and skylit painting galleries on the top floor) to be inserted behind the street faces of the building, and vaulted corridors (which Watkin labeled "cloisters") to ring the courtyard. Watkin did not try to extend Cram's Byzantine architectural narrative with the design of the Museum of Fine Arts. Instead, its street fronts were detailed in the Greek neoclassical style, the architectural genre identified with public art museums since the 1820s and 1830s, when the earliest purpose-designed museum buildings were built in European cities. As in his design of the Chemistry Building at Rice, Watkin's approach to design was more conventional than Cram's.

What is Rice-like about the Watkin building is the way in which it spatially reinforces the intersection of Main and Montrose. The front of the museum (and it was all there was of the building until the early 1950s) architecturally reciprocates the channeling of space the oak trees constructed as they matured. Like the Administration Building at Rice, the Museum of Fine Arts worked with the constructed landscape to frame, shape, and give form (and implicit meaning) to the formlessness of the landscape in its pre-urban condition. During the 1930s, the Garden Club of Houston, another elite women's organization, had the Houston landscape architect Ruth London design a modest garden at the Point, the triangular lawn in front of the museum. Miss London installed planting to reinforce the symmetry of the building while accommodating mature trees, which predated the building on the site. In 1936 the Garden Club of Houston commissioned William Ward Watkin to design the limestone balustrade and bench at the tip of the Point. As an architectural element in the landscape, it framed views, reinforced axial projection, and served as a landmark, a ceremonial threshold distinguishing between in-here and out-there. William McVey, an instructor of sculpture at the museum's art school from 1936 to 1938, was responsible for the relief panels on the balustrade. These depict the four arts: painting, music, sculpture, and flower arranging. In 2000, what remained of Ruth London's garden was replaced by a schematic design that de-layered the site and, although symmetrically composed, subverted the centrality of the museum building to emphasize the divergence of the two boulevards.

At 1001 Bissonnet Avenue, behind Watkin's neoclassical front, is the greatest work of modern architecture in Houston: the Brown Pavilion and Cullinan Hall of the Museum of Fine Arts, additions to the museum designed in 1954 by the German-American architect, Ludwig Mies van der Rohe. At the end of Chillman's tenure as director, the museum had added a single gallery, the Robert Lee Blaffer Memorial Wing of 1953 by the Houston architect Kenneth Franzheim. The next year, Nina J. Cullinan, whose parents had been donors of the museum site and were major contributors to the construction of the original building, provided funds to build a gallery for traveling exhibitions in their memory. Miss Cullinan specified that an architect "of outstanding reputation" be commissioned for the gallery. An architect selection committee, whose members included the young modern architects Hugo V. Neuhaus, Jr., Preston M. Bolton (Howard Barnstone's partner in the 1950s), and Anderson Todd, then an assistant professor of architecture at Rice and the husband of Miss Cullinan's niece, considered Harrison & Abramovitz, Edward Durell Stone, Pietro Belluschi, Eero Saarinen, and Louis I. Kahn among others, before recommending Mies. In June 1954 Mies and his assistant David Haid presented the museum's trustees with a scheme for completing the Watkin building. This entailed adding a thirty-foot tall, single-story gallery for traveling exhibitions in what was to have been the courtyard of the Watkin design, then ringing it with a north-facing, two-story gallery wing. The first phase of this plan, Cullinan Hall, was completed in 1958. The design of the second phase, the

Brown Pavilion, was completed just weeks before Mies's death in 1969. It was built in 1971–73, with the Office of Mies van der Rohe, Mies's successor firm, as architect.

Mies, as one of the seminal figures of the modern movement, first in Berlin in the 1920s and 1930s, and after 1938 in Chicago, endowed the raw materials of twentieth-century industrial construction, principally structural steel and plate glass, with the precision and refinement of classical architecture. Formally, Mies could not have been more unlike Ralph Adams Cram. Philosophically, they shared a deep reverence for the philosophy of St. Thomas Aquinas. By virtue of his layered, "Gothic" articulation of construction, Mies invested exposed steel frame construction with the subtlety and depth of Cram's monolithic masonry architecture. Additionally, Mies produced interior spaces that profoundly moved those who experienced them. Mies demonstrated his virtuosity by making his radically different additions fuse so smoothly with Watkin's very conventional museum building. Even Mies's choice of paving, a polished Venetian terrazzo is remarkable. The paving calls no attention to itself, yet in spaces that otherwise possess very little "architecture," it provides a sense of material richness and reflective depth (the kind of "negative" detailing visible in the Administration Building). The entrance to the Mies building from Bissonnet, the ascent into Cullinan Hall, and the sweep of space in the Upper Brown Gallery are awesome.

The magnitude of Mies's interiors has challenged the museum's curators. From 1961 until 1967 James Johnson Sweeney was director of the Museum of Fine Arts. A renowned curator of modern art, Sweeney had been a friend of Mies van der Rohe's since the 1930s. During his tenure, Sweeney suspended paintings from the grid of structural points Mies installed in the ceiling of Cullinan Hall. In the charged, luminous ambiance of Cullinan Hall, the paintings appeared to float above the Venetian terrazzo floor. Sweeney's installations were transcendent; they reinforced the emancipatory spatiality of Mies's architecture and of the modern art that Sweeney most often exhibited. Another renowned American curator, Jermayne MacAgy, organized exhibitions in Cullinan Hall that are legendary in Houston for their subject matter and inventive installation. Sweeney and MacAgy came to Houston under the auspices of Dominique and John de Menil. Both curators encountered opposition; Mrs. MacAgy in fact had to resign after four years as the first professional director of Houston's Contemporary Arts Museum in 1959 because of conflict with a segment of the membership who wanted exhibitions to be organized by members rather than by a director. Mr. and Mrs. de Menil established the art and art history program and art gallery at the University of St. Thomas for her in 1959. After Mrs. MacAgy's sudden death in 1964, Dominique de Menil took on the role of director of the gallery and the program. This became the Institute for the Arts after the Menils moved it to Rice in 1969.

of Cullinan's persistent lobbying that Kessler was retained as consulting landscape architect to the city's board of park commissioners in early 1915. Cullinan began negotiations with George Hermann about buying the Shadyside tract shortly before Hermann's death in 1914. In early 1916 Cullinan bought the property from the trustees of the Hermann Estate. He worked with Kessler and the Houston civil engineer Herbert A. Kipp to subdivide and improve the Shadyside tract, which was platted in October 1916.

Shadyside is a "private place," a distinct type of elite neighborhood especially associated with the private streets of St. Louis, where Kessler's practice was based. Since 1902, new elite Houston neighborhoods had emulated the private streets of St. Louis. They adopted discontinuous street layouts, ceremonial gate piers marking the entrance to the neighborhood, and, most important, restrictive covenants regulating land use and building in each neighborhood, to be enforced by a property owners' association. Because Houston, alone among large U.S. cities, never adopted a zoning code, restrictive covenants are still the legal instrument used to maintain the integrity of elite Houston neighborhoods. In 1983 the Shadyside property owners' association bought its two interior streets, Remington Lane and Longfellow Lane (named for the Cullinan family's favorite American artist and writer), from the City of Houston and installed street gates between the ceremonial gate piers. Therefore, Shadyside is not usually publicly accessible. That the brick and cast stone gate piers facing Main Boulevard, built in 1918 to the designs of the St. Louis architect James P. Jamieson, bear the inscriptions "Shadyside / Main Boulevard" on one face and "Remington Lane (or Longfellow Lane) / Private Way" on the other indicates that there was always ambivalence about the extent to which Shadyside was to be integrated with the Main Boulevard civic arena.

As can be seen from the Remington Lane entrance, Remington curves out of alignment with the right-angled geometry of Houston's nineteenth-century street grid. Kessler respected Cullinan's desire to differentiate the interior of Shadyside from the Main Boulevard parkway by inscribing it with a more episodic spatiality—which also resolved the site planning problem of how to efficiently subdivide the triangular-shaped tract. Cullinan decided not to plant street trees in uniform rows and to supplement the existing tree cover with oak species other than live oaks, since Spanish and pin oaks were the types of oak trees already on the site. The lack of allées of live oaks framing Shadyside's streets and the preference for other oak species, along with the curve of Remington, give Shadyside a "community" spatiality that distinguishes it from the "civic" spatiality of Main Boulevard. As at Rice, the production of spatial distinctions systematically integrated Shadyside into the larger civic landscape while preserving its domestic, communal identity, an identity constructed through a series of dialectical oppositions. Visible at the end of Longfellow (from the Longfellow gate on Main) is a landscaped court, around which the street divides. Facing the court is a symmetrically composed house that engages the axis of the street and the landscaped court reciprocally. The systematic integration of site planning and architecture permitted raw suburban space to be composed ceremonially so that it focused, framed, and constructed sequences of spatial order, grounding and stabilizing the "domestic" departures from public formality visible in the curvature of Remington and the rejection of allées.

Shadyside became the preserve of Houston's new oil elite. Cullinan made lots available to family members, friends, and business associates. Two of Cullinan's children, Craig F. Cullinan and Margaret Cullinan Wray, built houses for their families in Shadyside, and a third, Mary Cullinan Cravens, bought a house there. Three of the co-founders of the Humble Oil & Refining Company—Robert Lee Blaffer, Harry C. Wiess, and William S. Farish—built houses in Shadyside. Blaffer and Wiess served as trustees of Rice in the 1930s and 1940s. Farish was married to Libbie Rice, the great-niece of William M. Rice. Mrs. Farish's cousin, Kate Rice Neuhaus and her husband, the investment banker Hugo V. Neuhaus, built their house in Shadyside. The Neuhaus's eldest son was the modern architect Hugo V. Neuhaus, Jr., who participated in recommending Mies for the design of Cullinan Hall (and in 1953 designed an exquisite Miesian courtyard house for Nina Cullinan, the only one of Cullinan's children who didn't live in Shadyside). The Cullinan, Wiess, Blaffer, Farish, and Neuhaus families were significant supporters of the Museum of Fine Arts.

Architecturally, Shadyside exhibits Rice connections. At 5301 Bayard Lane (facing Montrose at the Montrose-Bissonnet intersection) is a two-story postmodern house by William T. Cannady, professor of architecture at Rice, of 1991. At 1 Remington Lane, just to the left of the Main Boulevard gate, is a two-story, white-painted brick house with a double-height Tuscan portico. This was built by Allie May Autry and Edward W. Kelley, Jr. Mrs. Kelley was the donor of the Autry Court at the Rice Gymnasium. Her father, Judge James L. Autry, had been J. S. Cullinan's lawyer and the first general counsel of Texaco. The Kelley House, built in 1938, was designed by Stayton Nunn-Milton McGinty. Stayton Nunn (Class of 1921) was William Ward Watkin's associate during the 1920s and an instructor in architecture at Rice from 1928 to 1942. William Ward Watkin designed the stucco-faced, tile-roofed Heitmann House at 1 Longfellow Lane, just to the left of the Main Boulevard entrance gate, in 1923.

Shadyside is most significant architecturally for the four houses designed there by the New York architect Harrie T. Lindeberg. The D. D. Peden House of 1924 at 2 Longfellow Lane, to the right of the Main

Boulevard entrance gate, is the Lindeberg house most clearly visible from Main. Lindeberg designed the Neuhaus House at 9 Remington Lane of 1923, the Kenneth E. Womack House at 8 Remington Lane of 1923, and the Farish House at 10 Remington Lane of 1925. The Farish House is the symmetrically composed house at the end of Longfellow Lane, visible from Main Boulevard. Just as Cram had sent William Ward Watkin from Boston to administer the construction of Rice's initial buildings, so Lindeberg sent John F. Staub from New York to administer construction of the Shadyside houses. Staub remained in Houston to become its foremost domestic architect of the 1920s and 1930s. In 1938 Staub designed the house of Margaret Cullinan and Andrew J. Wray at 3 Remington Lane.

The only house in Shadyside to have been demolished was J. S. Cullinan's at 2 Remington Lane, to the right of the Main Boulevard gate (today the site of two stucco-faced, tile-roofed houses of 1999 by Eubanks/Bohnn Associates). Completed in 1919 and designed by James P. Jamieson, it was demolished in 1971–1972 by its second owner Oveta Culp Hobby, widow of former Texas governor William P. Hobby, publisher of the *Houston Post*, head of the Women's Army Corps during World War II, the first Secretary of Health, Education and Welfare, and a trustee of Rice University from 1967 to 1974.

More explicitly than Rice or the Museum of Fine Arts, Shadyside socially constructed Main Boulevard as power space in early twentieth-century Houston. Typical of this City Beautiful landscape complex of parkway boulevards, parks, museums, university campuses, grand churches, modern hospitals, and elite residential enclaves, the Main Boulevard civic arena does not frame and highlight the downtown office buildings, ship channel refineries, or gasoline service stations that were the more obvious embodiment of the architecture of oil in Houston during the 1910s to 1930s. The progressive era civic landscape of Houston omitted those activities and portions of the population that in the consensus of Houston's elite were inharmonious and undesirable; these were subject instead to the reverse of systematic integration: systematic segregation. The shortcoming of the Main Boulevard civic arena was not what it included, but how much of Houston it excluded. That the beauty, coherence, and prestige of Main Boulevard and Rice were conditioned on such exclusions perhaps explains why the vision of Houston that they represent remains a spatial exception to the city Houston became in the twentieth century.

57. Wiess House

William Ward Watkin, 1920; Harrie T. Lindeberg, 1926; John F. Staub, 1935

Olga Keith and Harry C. Wiess came to Houston from Beaumont, Texas, in 1919. Both were members of elite Beaumont families. As one of the founders of the Humble Oil & Refining Company in 1917, Harry Wiess built Humble's Baytown Refinery along the Houston Ship Channel. William Ward Watkin had already designed houses in Beaumont for Wiess's half-brother and sister; the Italian villa-style house Watkin designed for Mr. and Mrs. Wiess at 2 Sunset Boulevard (facing Main Boulevard across from Entrance One to the Rice campus) was his first grandly scaled country house.

Watkin's planning seems to owe something to Cram & Ferguson's unbuilt 1916 design for the President's house at Rice. The Italian villa style, with stucco walls and tile roofs, had been suggested to J. S. Cullinan in 1916 as a unifying architectural style for Shadyside by Ima Hogg, the sister of Cullinan's business associate Will C. Hogg. Cullinan was intrigued by her suggestion but did not pursue the idea. Watkin, although he may have known nothing of Miss Hogg's recommendation, did. In the Wiess House and the adjoining Heitmann House, Watkin constructed continuity with the buildings of the Rice Institute by architecturally emphasizing urban coherence rather than individual difference. In the Main Boulevard civic arena, largely as a result of Watkin's efforts, Mediterranean architecture was elevated to the status of a unifying civic style that coded the district as cultured, refined, and rooted in its setting.

After having Watkin make several minor additions to the house, Mr. and Mrs. Wiess turned to Harrie T. Lindeberg in 1925 to reorganize the ground-floor public rooms and add a wing parallel to Sunset Boulevard, to contain a very grand living room and a new master bedroom. Lindeberg moved the front door from Sunset to Main and installed the hooded canopy above the Main Boulevard terrace to mark the new entrance. Lindeberg's sense of composition and proportion were very different from Watkin's, as can be deduced from the lower, more horizontal, less ornamented elevations of the Sunset wing. In the mid-1930s the service wing was expanded by John Staub, who also designed the stucco-faced garden walls along Main and Sunset (the first such walls in Shadyside) and installed one of the earliest residential central air-conditioning systems in Houston. At the same time the landscape architect Ruth London planned new gardens for Mr. and Mrs. Wiess.

Olga Wiess gave her house to Rice University in 1974 with the hope that it would become a house for the president. For twenty-five years the university rented the house or let it stand vacant and deteriorating. In 1999 Houston preservationists, led by Phoebe Tudor, appealed to the board of governors to rehabilitate the Wiess House or sell it. A committee of the

board, led by the trustee Lee Hage Jamail, determined that it was feasible to
rehabilitate the house as a residence for President and Mrs. Malcolm Gillis,
especially since it would provide much more space for entertaining than the
President's House of 1949 on the campus. Conversion of the Wiess House to
the president's house would also be in conformity with Shadyside's restrictive covenants, which mandate single-family residential occupancy as the
only permissible use of property. The Houston architects W. O. Neuhaus
Associates will carry out the rehabilitation of the Wiess House.

Adjoining the Wiess House on the west, facing Sunset Boulevard
and across from Brown College at Rice, is the house that Sarah Campbell
and R. Lee Blaffer built in 1920, now the oldest house in Shadyside. The
Blaffer House was designed by the Houston architect Birdsall P. Briscoe.
Like Mr. and Mrs. Wiess, Mr. and Mrs. Blaffer expanded their house on several occasions during the 1920s. Briscoe was the architect for all the alterations and additions. This was the childhood home of Jane Blaffer Owen, a
significant patron of Philip Johnson in the 1950s and Richard Meier in the
1970s. Mrs. Owen spent the second half of the twentieth century restoring
the historically significant town of New Harmony, Indiana, her husband's
family's hometown. As can be seen, J. S. Cullinan and the Rice Institute
lined Sunset Boulevard with live oak trees. Where Sunset widens, as
between the Wiess and Blaffer houses, there were originally traffic islands
in the center of the street containing trees that predated the street. The
trees, considered traffic hazards, were eventually removed.

The Blaffer House adjoins Remington Lane, whose intersection
with Sunset is marked by another Shadyside street gate. Visible from
Sunset is the small, French Breton-style house of 1924 that Birdsall P.
Briscoe designed for Mr. and Mrs. Henry W. Stude. It is located at 14
Remington Lane. The Stude House backs up to a much larger stucco and
timber-faced English manorial style house by Birdsall P. Briscoe, built in
1926 for Judge and Mrs. Walter E. Monteith at 16 Sunset. Briscoe added the
wall along the Sunset front of the property in 1948. Next to the Monteith
House, at 18 Sunset Boulevard, is a one-story house of 1965 designed by
the Dallas architect Frank D. Welch for Helen Cummings and Ghent Graves.
A modern house, the Graves House is raised on a high grass berm, as were
several of the early houses in Shadyside. Its pyramidal roof and encircling
gallery evoke Texas regional architectural prototypes.

58. Edward Albert Palmer Memorial Chapel (now Palmer Memorial Episcopal Church)

William Ward Watkin, 1927; John F. Staub, 1930

At the same time that he designed Cohen House at Rice, Watkin designed the Edward Albert Palmer Memorial Chapel for the Episcopal Diocese of Texas. Palmer Chapel was built to serve as the collegiate chapel of Rice. It is not on the Rice campus, however, but faces it at 6221 Main Boulevard. Since 1929 it has functioned as a parish church.

The donor of the chapel, Mrs. Edwin L. Neville, specified that it be modeled on the late fifteenth-century church of Santa Maria dei Miracoli in Venice by Pietro Lombardo. Watkin had measured and sketched Santa Maria during an architectural tour of Europe after his graduation from Penn and before going to work for Cram, Goodhue & Ferguson. Ralph Adams Cram, like many Gothic revival architects, deplored the renaissance of classicism in European architecture. However, he specifically exempted Lombardo's Santa Maria from this condemnation. The interior of Palmer Chapel, with its chancel raised five-and-a-half feet above the nave floor and its vaulted ceiling, is much more like the Venetian church than the exterior. Watkin and his associate Stayton Nunn treated the exterior, including the 90-foot tall campanile, as a very abstract rendition of the Lombard Romanesque style, surfaced with stucco rather than brick. The cast stone portal framing the Main Boulevard entrance to Palmer Chapel and the rose window above it are detailed in the style of Pietro Lombardo. This mixing and matching of historical styles was much admired in the 1920s; it displayed the architect's virtuosity and freedom from dependence on historical models. The antique painted glass windows were designed by Karl Hackert and installed in the late 1940s. They are memorials to parishioners' families, including three generations of the Rice family; the rose window above the entrance portal is dedicated to Mr. and Mrs. James A. Baker.

Palmer Chapel was a collegiate chapel for less than a year before a group of Episcopalians, including Mrs. Neville and a number of the Shadyside families, petitioned the Bishop of Texas to authorize the organization of a parish there. In 1930 the newly constituted parish built a parish house stretching back to Fannin Street behind the chapel. Harry C. Wiess was chair of the parish's building committee; John F. Staub was the architect. Staub so carefully matched Watkin's simplified Lombard Romanesque style that no disparity between the two components is evident. To the left of the Main Boulevard front of the church and set back behind it is a separate entrance to the parish house. Staub designed the cast stone portal framing this entrance, which is surfaced with Romanesque ornament.

Photographs taken from Rice around 1930 show the campanile of Palmer Chapel, along with the tower of Cohen House and the bulk of Hermann Hospital, rising in the distance above the hedge parterres and

Edward Albert Palmer Memorial Chapel (now Palmer Memorial Episcopal Church)

Italian cypresses of the Academic Court. These images preserve the vision that perhaps motivated Watkin and his clients as they constructed, piece by piece, a new city along Main Boulevard—whose modernity was attested by the uniform application of what Peter C. Papademetriou cleverly described as the Main Boulevard Mediterranean style. The modernity of the historic genres constituting this Mediterranean meta-style lay in their capacity to advertise identity. For Houston's Main Boulevard elite, the Mediterranean genres represented high mindedness and high culture, even as Houston developers and their architects were building a suburban "Spanish village" of Mediterranean style retail buildings on Main between Richmond and Elgin. The proposition that uniform architecture expressed a shared public purpose in building the city gained currency. By the end of the 1920s civic idealism was conflated with commercial attraction and persuasion to imply that Mediterranean architecture could render shops "artistic" rather than mercenary. The ambivalence and instability of stylistic coding, when applied to social constructions in a democratic society (where sumptuary laws could not be invoked to restrict the use of styles and the meanings they construed socially), meant that by the 1930s the architecture of Palmer Chapel, Rice, and the civic arena would be derided by critics for its stylistic fictitiousness. The construction of urban order and cultural meaningfulness through stylistic coordination encountered limits as soon as it was achieved. By concentrating their own discourses on thematics and style, rather than spatial and urbanistic connections, architects of Cram's, Watkin's, and Staub's generations found themselves unable to defend their practices on the terms set by their modernist challengers and critics. The loss of confidence they experienced is exemplified by Staub & Rather's buildings of the postwar 1940s at Rice.

59. Autry House *Cram & Ferguson and William Ward Watkin, 1921*

Next door to Palmer Chapel, at 6265 Main Boulevard, is Autry House. This was built to be the "community house," a student center for Rice students, by the Rev. Harris Masterson, Jr., a priest who had formerly been the Episcopal chaplain at the University of Texas at Austin. Mrs. James L. Autry, for whom the Autry Court at Rice is named, donated funds to the Diocese of Texas to build Autry House as a memorial to her husband, James L. Autry. Their two children, James L. Autry, Jr. (Class of 1921) and Allie May Autry Kelley, were graduates of Rice.

In 1919 Father Masterson persuaded the Bishop of Texas to buy a square block of property along Main Boulevard opposite Entrance Three to the Rice campus. The shuttle car line that the Galveston–Houston Electric Company, the local streetcar company, extended south in 1910 to serve the Rice Institute and the suburban new town of Bellaire, Texas, was aligned along what is now Fannin Street. Its principal Rice stop was opposite Entrance Three. Father Masterson moved several surplus barracks from Camp Logan, Houston's World War I Army training camp, to the Rice carline stop to form the Emmanuel Community House. The community house offered hot lunches, a ready supply of bridge players, and a variety of services (a press shop, a barber shop) that students would otherwise have had to go into Houston to obtain. It also offered female students a place to study and socialize. Father Masterson screened films and sponsored dances there as well.

Indicative of the lack of such facilities at Rice (female students were particularly ill served; for several decades they were not even permitted to remain on campus after dark), the community house was instantly successful. In 1920 Father Masterson commissioned Cram & Ferguson and William Ward Watkin to prepare a master plan for development of the diocese's property. Cram & Ferguson proposed a permanent community house, a collegiate chapel (where Palmer Chapel was built), a dormitory for women students attending Rice, a dormitory for nurses working at the planned Hermann Hospital, and a house for the chaplain. Autry House was built immediately as the community house. It is a condensed version of the architecture associated with the Residential Group at Rice. The two-story, stucco-faced, tile-roofed building was picturesquely composed as a series of secondary spaces configured around a central, double-height common room. The common room contains a musicians' gallery at one end and a stage at the other incorporating an apsidal-ended chapel. The common room opens to a terrace on the south that overlooks Main Boulevard and Hermann Park, and, once, the walk from the trolley stop to Entrance Three

Interior, Autry House

at Rice. Above the fireplace in the common room is a bronze relief portrait of James L. Autry. A work of the Italian-American sculptor Pompeo Coppini, it was a gift of Will C. Hogg.

From its opening in 1921 until the completion of the Fondren Library in 1949, Autry House was the de-facto student center of Rice. Called "the fireside of Rice" (at least in published references), it was the center of student life for nearly thirty years. The first Archi-Arts Ball, the architecture students' Beaux-Arts ball, was held at Autry House in 1922. In the 1920s it was publicized within the Episcopal church as a model center for campus ministry. Autry House continues to function as an Episcopal chaplaincy to Rice and the schools of the Texas Medical Center. It is also home to the Autry Refectory, which serves lunch on weekdays. Autry House was rehabilitated in 1974–77 by Howard Barnstone and Bailey & Belanger.

At Autry House and Palmer Chapel, Watkin used architecture to imply a connection to Rice. This quintessentially Progressive desire to make connections, and to make urban architecture that embodied these connections, was reiterated all along Main Boulevard in the 1920s.

60.   Hermann Hospital   *Berlin & Swern and Alfred C. Finn, 1925*

When George Hermann died in 1914 he bequeathed the bulk of his estate (based on investment in real estate, some of which turned out to contain oil) to the endowment and construction of a modern hospital. Litigation over the management of his estate led to a long delay in planning, building, and equipping the new Hermann Hospital. The Chicago architects Berlin & Swern collaborated with Alfred C. Finn on the six-story building. Constructed at what is now 6411 Fannin Street, the corner of Fannin and North MacGregor Drive, it originally rose in open countryside amid the pine forest of Hermann Park. Despite alterations and additions, the exterior of the building and its ground-floor public spaces remain substantially intact. Hermann Hospital demonstrates how American architects of the 1920s constructed urbanity, even when designing a free-standing building in a rustic setting.

Like Watkin's art museum, Hermann Hospital is sited on the diagonal in relation to its street corner location, enabling it to frame open space urbanistically. The building spatializes its implied forecourt through composition and massing: twin towers flank a recessed, symmetrical facade, in front of which a projecting, one-story pavilion is faced with a monumental classical portal. Symmetry, centrality, and figuration construct an order that is developed volumetrically, despite the fact that this was a freestanding building on an open site. The systematic construction of reciprocal spatial relationships is carried inside the entrance portal. Visitors pass through a wrought-iron screen and entrance alcove into what was originally a shallow cloister. One can either follow the cloister under cover into the lobby or continue on axis into what was originally an open-air courtyard (today enclosed with a skylight and air-conditioned), and only then into the real front door. Once inside the hospital lobby, vaulted passageways reiterate the spatiality of the cloisters and, originally, led visitors to a reception desk, stairs, and elevators. The lobby is richly decorated with the most elaborate display of art tile work in Houston.

Despite being a modern, scientific medical building designed by architects who specialized in this building type, Hermann Hospital was conceived as a public building. Its massing and internal organization acknowledged this public-ness. Such attributes as its orientation toward the southeast and thin floor plates also enabled it to perform well in Houston's hot, humid climate. Berlin & Swern's use of stucco to finish the outside of the building, their Spanish Mediterranean ornament, and red tile roofs reinforced the hospital's identity as a public building and connecting to the Main Boulevard Mediterranean narrative. Rather than treating its specialized identity as a hospital as antithetical to its urbanistic obligations as a public building, Berlin & Swern gave Hermann Hospital shape, purpose, and meaning by resolving these differences architecturally.

The five-story wings that frame the original buildings are additions from the mid-1970s. Rising behind it is the immense Hermann Hospital Pavilion by Watkins Hamilton Ross of 1999. Construction of this big box annex entailed reconnecting the old lobby to the rest of the Hermann Hospital complex. In 1990 the Austin, Texas, architects David Hoffman and Wayne Bell were responsible for restoring the exterior and the public interiors of the 1925 building, now called the Cullen Pavilion.

In 1943 Houston voters authorized the sale of 133 acres of Hermann Park adjoining Hermann Hospital to a newly-chartered non-profit organization, the Texas Medical Center, Inc. Organized by a group of Houston business and professional men and financed by the M. D. Anderson Foundation, the Texas Medical Center was developed to diversify Houston's economy and free the city from total dependence on the oil industry. Today it is the largest concentration of health care, education, and research institutions in the world. Herbert A. Kipp, who had worked with George Kessler on the planning of Hermann Park and Shadyside and who was responsible for laying out the garden suburban community of River Oaks between 1923 and 1947, planned the Medical Center complex, which absorbed Hermann Hospital. Although conceived as a "campus," the Medical Center was planned and is operated on the model of a Houston residential subdivision. Institutions occupy their own plots on a network of streets, which curve to reconcile a shift in alignment between Main Boulevard and Holcombe Boulevard. Through the equivalent of restrictive covenants and a property owners association, the institutions police each other while remaining responsible for their own plots as long as the restrictions are adhered to.

Although the first generation of buildings constructed in the Medical Center in the late 1940s and early 1950s were designed along similar lines to Hermann Hospital, the Medical Center's underlying suburban conception thwarted the urban intentions of the early architecture, especially after a shift to modernist building typologies in the early 1950s led to the abandonment of symmetry, centrality, and figuration. Since the 1980s big-box typologies, frosted with postmodern architectural veneer, have dominated. In terms of urban spatiality, the Texas Medical Center is the anti-Rice. It is a microcosm of the kind of city Houston became after the middle of the twentieth century, in which clashing institutional and individual wills and a disposition to engineer impulsive responses to urban problems rather than resolve them through design produce a raw, frenetic urban landscape.

61. Hermann Professional Building

Kenneth Franzheim and Wyatt C. Hedrick, 1949; Kenneth Franzheim with John H. Freeman, Jr., 1957

Hermann Professional Building

The 15-story Hermann Professional Building at 6411 Main Boulevard, between Entrances Three and Four to the Rice campus, was the first high-rise office building in Houston to be constructed outside downtown. It was built by the Hermann Hospital Estate to attract physicians and surgeons to the Medical Center. The original portion of the building faces Fannin Street; the addition of 1957 was achieved by simply extruding the original slab westward through the block to Main. Until 1946 Fannin, as it came south from downtown parallel to Main, stopped at Hermann Park. It was cut through the park in 1947 to relieve congestion on Main. Fannin, not Main, became the main street of the Medical Center, especially after 1970 when high-rise professional buildings began to be constructed in emulation of the Hermann Professional Building, with their multi-story parking garages abutting Main Boulevard.

The Hermann Professional Building represents an alternative to this development. It reflects an approach to urban design typical of Houston architecture of the late 1940s. Although the design was very conventional (Franzheim described it as "conservative modern" in style), the building nevertheless demonstrated the feasibility of a garden city urbanism that reconciled density with a desire for broad, landscaped public spaces; this urbanism lay in the generous width of the Main and Fannin sidewalks, the preservation of the live oak trees on Main, and the careful detailing of the base of the building. The monumental entrance portal was framed by plate glass display windows with bull-nosed corners a slightly delirious abstract relief panel by the Finnish artist Mauno Oittenen. The red tile roof and vestigial Spanish cartouche near the top of the narrow street fronts of the building acknowledged the unifying Main Boulevard Mediterranean civic style.

Further up Main are two professional buildings, the Medical Towers Building and St. Luke's Medical Tower, that display a degree of attentiveness to the example set by the Hermann Professional Building. The Medical Towers at 1709 Dryden and Main of 1956 by Golemon & Rolfe of Houston with the New York office of Skidmore, Owings & Merrill represents the modernist challenge to the setback massing, corner windows, and historical ornament of the Hermann Professional Building. The eighteen-story slab, riding atop its own parking garage, was based on the model of Lever House, which Skidmore, Owings & Merrill had designed in New York in 1952. The ground level of the Medical Towers is occupied by commercial lease space facing the sidewalk, although its proportions are not as generous as Franzheim's nor were live oaks planted this far south on Main. Next door, at 6625 Main, the twenty-five-story St. Luke's Medical Tower of 1991 is César Pelli's postmodern conflation of the Hermann and Medical Towers buildings (in association with Kendall/Heaton Associates). Pelli combines the figured profile, generous scale, and spatially shaped interior of the Hermann Professional Building with the office-stacked-on-top-of-a-parking-garage organization of the Medical Towers. Neither building has urbane public space to work with. The lack of consensus on the importance of public space in Houston at the beginning of the twenty-first century strongly distinguishes even the most conscientious architecture of the Texas Medical Center from Rice.

The domination of Main Boulevard by buildings connected with the Medical Center did not occur until the 1970s. Since Main becomes U.S. Highway 90, the main road to San Antonio before construction of the freeway network in the 1950s and 1960s, Main Boulevard south of MacGregor Drive developed as a highway strip beginning in the 1920s. William Ward Watkin designed Ye Old College Inn for the restaurateur George Martin across from the old Field House in 1921. The stucco-surfaced arches and tile roofs of Watkin's original buildings integrated it into the civic arena. Drive-in

Detail, Hermann Professional Building

restaurants of the 1930s and 1940s along Main, such as Walter Wingate's and Bill Williams's, tended to be designed in the streamlined modernistic style. The development of the Medical Center prompted a boom in hotel construction, beginning with the legendary Shamrock of 1949 at Main and Holcombe. This eighteen-story, 1,100-room hotel, built by the independent oil operator Glenn H. McCarthy, was the largest hotel built in the U.S. in the 1940s and it epitomized popular stereotypes of Texan outrageousness. The Shamrock was acquired by the Texas Medical Center, Inc., and demolished in 1987. Its site is now a parking lot. Indicative of the suburban trend of the 1950s is the ex-Tidelands Motor Inn of 1958 at 6500 Main Boulevard and University, across from old Rice Stadium. Designed by the Austin architect Winifred O. Gustafson, the Tidelands in its heyday in the 1960s reproduced the Hollywood subtropical landscape theme of the Shamrock's swimming pool garden. From 1983 to 1999, the Tidelands was Rice's Graduate House. Rice demolished the Tidelands in 2000.

62. Congregation Emanu El Temple

MacKie & Kamrath and Lenard Gabert, 1949

Congregation Emanu El, a Reform Jewish congregation, retained Houston's first modernist architects, Fred MacKie and Karl Kamrath, to design a new temple complex in 1946 at 1500 Sunset Boulevard across from the Rice campus. The Houston architect Lenard Gabert (Class of 1917), a member of the recently organized congregation, recommended that MacKie & Kamrath be retained and associated with them. MacKie & Kamrath's use of symmetry and centrality makes Temple Emanu El intriguing with respect to Cram's buildings at Rice. Kamrath, the firm's designer, was devoted to the Usonian architecture of Frank Lloyd Wright. At Temple Emanu El, he produced a modern Usonian building that used symmetry externally to shape strong site relationships and internally to construct a sequence of spaces that transcend academic conventions of bilateral composition to achieve a sensation of spiritual liberation. MacKie & Kamrath's Usonian buildings tended to exhibit the layered vertical organization—with defined base courses, staged ascents, and strongly terminated rooflines—of academically composed buildings. They also constructed site relationships spatially, which became much rarer in Houston as modern architecture gained ground in the 1950s. Temple Emanu El is a suburban rather than an urban building, yet it contributes to the garden city urbanism of the civic arena because of its architectural civility. In addition, the architect's creation of spiritually elevating communal space makes it one of the most moving works of twentieth-century architecture in Houston.

Backing up to Temple Emanu El is the Rice Graduate Apartments at 1515 Bissonnet Avenue of 1999. This three-story garden apartment complex was constructed for the university by the Houston apartment developer Jenard M. Gross and designed by his architect, the Steinberg Collaborative. It replicates a typology that Gross successfully repeated in other Houston rental apartment complexes of the 1990s. While Rice builds residential colleges for undergraduates on campus costing between $25 and $30 million, it offers its graduate students speculative housing. This is a troubling disparity, not least because it demonstrates that once off-campus, Rice University is content to abandon its position as architectural patron and go with the flow of Houston's speculative real estate and building market.

63.   First Christian Church   *Brown & McKim, 1958*

Across the street from Temple Emanu El at 1601 Sunset Boulevard, the
First Christian Church exhibits certain parallels with the Rice Memorial
Chapel at Rice. Donald Barthelme (Class of 1928), professor of architecture
at the University of Houston and the first William Ward Watkin Professor of
Architecture at Rice, collaborated with Hamilton Brown and Charles McKim
on the design of what Barthelme called the "church without walls."
Barthelme withdrew from the project before construction began. Brown &
McKim maintained his image of a worship space in nature in their meticu-
lously detailed modern design. The high-ceilinged church is walled with
glass, sheltered beneath projecting concrete overhangs and screened from
Rice Boulevard by brick walls. The congregation looks out to the out-of-
doors. The floor of the church, which is paved with flagstone, slopes down
toward the chancel, so that the sightlines of many of the worshippers hover
near the ground plane. Laterally the church feels very open; vertically, it is
enclosed with a volume of ascending space. By adhering consistently to
Barthelme's idea of bringing the worshippers into contact with nature, the
First Christian Church is a more powerful expression of the romantic modernist notion of the spiritual beneficence of nature than is the Rice Memorial
Chapel, with its overlay of historical quotation. The Houston landscape
architect Ralph Ellis Gunn designed the grounds, forecourt, and gardens of
the First Christian Church. The artist Seymour Fogel installed the mural of
glazed brick and stained glass on the Cherokee Street front of the church.

64.   Southampton
William Ward Watkin, subdivision and landscape planner, 1923

In the early 1920s William Ward Watkin designed several residential subdivisions that contributed to the spread of the civic arena. While the most
exalted of these was Broadacres, an elite enclave off Bissonnet Avenue near
the Museum of Fine Arts, the largest was Southampton, a 160-acre subdivision along Rice Boulevard. Southampton was developed by E. H. Fleming
& Company. It was aimed at a middle-income market rather than an elite
market and was affordable enough for Rice faculty members to build or buy
houses there.

　　The largest house sites in Southampton are on Rice Boulevard
along the northern boundary of the Rice campus. Watkin outlined Rice
Boulevard with live oak trees to match those planted on the south side of
the street by Rice. Watkin extended this oak allée to Sunset Boulevard,
which is a divided boulevard in Southampton. It is the collective landscape
established with the live oaks rather than the architecture of individual

houses that gives Southampton its identity. By extending the armature of oak trees from Rice to Main Boulevard, then to surrounding subdivisions in the 1920s, Watkin systematically constructed urban space in the image of a modern garden city.

Since the 1920s, a number of Southampton houses have been designed by Rice architecture professors. One of the most distinctive is the flat-roofed, steel-framed courtyard house of 1994 by Anderson Todd with his wife and collaborator Iris G. Todd, located at 1932 Bolsover Road, one block from the Rice Boulevard-Hazard Street intersection.

65.   The Village   *1938*

The Village is a twelve-block shopping district two blocks west of Greenbriar Drive, which forms the west boundary of the Rice campus. The blocks between Rice Boulevard, University Boulevard, Morningside Drive, and Kirby Drive are its heart. The Village is a curious amalgam of auto-oriented strip shopping center and small-town downtown. Initially developed between the late 1930s and the mid-1950s, it represents the transposition of one-story retail storefronts from a downtown setting to the suburbs. Rather than being built up against sidewalk-lined streets, most shops and their sidewalks were pushed back to allow for off-street, pull-in parking. The developers Olson & Associates, who built many of the retail buildings, supplemented on-grade parking with rooftop parking decks accessible by ramps.

In the 1980s, Rice University began to buy real estate in the Village, especially along University Boulevard. Weingarten Realty Investors developed portions of this property in the 2400 and 2500 blocks of University for Rice with the Village Arcade, a three-block complex built in two phases (1992, 1995). The Village Arcade is a specialty shopping center within the Village. It repeats elements of the typologies of the 1950s, such as its canopy-covered sidewalks (the "arcade") set back from surrounding streets behind two rows of parking. However, each phase covers a full-block site and in order to incorporate a parking garage in the second phase, one block of Amherst Street was privatized. The design of the complex by O'Brien-Dietz & Associates of Dallas features postmodern pediments and columns with brick banding, which was intended to relate it to Rice.

Rice architectural connections of a different kind are represented by Village Square at 2365 Rice Boulevard, a two-story, retail "tin house" by William T. Cannady & Associates of 1995, and a three-story house at 6136 Kirby Drive of 1996 by Wittenberg Architects that is spatially inflected toward the Village rather than insulated from it. Like William Cannady, Gordon Wittenberg is a professor of architecture at Rice.

The unpretentious liveliness of the village underscores Rice University's lack of spatial connection to it. Although the armature of live oak trees relates the university to its setting on three sides, on the west the stadium parking lot is a gulf separating the campus and the Village. From the Village, Rice seems like an insular presence. The power of the university to reshape Village real estate and retailing practices (the major tenants of the Village Arcade are up-market national chains) was not matched in the 1990s by any sense of commitment to proposing new forms of community or commissioning architecture that goes beyond the calculations of the real estate market.

66.   Shorthand House   *François de Menil, 1997*

The Shorthand House, a single-family house at 2233 University Boulevard, was built in the subdivision of Southgate, across from Rice Stadium. Since Southgate was put on the market in 1930, housing construction did not being in earnest until the mid-1930s. Stayton Nunn was the architect for the original development corporation. It was Claude E. Hooton (Class of 1927), however, an instructor in architecture at Rice from 1931 to 1941, who had the most influence on Southgate's architectural evolution in the 1930s. Hooton designed houses for the developer, R. W. Gillette, as well as for private clients. The most notable was his house for the interior decorator

Shorthand House

Shorthand House

Virginia West and her husband, the contractor Randolph C. West, of 1936 at 2435 Dryden. Hooton's own house, a flat-roofed, white stucco-surfaced modern house, was built on this site in 1936. Several years after the Hooton House was demolished, the client purchased the site for this house. The New York architect François de Menil, the youngest son of Dominique and John de Menil, designed a self-effacing, flat-roofed, white stucco-surfaced house, offset by a one-story garage. Proportions and the treatment of the front yard as a graveled motor court give the house an urbane presence. Operable louvered shutters on east-facing second-floor windows regional-ize it. Its nickname "shorthand" derives from Menil's clever organization of interior spaces with pivoting and sliding wall panels, which allow rooms to be reconfigured for different conditions of use. William Hartman of Houston was the landscape architect.

Bibliography

Collections

Woodson Research Center, Fondren Library, Rice University
Architectural Records Collection, Department of Facilities and
Management, Rice University
Houston Metropolitan Research Center, Houston Public Library
Archives, The Museum of Fine Arts, Houston

Rice University Periodicals

The Campanile
The Cornerstone   www.ruf.rice.edu/~rhs/corner/corner.html
The Flyleaf
Institute for the Arts Newsletter
Rice Alumni Magazine
Rice News   riceinfo.rice.edu/projects/reno/index.shtml
Rice Thresher   www.rice.edu/projects/thresher
Rice University Review
The Sallyport

Websites

"Campus of Rice University"
           www.rice.edu/Fondren/Woodson/buildings.html
"Geology of Rice Buildings"   www.geophysics.rice.edu/~ezenker/buildings
"Rice Campus Maps"   dacnet.rice.edu/maps/space
"Rice Facts"   www.ruf.rice.edu/~instresr/ricefacts/
Rice University   www.rice.edu

Publications

Adams, Celeste Marie, editor. *The Museum of Fine Arts, Houston: An Architectural History, 1924–1986.* "Architecture 1959—First Honor Awards: Laboratory Buildings for Rice Institute, Houston, Designed by George Pierce-Abel B. Pierce, Architects, Houston." *Texas Architect* 9 (November 1959): 11.

Arnell, Peter, and Ted Bickford, editors. *James Stirling Buildings and Projects, James Stirling Michael Wilford.* Introduction by Colin Rowe. New York: Rizzoli, 1984.

Barna, Joel Warren. "Research and Jobs." *Texas Architect* 41 (May–June 1991): 35–36.

———. "Shepherd School at Rice." *Texas Architect* 42 (January–February 1992): 62–63.

———. "Understated at Rice." *Progressive Architecture* 73 (January 1992): 24, 26.

Barnstone, Howard. *The Architecture of John F. Staub: Houston and the South.* Austin: University of Texas Press, 1979.

Barrick, Nolan. *Texas Tech: The Unobserved Heritage.* Lubbock: Texas Tech Press, 1985.

Boles, John B. *Rice University and the 1990 Economic Summit of Industrialized Nations.* Houston: Rice University, 1991.

The Book of the Opening. Houston: The Rice Institute, 1914.

Brownlee, David B., and David G. DeLong. *Louis I. Kahn: In the Realm of Architecture.* Introduction by Vincent Scully. Photography by Grant Mudford. Los Angeles: The Museum of Contemporary Art, and New York: Rizzoli, 1991.

"Buildings in a Context: Master Plan for Growth." *Architecture for the Emerging American City.* Center, A Journal for Architecture in America, No. 1. Austin: Center for the Study of American Architecture, 1985: 124–131.

Bulletin of The Museum of Fine Arts, Houston. New series vol. 15. April 1992.

Burchard, John, and Albert Bush-Brown. *The Architecture of America: A Social and Cultural History.* Boston: Little, Brown, 1961.

Camfield, William A. *Michael Heizer, 45 Degrees, 90 Degrees, 180 Degrees: A Sculpture for Rice University.* Houston: Rice University Farish Gallery, 1985.

"Consultation Among Institutions Precedes Library Design." *Architectural Record* 107 (June 1950): 138–42.

Cram, Ralph Adams, "Have I a 'Philosophy of Design?'" *Pencil Points* 13 (November 1932): 729–734.

Cram, Ralph Adams. *My Life in Architecture.* Boston: Little, Brown, 1936.

Curtis, William J. R. *Modern Architecture Since 1900.* Saddle River: Prentice Hall, 1996.

Dillon, David. "Combining Adventure and Respect: Herring Hall, Rice University." *Architecture* 74 (May 1985): 174–181.

———. "Expanding 'an Extraordinary Spectacle:' Planning and Design of the Rice University Campus." *Architecture* 77 (February 1988): 63–67.

Doody, Terrence. "Is Rice a City?" *Cite 35, Architecture and Design Review of Houston* (Fall 1996): 17–18.

Edgell, G. H. *The American Architecture of To-day.* New York: Charles Scribner's Sons, 1928.

"Extension of the School of Architecture, Rice University, Houston, Texas, 1979–1981." *Architecture + Urbanism 194* (November 1986): 44–46.

Fox, Stephen. "BioMass: Cambridge Seven's Recombinant Addition to the Rice Campus." *Cite, Architecture and Design Review of Houston* (Spring–Summer 1989): 14–15.

———. *The General Plan of the William M. Rice Institute and Its General Development.* Architecture at Rice 29. Houston: School of Architecture, Rice University, 1980.

———. "Enlightened Hindsight: Pelli's Herring Hall." *Arts and Architecture* 4 (July 1985): 78-83.

———. "Music Mall: Ricardo Bofill's Building for the Shepherd School of Music." *Cite, Architecture and Design Review of Houston* (Fall 1988): 8-11.

Fuller, Larry Paul. "Stirling at Rice: A Study in Contextualism." *Texas Architect* 32 (January–February 1982): 54–56.

Gebhard, David. "Critique." *Progressive Architecture* 62 (December 1981): 60–61.

Girouard, Mark. *Big Jim: The Life and Works of James Stirling.* London: Chatto and Windus, 1998.

Greene, Alison de Lima. "45 Degrees, 90 Degrees, 180 Degrees." *Cite, Architecture and Design Review of Houston* (Spring 1985): 6–7.

Gutheim, Frederick. *One Hundred Years of Architecture in America.* New York: Reinhold Publishing, 1957.

Hegemann, Werner, and Elbert Peets. *The American Vitruvius: An Architect's Handbook of Civic Art*. New York: Architectural Book Publishing, 1922.

Henry, Jay C. *Architecture in Texas, 1895–1945*. Austin: University of Texas Press, 1993.

Hewitt, Mark A. "Two Campuses: Lessons from Rice and the University of Houston." *Texas Architect* 34 (September–October 1984): 66–72.

"High Voltage Laboratory, Rice Institute, Houston, Texas, George F. Pierce and Abel B. Pierce, Architects." *Architectural Record* 121 (March 1957): 189, 191.

Hitchcock, Henry-Russell. *Architecture, Nineteenth and Twentieth Centuries*. Baltimore: Penguin Books, 1958.

Hoffman, Gilbert. "Bofill Opens 'Design Dialogues.'" *Texas Architect* 40 (May–June 1990): 15.

Ingersoll, Richard. "Houston's Academic Enclaves: Four Campuses in Three Acts." *Cite 35*, *Architecture and Design Review of Houston* (Fall 1996): 12–16.

Ingersoll, Richard. "Quasimodo Returns: John Outram's Computational Engineering Building at Rice." *Cite 32, Architecture and Design Review of Houston* (Fall 1994–Winter 1995): 6–7.

Irace, Fulvio. "Una questione di pelle: Architettura." *Ottogano 21* (June 1986): 60–65.

"Jesse H. Jones Graduate School of Administration, Rice University, Houston, USA." *Architektur und Wettbewerbe 123* (September 1985): 26–27.

Kidney, Walter C. *The Architecture of Choice: Eclecticism in America*. New York: George Braziller, 1974.

Klauder, Charles Z., and Herbert A. Wise. *College Architecture in America and Its Part in the Development of the Campus*. New York: Charles Scribner's Sons, 1929.

Larson, Jens Frederick, and Archie MacInnes Palmer. *Architectural Planning of the American College*. New York: McGraw-Hill, 1933.

"Ley Student Center Expansion, Rice University, Houston, Texas, 1986." *Architecture + Urbanism 233* (February 1990): 122–29.

McMichael, Carol. *Paul Cret at Texas: Architectural Drawings and the Image of the University in the 1930s*. Introduction by Drury Blakeley Alexander. Austin: Archer M. Huntington Gallery, College of Fine Arts, The University of Texas at Austin, 1983.

"Machine Shop for Art." *Architectural Forum* 131 (July–August 1969): 95.

Meiners, Fredericka. *A History of Rice University: The Institute Years, 1907–1963*. Houston: Rice University Historical Commission and Rice University Studies, 1982.

Micou, Paul. *The Church's Inquiry into Student Religious Life*. New York: National Council, Protestant Episcopal Church, Department of Religious Education, 1923.

Mitchell, O. Jack. *Parking Study, Rice University, Houston, Texas, 1991*. 1991.

Morehead, James C., Jr. *A Walking Tour of Rice University*. Houston: Rice University Press, 1990.

Moorhead, Gerald. "Classical Music: Alice Pratt Brown Hall, Shepherd School of Music, Rice University, Houston, Texas." *Architectural Record* 180 (March 1992): 74-83.

———. "In Cram's Footsteps." *Texas Architect* 49 (January–February 1999): 64-66.

———. "New College Buildings: A Building Boom is Reshaping Texas Campuses." *Texas Architect* 44 (May–June 1994): 34–36.

Muir, Andrew Forest. *William Marsh Rice and His Institute*. Edited by Sylvia Stallings Morris. Rice University Studies 58 (Spring 1972).

"New Stadium Design Reduces Construction to Nine Months, Simplifies Problem of Handling Crowds." *Architectural Forum* 96 (June 1952): 126–29.

Oliver, Richard. *Bertram Grosvenor Goodhue.* New York: Architectural History Foundation, and Cambridge: MIT Press, 1983.

"Ornamente und Schmuck: ein Mittel zur Interpretierung Uberspielung tragender Elemente." *Baumeister* 82 (December 1985): 50–59.

Papademetriou, Peter C. "Pattern and Principle." *Progressive Architecture* 66 (April 1985): 86–97.

———. "Pelli at Rice: Part Two." *Progressive Architecture* 67 (May 1986): 27

———. "Pelli Continues a Rice Tradition." *Progressive Architecture* 63 (December 1982): 31–32.

———. "Pelli Crams Old and New Ideas into Rice's Future." *Cite, Architecture and Design Review of Houston* (Winter 1984): 14–15.

———. "Ricardo Bofill at Rice." *Progressive Architecture* 69 (January 1988): 29.

———. "Rice Reprise: Ley Student Center, Rice University, Houston, Texas." *Progressive Architecture* 69 (February 1988): 72–75.

———. "Stirling at Rice: School of Architecture, Rice University, Houston, Texas." *Architectural Review* 171 (February 1982): 50–67.

———. "Stirling in Another Context: School of Architecture Addition, Rice University, Houston, Texas." *Progressive Architecture* 62 (December 1981): 53–59.

Papademetriou, Peter C., and Paul Goldberger. "School of Architecture, Rice University, Houston, Texas." *GA Document 5* (1982): 50–71.

Pelli, César. *César Pelli, Buildings and Projects, 1965–1990.* Introduction by Paul Goldberger. New York: Rizzoli, 1990.

———. *César Pelli, Current and Selected Works.* Introduction by Michael J. Crosbie. Mulgrave, Australia: Images Publishing Group, 1993.

———. *Observations for Young Architects.* New York: Monacelli Press, 1999: 192–203.

Pelli, César, & Associates. *William Marsh Rice University: Master Plan for Growth.* September 1983.

Ralph Adams Cram, Cram & Ferguson. Contemporary American Architects. Introduction by Alfred Tappan North. New York: Whittlesey House, 1931.

Predock, Antoine. *Antoine Predock Architect 2.* Edited by Brad Collins and Elizabeth Zimmermann. New York: Rizzoli, 1998.

Reed, Cleota. *Henry Chapman Mercer and the Moravian Pottery and Tile Works.* Philadelphia: University of Philadelphia Press, 1987.

"Revivalism at Rice: Seely G. Mudd Computer Science Laboratory." *Architectural Record* 171 (November 1983): 90–95.

The Rice Institute, A Community Asset, undated (circa 1952).

"Rice Institute, Cram, Goodhue & Ferguson, Architects," *Western Architect* 19 (February 1913): 20–22.

Rice Institute Looks Forward, 1946.

"Rice University School of Architecture Renovation and Expansion Project." *Architectural Design 50* (7–8, 1980): 50–55.

Robinson, Willard M. "Temples of Knowledge: Historic Mains of Texas Colleges and Universities." *Southwestern Historical Quarterly* 77 (April 1974): 445–480.

"Ryon Engineering Laboratory, Rice University, Houston, Texas." *Texas Architect* 17 (February 1967): 5–7.

Schuyler, Montgomery. "The Work of Cram, Goodhue & Ferguson." *Architectural Record* 29 (January 1911): 30.

"Sid W. Richardson College, Rice University, Houston, Texas." *Texas Architect* 22 (June 1972): 15–16.

Sorkin, Michael. "Anderson Hall Expansion, School of Architecture, Rice University." *Arts and Architecture* 1 (Winter 1981): 4749.

Speck, Lawrence W. *Landmarks of Texas Architecture*. Photographs by Richard Payne. Austin: University of Texas Press, 1986.

Stephens, Suzanne. "Reconstructing Rice." *Skyline* (November 1981): 19–21.

Stern, William F. "Robert R. Herring Hall." *Cite, Architecture and Design Review of Houston* (Spring 1985): 20–21.

Stirling, James, AD Architectural Design Profile. London: Academy Editions, St. Martins Press, 1982 (includes Paul Goldberger, "Buildings in Context," 180–81).

Tallmadge, Thomas E. *The Story of Architecture in America*. New York: W. W. Norton, 1927.

Tilley, Ray Don. "Mortared Logic: George R. Brown Hall, Rice University, Houston, Texas." *Architecture* 81 (April 1992): 62–67.

Tucci, Douglass Shand. *Ralph Adams Cram, American Mediaevalist*. Boston: Boston Public Library, 1975.

Turner, Drexel. "Powers of Tin." *Cite 31, Architecture and Design Review of Houston* (Winter–Spring 1994): 38–44.

———. "Slouching Towards Byzantium: About Face at the Rice Library." *Cite 28, The Architecture and Design Review of Houston* (Spring 1992): 26–30.

———. "Stirling Example." *Cite 29, Architecture and Design Review of Houston* (Fall 1992–Spring 1993): 3.

———. "W(h)ither the Rice Museum?" *Cite, Architecture and Design Review of Houston* (Fall 1986): 23.

Turner, Paul V. *Campus, An American Planning Tradition*. New York: Architectural History Foundation, and Cambridge: MIT Press, 1984.

Vogliazzo, Maurizio. "Ley Student Center, Houston, Texas." *Arca 17* (June 1988): 46–51.

Watkin, William Ward. "Architectural Development of the William M. Rice Institute, Houston, Texas." *Southern Architectural Review* 1 (November 1910): 110-115.

Watkin, William Ward. "Architectural Traditions Appearing in the Earlier Buildings of the Rice Institute." *The Slide Rule* (June 1953): 5–10.

Wilford, Michael. *James Stirling Michael Wilford Associates, Buildings and Projects, 1975–1992*. Introduction by Robert Maxwell. London: Thames and Hudson, 1994.

"William M. Rice Institute, Houston, Texas." *American Architect* 102 (December 1912): 207–08.

Winkler, Franz, "The Administration Building of the Rice Institute, Houston, Texas." *The Brickbuilder* 21 (December 1912): 321–24.

The Work of Cram & Ferguson, Architects, Including the Work of Cram, Goodhue & Ferguson. Introduction by Charles D. Maginnis. New York: Pencil Points Press, 1929.

This guide reflects the enthusiastic support and encouragement of many people at Rice University and in Houston. President Malcolm Gillis generously committed university resources to underwriting publication of the guide. Without the efforts of John B. Boles, William P. Hobby professor of history and historian of Rice University, and the Rice Historical Society, especially Helen Lawrence-Toombs, Greg Marshall, and Neal Heaps, the university's commitment to this project would not have been forthcoming. Dean W. Currie, vice president of finance and administration, made it possible for me to look into the near future of architecture at Rice. The Fondren Library, Charles Henry, librarian and vice provost, and especially Nancy Boothe, university archivist and head of the Woodson Research Center, Lee Pecht and Joan Ferry, archives associates, Jett Prendeville, art and architecture librarian, and Sharon Link provided access to the published and archival sources of information on which this book is based. The Facilities and Engineering department, William G. Mack, associate vice president, allowed me to review its architectural records file; special thanks are due to Joseph L. McGrath, architectural records analyst, and Paul Sanders, Jr., staff architect. Paul Harcomb, professor of ecology and evolutionary biology, was of great help. The support of Lars Lerup, dean of architecture, John J. Casbarian, associate dean, Doris Anderson, architecture school administrator, and Janet Wheeler, Kathleen Roberts, Elaine Sebring, and Diania (SP?) Williams of the school of architecture was invaluable. William T. Cannady, professor of architecture, and Anderson Todd, Gus S. Wortham professor emeritus, deserve special recognition. Thanks to David Kaplan of *Rice News* and Christof Spieler, formerly of the *Rice Thresher*. I am grateful for the support of the Rice Design Alliance.

Special thanks are due to Susan Booth Keeton for generously and patiently sharing her knowledge of horticulture and landscape history, and to Charles Tapley. The Texas and Local History Collection and Architectural Collection of the Houston Public Library's Houston Metropolitan Research Center provided much needed documentation. The late O. Jack Mitchell, James C. Morehead, Jr., Howard Barnstone, John F. Staub, and H. Malcolm Lovett were important sources of information. I am grateful to Douglass Shand-Tucci for insights into Cram's architecture. The Rev. John D. Worrell, retired chaplain of Autry House, encouraged my research on the architectural history of Main Boulevard as did Peter C. Papademetriou, Richard Ingersoll, Harold Hyman, William P. Hobby professor emeritus, and Celeste Marie Adams. Thanks are due to the Gerald D. Hines College of Architecture at the University of Houston and to two individuals who have long encouraged knowledge of the historical and architectural heritage of Rice, Ray Watkin Strange and Drexel Turner; I am the beneficiary of their support and encouragement.

The Anchorage Foundation of Texas made possible my involvement in this project. I am indebted to its president, Anne S. Bohnn, its directors LeRoy Melcher III, Pierre S. Melcher, Marc Melcher, Pierre M. Schlumberger, and Jody Blazek, and its staff member, Diana Hall.

Jan Cigliano of the Princeton Architectural Press was unfailing in her patience and support.

An author could not hope for a more gifted and insightful photographer than Paul Hester.

Stephen Fox
Anchorage Foundation of Texas
Houston, Texas

Index

(Italics indicates a photograph.)